BLACK&DECKER®

THE COMPLETE GUIDE TO

WINDOWS & ENTRYWAYS

- Repair
- Renew
- Replace

by Chris Marshall

Creative Publishing
international

MINNEAPOLIS, MINNESOTA
www.creativepub.com

Creative Publishing
international

Copyright © 2008
Creative Publishing international, Inc.
400 First Avenue North, Suite 300
Minneapolis, Minnesota 55401
1-800-328-3895
www.creativepub.com

Printed in China

10 9 8 7 6 5 4 3 2 1

Library of Congress Cataloging-in-Publication Data

Marshall, Chris.
 The complete guide to windows & entryways : repair, renew,
replace / by Chris Marshall.
    p. cm. -- (Complete guide)
  At head of title: Branded by Black & Decker
  Summary: "Includes inspiration, design, installation and main-
tenance information for both windows and doors"--Provided by
publisher.
  ISBN-13: 978-1-58923-375-1 (pbk.)
  ISBN-10: 1-58923-375-1 (pbk.)
 1. Doors--Design and construction. 2. Windows--Design and
construction. 3. Entrance halls--Design and construction. I. Black &
Decker Corporation (Towson, Md.) II. Title. III. Title: Branded by Black &
Decker. IV. Title: Complete guide to windows and entryways. V. Series.

TH2270.M33 2008
690'.1823--dc22   2007039142

President/CEO: Ken Fund
VP for Sales & Marketing: Peter Ackroyd

Home Improvement Group

Publisher: Bryan Trandem
Managing Editor: Tracy Stanley
Senior Editor: Mark Johanson
Editor: Jennifer Gehlhar

Creative Director: Michele Lanci-Altomare
Senior Design Manager: Brad Springer
Design Managers: Jon Simpson, Mary Rohl

Lead Photographer: Steve Galvin
Photo Coordinator: Joanne Wawra
Shop Manager: Bryan McLain
Shop Assistant: Cesar Fernandez Rodriguez

Production Managers: Linda Halls, Laura Hokkanen

Author: Chris Marshall
Page Layout Artist: Laura Rades
Photographers: Peter Caley, Andrea Rugg, Joel Schnell
Shop Help: Dan Anderson, Scott Boyd, John Haglof,
    Mark Hardy, David Hartley
Cover photo © Peachtree Doors and Windows

The Complete Guide to Windows & Entryways
Created by: The Editors of Creative Publishing international, Inc., in cooperation with Black & Decker.
Black & Decker® is a trademark of The Black & Decker Corporation and is used under license.

NOTICE TO READERS

For safety, use caution, care, and good judgment when following the procedures described in this book. The publisher and Black & Decker cannot assume responsibility for any damage to property or injury to persons as a result of misuse of the information provided.

The techniques shown in this book are general techniques for various applications. In some instances, additional techniques not shown in this book may be required. Always follow manufacturers' instructions included with products, since deviating from the directions may void warranties. The projects in this book vary widely as to skill levels required: some may not be appropriate for all do-it-yourselfers, and some may require professional help.

Consult your local building department for information on building permits, codes, and other laws as they apply to your project.

Contents

The Complete Guide to Windows & Entryways

Introduction

Windows and doors are your home's primary points of entry, but they also have a major impact on its appearance. They must allow free passage to desired elements—friends and family members, sunlight, and fresh air—but they also need to protect against elements you don't want, such as human intruders, animal pests, or inclement weather.

Few remodeling jobs have a greater impact on the livability and value of your home than replacing, adding, or repairing windows and doors. There are many paybacks: improved home value, better security, lower energy costs, increased light and ventilation, and added curb appeal. Best of all, if you have moderate tool skills, window and door projects are well within your reach, saving you considerable costs over having the work done by contractors.

The Complete Guide to Windows and Entryways is a comprehensive guide to all aspects of window and door work—from initial planning and site preparation through installation, repair, and weatherizing. The book is arranged in 10 chapters to make it easy to use:

"Gallery," the first chapter, includes many inspiring photos that show how windows and doors can enhance the architectural style of your home and create the mood and setting you desire.

The second chapter on "Selection" will help you clarify your window and door needs and choose from a wide variety of styles, material compositions, and hardware. It will also help you review the basic issues of light, ventilation, and home security you'll need to consider, make project plans, and collect the tools you'll need to do the projects covered here.

"Replacing Windows" and "Replacing Doors" take you right into some popular projects. In full step-by-step detail, you'll learn how to frame window and door openings and install 16 different types of windows and doors. "Finishing Techniques" covers the basics of trim carpentry, so you can give your projects the crowning touch with the appropriate trim details, locksets, deadbolts, and security hardware.

Next comes a chapter on "Entryway Additions" that will show you how to enhance your home with three decorative masonry and tile projects.

"Garage Doors and Openers" expands your project options even further to include replacing sectional garage doors and openers—two projects you may not have considered "DIY" before now.

The next two chapters show you how to maintain and weatherize the windows and doors you already have so you can extend their serviceable life and lower your energy costs. Finally, we've included an extended appendix at the end of this book on "Preparation." If you're relatively new to patching wallboard, removing vinyl siding, or adding a temporary support wall, this section will provide a helpful primer for those necessary skills.

Thank you for choosing *The Complete Guide to Windows and Entryways*. We hope it becomes an essential reference guide for many successful projects to come.

Gallery

The perfect door is more than a hardworking, well-used part of your home. An entry door often makes a style statement, in addition to its main function as an opening to your home. An interior passage door serves to provide security and privacy while echoing elements of the home's architectural style.

In the same way, the perfect window does more than just let in light. It adds personality and charm to a room's decor as it controls exposure to air and sunlight. Your needs for privacy, energy efficiency, and traffic patterns will influence the type, style, and placement of the windows in your home.

The dazzling photographs in this section feature many types and styles of windows and doors in creative and dramatic displays. They are sure to spark your imagination and help you make choices that will meet your remodeling needs perfectly.

An entry door extends a message to all visitors, either familiar or new. Whether that message is "You're welcome here" or "Please leave" can depend on how attractive and inviting your entryway appears.

When fiberglass doors entered the market, their flat, staid styling left much to be desired. Now, fiberglass doors are available in a wide variety of designs to match their wooden or steel counterparts. Sizes, surface textures, finish colors, and window arrangements can be combined to suit most any architecture.

Glass details, such as the intricate scrollwork design shown here, create a dazzling visual display for every visitor that comes calling.

Leaded glass and a dark finish add old-world charm to this double sidelight entry door. A handsome iron lockset is a fitting detail to this attractive entryway.

Steel, six-panel entry doors still dominate the entry door market. They're relatively inexpensive, stand up to the elements, and offer excellent security. By itself, a conventional six-panel can look drab, but a pair of fashionable sidelights and a matching transom window transform it into a stately entry.

The right entry door system can turn a traffic area into a spectacular space all its own. Here's a spot tailor-made to hang those memorable family photos or decorate for the holidays.

These triple-sash, double-hung windows create walls of light and a lovely interplay of sunlight against dark woodwork. It softens the formality of the space and invites conversation, a good book, or even a nap.

The decision to replace old, drafty windows or a dilapidated door doesn't have to compromise historical preservation. Notice how the expansive, double-hung windows of this Southern plantation home tie in perfectly with the existing paneled wainscot and trim details. The windows look as though they've been part of the home from the start.

A captivating view does more to impress than any wall hanging or artwork ever could. Make the most of it with a well-planned window system. These energy-efficient and largely maintenance-free windows will guarantee spectacular views for decades.

Regardless of styling or size, most operable windows have sash that unlock and tilt in for easy cleaning. Window washing will never again be the chore it once was, and you can tackle it from inside without a ladder.

Floor-to-ceiling, grille-less sash promote an almost panoramic view of the garden in this dining area. They also maximize natural light and give the space an open, airy atmosphere.

A bank of skylights flood this deck and lap pool with sunlight and warmth, while keeping the undesirable aspects of bad weather or cooler temperatures outside.

What could be more luxurious than a deep tub with an ocean view? Even if your bath is on the first floor, several window manufacturers offer privacy glazing that permits one-way viewing for situations like this.

In terms of sheer functionality, this outswing French patio door is hard to beat. With both doors open, it provides excellent passage for bringing in oversized appliances or furniture.

The same outswing patio door also has aesthetic benefits. Its large expanses of glass provide unobstructed views of the terrace and hillside beyond. Imagine the sunrise or sunset views from this vantage point.

Multiple patio doors turn a spacious patio into an ideal gathering place for larger groups by reducing congestion in the doorway.

Who says an entryway has to be conventional? This minimalist steel-and-glass door system works well for secluded access to this home, and its wide side windows brighten what could be an otherwise dark foyer area.

Selection

Shopping for new windows and doors isn't something we do very often. Yet, when the time comes to make these improvements, the investment can be substantial, so it pays to shop carefully and choose wisely. That new foyer entry door or bay window in your living room is probably going to be there for a long while, so you want to be happy with nuances of style, color, and other features for the life of that item. Of course, you also want windows and doors to function in a way that makes daily living a little bit better. Windows should be easy to open and to clean, providing plenty of light and ventilation. Doors should enhance rooms or entryways and create a weather-tight seal to keep out winter's chill or summer's swelter.

If it's been a while since you've shopped for new doors, windows, and door hardware, you may be excited to learn that your choices of style, size, and functionality are almost limitless. Windows and doors are a lucrative part of the housing industry, which works to consumer advantage. However, all the choices may make the process of selecting the right products more challenging, if not downright overwhelming.

This chapter includes:
- Choosing Windows, Doors & Hardware
- Materials

Choosing Windows, Doors & Hardware

Because windows and doors serve very basic purposes, consider your options carefully before making any purchases. Your design considerations will affect which styles you select. Keep in mind the size and strength of those who will operate the windows, and remember that the hardware must be reachable by those users.

Window considerations: Casement windows offer many attractive design features. Well-built models are easy to operate, and some come equipped with tandem latches or single-lever locking systems. Unfortunately, most casement windows do not accept window air conditioners.

Many horizontal sliding sash windows have improved in recent years. Some manufacturers now produce models with quality sliding mechanisms and offset hardware. These windows can accept air conditioners and screens.

Double-hung windows (or vertical sliding sash windows) are good options due to their availability and affordability, and they accept air conditioners and screens. High-quality models are easy to operate, and many come with convenient features such as tilt-in design for easy cleaning.

Window hardware is often determined by the type of window you select. Tandem latches, which operate multiple locks on a window with one motion, may be optional on some models; they simplify use considerably. Where possible, opt for larger handles or automatic openers. For other types of hardware, investigate adapters that make windows easier to operate.

Door considerations: A hinged door requires swing space equal to the width of the door plus 18" to 24" of clear space on the latch side for maneuvering (see page 41). Consider the swing direction, available swing space, and whether the swing of the door will interrupt the flow of traffic in a hallway. Many

Casement windows are easy to open and close, using their single-lever latches. Automatic openers can also be fitted to most models.

Sliding windows are a snap to open and close, requiring minimal strength and no extra dexterity.

experts recommend that hinged bathroom doors swing outward, so a person who has fallen inside the bathroom cannot block the door.

Choose entry doors with low thresholds or no thresholds (see pages 238 to 241). The front edge of the threshold should be no more than ¼" high if it's square, ½" high if it's beveled. A hinged sidelight makes a front entry door easier to navigate, especially when moving large objects.

Because glass doors can appear to be open when they are closed, glass doors—sliding or hinged—are dangerous to some people.

Sliding doors can be difficult to operate from a seated position, and as these doors age and dirt accumulates in the tracks, they become even more difficult to open. Also, thresholds on sliding doors typically are high, which creates barriers for walkers and wheelchairs. French doors may be a better alternative, as long as each door is at least 32" wide. There are many styles of this type of glass door (see pages 118 to 121).

Lever handles require less exacting hand placement and are easier to use than knobs or pulls. Locks vary widely. For exterior locks, a keyless entry system is an ideal way to eliminate fumbling with keys in cold weather. For interior locks, slide bolts typically are preferred over standard deadbolts, because they are easier to operate. You can gain space in all hinged-door openings by installing swing-clear hinges. These have L-shaped leaves that allow the door to swing away from the jamb, increasing the clear opening by the thickness of the door.

A swinging door with no latch requires swing space on both sides. Because they require no hardware to open and close, swinging doors may be a good option in situations where latches or locks are unnecessary. As with a standard hinged door, consider the door's swing space and whether the swing will interrupt traffic flow.

Perhaps the best alternative to a hinged or sliding door is a pocket door. It saves space, requires no threshold, and can be equipped with hardware that is easy to use. Pocket doors require special framing considerations; because the door slides into the wall, the rough opening is about twice the width of a standard door opening.

Standard recessed hardware for pocket doors is difficult to use, so install D-pulls instead (page 115). They also provide more room for fingers when the door is closed. Pocket door units can be custom-built or purchased as prehung units.

Lever door handles on hinged passage doors facilitate access to other rooms of the home. The handles come in a variety of sizes and design.

Double-hung windows can be used with most home styles and come in many sizes and shapes.

Window & Door Styles

The following pages contain examples of some of the types of windows and doors you may consider for your home. Your imagination may lead you to other options and combinations of options.

Casement windows pivot on hinges mounted on the side. They have a contemporary look and offer good ventilation. Whether your window has exposed or concealed sash locks, casements have a reputation for weather-tight construction.

Double-hung windows slide up and down and have a traditional appearance. The newer-style, spring-mounted operating mechanism is virtually trouble-free. The dividers (muntins) may divide individual panes of glass or snap on for decoration.

Bay windows consist of three parts: a central window, usually fixed, parallel to the existing wall, and two side windows (often casements or double-hungs), each set at a 30°, 45°, or 60° angle. The deep sill area makes a handy shelf space.

Bow windows have four or more units set at incremental angles to one another. The effect is a subtle, curved look. When large units are used, the bow window may become an extension of the room, even taking the place of a wall.

Garden windows bring the outside in by creating shelf space and letting in sunshine as well as fresh air. Many types are easy-to-install kits that fit into an existing window space. They can be added to any room in the home.

Sliding windows are inexpensive and require little maintenance, but they provide restricted ventilation since only half the window can be open at one time. However, that may be an acceptable tradeoff for a large, unobstructed view.

Awning windows pivot on hinges mounted at the top. Awning windows work well in combination with other windows, and because they provide ventilation without letting moisture in, they are a good choice in damp climates.

Fixed windows do not open, and they can be any size and shape used in any room. They may be flanked by other fixed windows or opening styles such as awning, casement, or double-hung.

Window groupings in an endless number of shapes and sizes may be used to dramatic effect in a home. They can become the focal point of a room, serving to highlight a spectacular view and let in lots of sunshine.

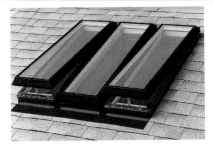

Skylights introduce extra light into rooms that have limited wall space. Skylights serve as solar collectors on sunny days, and those that also can be opened improve ventilation in the home.

Sliding patio doors offer good visibility and lighting. Because they slide on tracks and require no floor space for operation, they are a good choice for cramped spaces where swinging doors do not fit.

French doors open on hinges, so your room design must allow space for them to swing. Weather-tight models join indoor and outdoor living areas, while indoor models link two rooms.

Interior panel doors are also known as raised-panel, stile-and-rail doors. They have a traditional look and are available in many panel designs and configurations.

Pocket doors can be of flush or raised-panel design. One advantage is that they save floor space in tight quarters. They also allow you to hide the door when it's not in use.

Bifold doors are very convenient where there is little room for the swing space of a hinged interior door. The sections' surfaces can be flush, paneled, even partially or completely louvered to assist with airflow.

Entry doors may be made of steel, wood, fiberglass, or a range of new composite materials. Each appeals to the buyer in different ways—from energy efficiency to practicality, cost, or durability.

Entry doors with sidelights brighten a dark entry hall and give an inviting look to your home. The sidelights often contain tempered, double-pane glass for better security and energy efficiency.

Storm doors can improve the energy efficiency and appearance of your entry. A storm door prolongs the life of an expensive entry door by protecting it from the elements.

Garage Door Styles

There's no reason a garage door needs to be merely a utilitarian aspect of your home. Here, the translucent panels of this door give the impression that it's actually another window without compromising the security a garage requires.

Premium wood garage doors can be ordered in several styles and wood species to complement other exterior trimwork of your home. This sectional door also includes a panel of windows to brighten up a dark parking space.

This garage door's coach-house styling with faux hinges and two-tone paint scheme help conceal its true construction... it's actually a sectional door (one which is in two pieces and, usually, opens in center).

Garage doors contribute substantially to your home's curb appeal, mostly due to their placement and sheer size. Details such as divided lights, frame-and-panel construction, and rich wood finishes can elevate their status from functional to elegant and enhance your home's charm.

Hardware

Windows generally are purchased with what little hardware they require already included. But doors, on the other hand, normally are sold without hardware and thus present a much greater opportunity to impact the appearance of your house. Prehung doors come installed in jambs with hinges, but if you buy a slab door you'll need to select hinges along with a lockset and a deadbolt (on exterior doors). You can add embellishments, such as a fancy brass doorknocker or a shiny kickplate, to an entry door.

Door hardware can be plain and utilitarian or lavish and mostly decorative. In addition to the general type (contemporary versus Victorian, for example), you'll need to make choices about finish and overall quality. For instance, all-brass hardware is more durable than brass-plated versions, but it is considerably more expensive.

If you live in a larger city, the chances are good that you'll have access to at least one specialty store that focuses almost exclusively on decorative hardware. There are numerous websites dedicated to door hardware, too, and many mail order catalogs that offer a vast array of choices. Also consider architectural salvage yards for unique door hardware. You probably won't save any money going this route, but you may discover that one-of-a-kind conversation starter that sets your house apart in a wonderful way.

Various metal finish options are available for most door hardware, including knobs, locksets, handles, and hinges. The selection may include antique finish (A), bright brass (B), brushed nickel (C), polished chrome (D), or brushed steel (E).

Knob Styles

Door knobs are manufactured in a variety of shapes, styles, and materials, including plated metal (A), solid metal with brushed or polished finishes (B), glass (C), or porcelain (D). These are just a few of the styles and shapes available; each manufacturer will offer its own unique lines of knob options.

Handle Sets & Backplates

Another option for door hardware is to use a handle set instead of a knob. For simple passage doors that don't require a lock, you can use a handle only (A) or a handle combined with a thumb lever (B). Handle sets with integral or separate deadbolts (C) are also available for greater security. Doorknobs with decorative backplates (D) are perfect for historical preservation or simply to add a special touch.

Knob Functions

Door knobs are designed for three basic functions. A non-locking knob (A) is intended for interior passage doors or closets where security is not a concern. Knobs with keyed locks (B) are designed for entry doors. A privacy knob (C) with a pin lock on the room-side knob is a good choice for bathrooms or bedrooms.

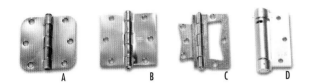

Door hinges are manufactured in several styles, including those with radiused or square-cornered leaves (A, B), non-mortising hinges (C), and spring-activated self-closing hinges (D).

Stylized hinges can add a subtle touch of charm to a historical home. Some have decorative finials or balls on the hinge pin (E); others are detailed with elaborate etched or carved leaves (F, G). If you can't find a new, stylized hinge that quite suits your door project, check for architectural salvage stores in your area—they're sure to have many ornate or period hinges to choose from.

Security Hardware

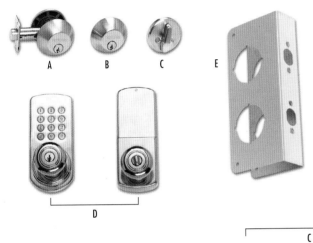

A variety of hardware items can help improve door security, including deadbolt locks (A) with either keyed (B) or lever-style (C) activation. Keyless entry deadbolts (D) are ideal for those times when you forget your key or when children need to have a secure way of unlocking the front door. A door reinforcer plate (E) surrounds locksets and prevents intruders from prying a door open.

Miscellaneous Door Hardware

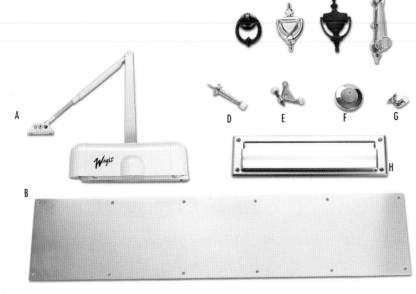

Additional hardware items are available to make entry doors more versatile, accessible, and durable. They include automatic door closers (A), metal kickplates (B), decorative doorknockers in many styles (C), and doorstops in wall-mounted (D, E), floor-mounted (F), or hinge-mounted (G) varieties. Pass-through mail slots (H) are designed in both horizontal and vertical styles when a separate mailbox isn't an option.

Materials

Window & Door Materials

Before buying new windows, you need to decide on a window style, choose framing and glazing (glass) materials, and compare energy efficiency ratings. You'll also find that several manufacturers offer a variety of decorative treatments, including beveled and stained-glass panels.

Installing a skylight may be another option. Skylights can be operable (capable of being opened) or fixed (non-opening).

If you don't like the window style you're replacing or you want to add some windows, look for new ideas by studying other homes similar to yours or by asking a window dealer or contractor for advice.

When buying new doors—whether for the interior or exterior of the home—most people choose prehung units with the door already attached to the jambs. Installing a prehung door is usually easier than installing a door and jambs separately, but both

projects can be frustrating if you don't take time to be sure the door is plumb, square, and level throughout the project.

Interior passage doors are not only a focal element of interior design, but also a hardworking and often-used feature of the home.

Replacing inexpensive hollow-core interior doors with new solid-core ones makes a noticeable difference. A solid-core door feels more substantial, closes with less rattle, insulates against sound more effectively, and withstands hard use more readily. However, a solid-core door almost always costs considerably more than a hollow-core model. Your budget may help you make the decision.

Exterior entry doors are usually the most expensive door in the home. Whatever material your entry door is made of, the added protection of a storm door will extend its life and keep it looking new.

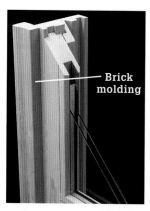

Wood frames are a good choice for windows and patio doors used in remodeling projects. Their preattached exterior brick moldings blend well with the look of existing windows.

Brick molding

Aluminum or vinyl shell

Clad-frame windows and doors feature an aluminum or vinyl shell on the exterior side of the window. Most are attached with nailing flanges that fit underneath the siding.

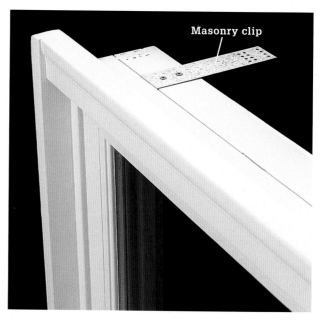

Masonry clip

Polymer coatings are optional on some wood-frame windows and doors. Polymer-coated windows and doors are available in a variety of colors and do not need painting. To avoid using casing nails, which would pierce the weatherproof coating, anchor polymer-coated units with masonry clips that are screwed to the jambs and to the interior framing members (page 57).

Several types of glass are available from window and door manufacturers. Single-pane glass (A) is suitable only in very mild climates. Double-panes (B) have a sealed air space between the layers of glass to reduce heat loss. They are available in several variations with improved insulating ability, including "low-E" glass with an invisible coating of metal on one surface, and gas-filled windows containing an inert gas such as argon. In southern climates, double-glazed tinted glass (C) reduces heat transfer. Tempered (or "safety") glass (D) has extra strength for use in patio doors, storm doors, and large picture windows.

Whatever the type of framing or glass in your window, the pane can be one piece or divided into smaller panes by muntins. True muntins actually hold individual pieces of glass, while snap-on muntins can be easily removed for cleaning the glass or to change the look of the window.

Window & Door Inspection Tips ▸

Here are a few things to look for when you inspect your new window or door before you begin the installation:

- Hardware is sturdy and all pieces are present.
- Sash lock or opening mechanism is operable.
- There are no glass cracks or cloudy areas.
- The window weather stripping is uniform and "tight."
- All door hinges operate easily.
- The doorknob hole is correctly positioned.
- There are no unsightly wood-grain blemishes.
- Each has a seal of quality from one or more of these industry testing organizations: National Woodwork Manufacturers Association, Architectural Aluminum Manufacturers Association, American National Standards Institute, American Wood Window Institute. The National Fenestration Rating Council tests windows and doors for heat loss (U-value), R-value, and solar heat gain.

ENERGY DATA WOOD CASEMASTER	Air Space in mm	Center of Glass U Value	Unit "U" Value	Unit "R" Value	Air Infiltration Per CFM/Ft
Single Glass					
Single Glass plus Energy Panel		0.89	0.89	1.12	.03
Single Low E plus Energy Panel	24	2.00	0.45	2.22	.03
Insulating Glass	24	2.38	0.39	2.56	.03
Insulating Low E	13	2.04	0.46	2.17	.03
Insulating Low E with Argon	13	3.23	0.34	2.94	.03
	13	4.00	0.29	3.45	.03

All calculated values based on Lawrence Berkeley Labs Window 3.1 program using ASHRAE Standards.

R-values of windows and doors, listed in manufacturers' catalogs, indicate the energy efficiency of the unit. Higher R-values indicate better insulating properties. Top-quality windows can have an R-value as high as 4.0. Exterior doors with R-values above 10 are considered energy-efficient.

(continued)

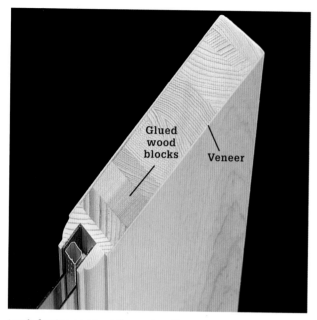

Look for "core-block" construction when choosing exterior wooden doors. Core-block doors are made from layers of glued or laminated wood blocks covered with a veneer. Because the direction of the wood grain alternates, core-block doors are not likely to warp.

Before ordering, find your wall thickness by measuring the jamb width on an existing window or door. Manufacturers will customize the frame jambs to match whatever wall construction you have. Many companies also build custom doors up to 14 ft. tall and 5 ft. wide.

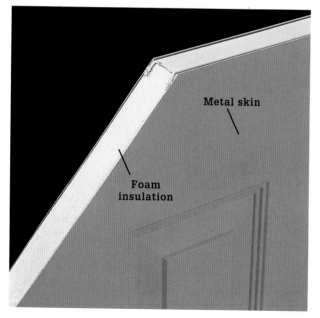

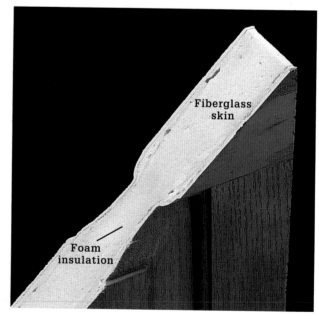

Steel entry doors are well insulated. Steel doors are less expensive than wooden doors and require little maintenance. Although steel is susceptible to dents and rust, it is used for about 70% of all exterior doors sold to homeowners.

Fiberglass doors are expensive, but they are sturdy, have excellent insulating values, and require little maintenance. The fiberglass surface is designed to have the texture of wood and can be stained or painted different colors.

Garage Door Materials

Aluminum and glass garage doors turn an otherwise dull door opening into an attractive curb feature in its own right. Translucent glass allows sunlight through to brighten up the garage interior, but it doesn't advertise the contents inside to passersby.

Wood garage doors offer excellent durability, security, and aesthetic appeal. They're available in a range of styles and wood types. The only drawback to wood, however, is that you'll need to periodically strip and refinish those that are stained and varnished rather than painted.

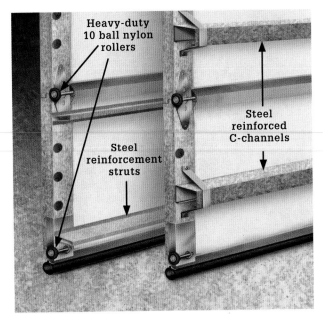

Heavy-duty 10 ball nylon rollers

Steel reinforced C-channels

Steel reinforcement struts

Insulated steel garage doors are the popular choice by most homeowners. State-of-the-art metal finishes mean that today's steel door will resist fading and corrosion for many years and, depending on quality, even the full life of the door.

Depending on where you live, your garage doors may need to withstand high winds, wind-driven rain, or heavy snowfalls. Be sure to invest in garage doors reinforced with heavy-duty rollers, reinforced bracing, and struts. These features are also important on oversized or frequently used doors.

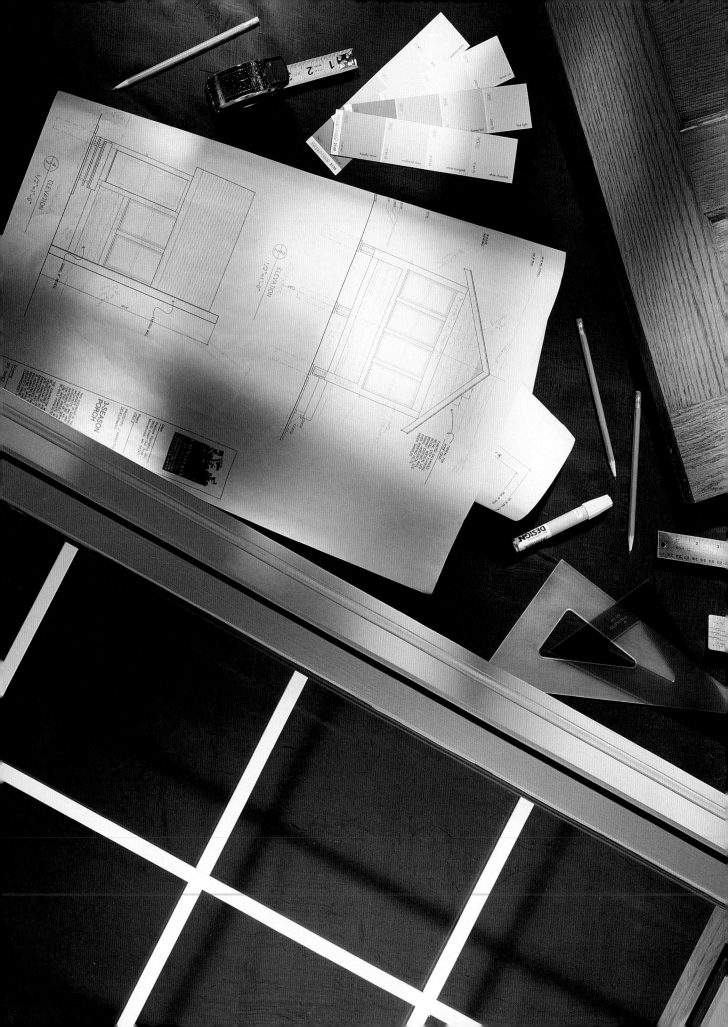

Planning for Windows & Entryways

Once you've got a feel for the style of windows or doors you'd like to add to your home, the next step involves careful planning. In terms of the "product" side of your project, you'll need to consider how a new door or window meets your needs for energy efficiency, durability, ease of maintenance, and security.

There's also the equally important matter of how a new window or door will impact your home's livability. Will it face a direction that takes advantage of sunlight and prevailing breezes or make the room stifling hot in mid July? Adding a window to a living space also brings matters of egress into consideration. Building codes mandate that your project window must satisfy these requirements. Likewise a new doorway into a room can improve traffic patterns, but it can also make furniture more difficult to arrange in the space.

This chapter will help you plan wisely so that your new project truly satisfies you and benefits your home.

This chapter includes:

- Getting Started
- Evaluating Your Needs
- Universal Design
- Planning & Preparation
- Tools Needed
- Framing Anatomy

Getting Started

Windows and doors link your home to the outside world and are the most important design elements in any remodeling project. Adding new windows makes your home brighter and makes living spaces feel larger. Replacing a shabby entry door can make your home more inviting to guests and more secure against intruders. Interior passage doors can be used to accent a decorating style as well as ensure privacy between the rooms they divide.

When planning your remodeling project, remember that the choice and placement of windows and doors will affect your lifestyle. For example, a room with too many windows may let in wonderful natural light and a great view, but make furniture placement difficult. Installing a large patio door is a good way to join indoor and outdoor living areas, but it also changes the traffic patterns through your home and affects your personal privacy. Rooms with too many doors seem smaller because much of the floor space is used for traffic patterns and must be reserved for the doors to swing freely.

Window combinations can be custom-ordered from the manufacturer. Unusual shapes work well in contemporary-design homes, and they can also help create a visual accent in traditional-design homes.

In addition to style, consider the size and placement of any windows and doors as you plan the project. Most homeowners install new windows to provide a better view, but remember that a well-positioned window can also reduce heating and cooling bills by serving as a passive solar collector in the cooler months and by improving ventilation in the summer.

Balanced

Mismatched

Choose new windows and doors that match the style and shape of your home. For traditional home styles, strive for balance when planning for windows and doors. In the colonial-style home shown on the top, carefully chosen window units match the scale and proportions of the structure, creating a pleasing symmetry. In the home on the bottom, mismatched windows conflict with the traditional look of the home.

Evaluating Your Needs

There are many good reasons a homeowner may choose to replace windows and doors. Some of the options discussed in this section might apply to your project, or you may have other reasons. Those reasons may change as your living situation changes, producing new opportunities to use different products.

Especially in older homes, the need to reduce energy loss is high on the list. This section discusses many of the telltale signs that indicate a home is not as efficient as it could be. Installing the newer styles of window with the advanced technology of low-E glass and increased insulation factors is certainly one way to lower energy costs year-round. Entry doors can be a source of energy loss also, and today's variety of well-insulated units can satisfy almost any need.

Weatherizing your existing windows and doors is an instant way of making your home more energy-efficient. See pages 254 to 263 for some easy weatherizing tips.

Increasing light and ventilation are other ways new windows can enhance the comfort and usability of your home. Well-placed windows can take advantage of natural exposure and prevailing breezes. They can also work to limit those factors, as you wish. Doors with glass panels offer stylish new ways to connect rooms within the home. They can make rooms seem more accessible while still providing separation.

Perhaps a room needs an additional exit. A new door can certainly provide another avenue to the rest of the home. A window can increase the use of a basement area. For example, by meeting the code requirements for egress windows, a basement room can legally function as a bedroom.

For many people, security is a concern. New windows and doors with state-of-the-art construction and locks can help put your mind at ease. There are also a multitude of ways to make your home more secure without replacing windows and doors. Pages 168 to 179 discuss several tips and illustrate how to install various safety devices.

Improving the usability of a space warrants adding or replacing windows and doors. Sometimes the sheer aesthetics of having a new unit is all the reason you need.

Windows play an integral part in the interior design of your home. They can enhance your lifestyle by influencing the way you use a room, making the outdoors seem to come inside and become a focal point of the room. A new entry door can certainly make a home more inviting to guests, as well as to the residents.

As with any remodeling project, be sure to check with your local building inspector to find out whether you need permits before beginning the work.

Before making a substantial investment in a new window or door, think carefully about why you're replacing it, the features you want, and how it will impact the room it's destined to improve.

Windows and doors are portals to the outside world, improving access to natural light and ventilation while safeguarding against intrusion.

Natural Light & Ventilation

Here are a few guidelines to keep in mind if you are considering new windows to increase the light and ventilation in a room:

- Windows must open and operate from inside, and they must exit to a street, alley, yard, court, or porch.
- Windows must equal at least 8% of the floor area in habitable rooms. The minimum openable area of a window must equal at least 4% of the room's floor area.
- In bathrooms, windows must be at least 3 sq. ft., and at least half of the window must open.
- Glass block, frosted, leaded, and stained glass are specialty glasses that also can be used to bring in natural sunlight, while preserving privacy.
- Casement windows are best for ventilation; they circulate the most air because the entire window opens.

Home Security

When thinking about the security of your home, the most obvious component is the exterior entry door. It should have secure hinges and a good lockset attached; a deadbolt is best. You should also have at least one way to see who is outside the door. If the door does not have a window that provides a clear view of visitors, then add a sidelight or a peephole.

Specialty doors, such as sliding patio doors and French doors, have some unique security challenges because of their large size and the fact that they are mostly glass. Think of them as big windows. Add extra locks and install screws to prevent the panels from being pried from their tracks.

Most local hardware or home stores carry a large variety of inexpensive locks and security devices available for any type of window or door you may have in your home.

Building Codes & Permits

Building permits are required for any remodeling project that involves a change or addition to your home's structure or mechanical systems.

Most simple window and door replacements do not require building permits. Check with your local building department if you're unsure about how the regulations might apply to your project.

Building permits are issued to ensure your remodeling project meets local building codes, which establish material standards, structural requirements, and installation guidelines for your project. In short, they ensure that your work is done properly.

Building permits are required by law, and getting caught without them can result in fines from the city and possibly trouble with your insurance company.

Also, work done without permits can cause problems if you try to sell your home.

Most local building codes follow the national codes, such as the National Electrical Code, but they are adapted to meet the demands of local conditions and legislation. Keep in mind that local codes always supersede national codes.

Before issuing permits, your local building department will require plans and cost estimates for your project. After your plans have been approved, you must pay permit fees, which are based on the cost of the project. You'll also learn what inspections are required and when you should call for them.

Once issued, a building permit typically is good for 180 days.

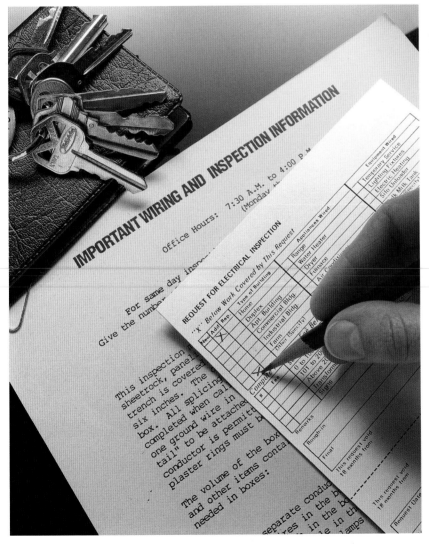

Before embarking on a window or entryway project, be sure to contact your local building department to see if you'll need an approved permit.

Egress Window Considerations

If your home has an unfinished or partially finished basement, it's an enticing and sensible place to expand your practical living space. Another bedroom or two, a game room, or maybe a spacious home office are all possibilities. However, unless your basement has a walk-out doorway, you'll need to add an egress window to make your new living space meet most building codes. That's because the International Residential Code (IRC) requires two forms of escape for every living space—an exit door and a window large enough for you to climb out of or for an emergency responder to enter.

Code mandates that a below-ground egress window will have a minimum opening area of at least 5.7 square feet. There are stipulations about how this open area can be proportioned: The window must be at least 20" wide and 24" high when open. Additionally, the installed window's sill height must be within 44" of the basement floor to permit easy escape. Standard basement windows do not meet these requirements. A large egress window requires an oversized window well. The well must be at least 36" wide and project 36" or more from the foundation. If the window well is deeper than 44", it must have a fixed ladder for escape.

What does this all mean for the ambitious do-it-yourselfer? The good news is that if you've got the nerve to cut an oversized opening in your home's foundation, and you don't mind spending some quality time with a shovel, installing a basement egress window is a manageable project. Here's a case where careful planning, a building permit, and some help can save you considerable money over hiring the work done by a contractor. To see a complete step-by-step egress window and well installation, see pages 92 to 97. Contact your local building department to learn more about specific egress requirements that apply to your area.

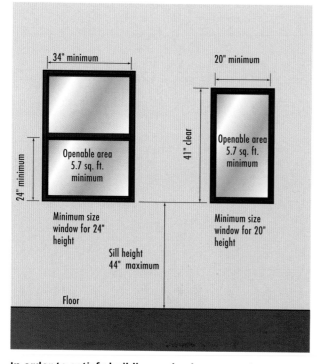

In order to satisfy building codes for egress, a basement window must have a minimum opening of 5.7 sq. ft. through one sash, with at least 20" of clear width and 24" of clear height. Casement, double-hung, and sliding window styles can be used, as long as their dimensions for width and height meet these minimum requirements.

Egress window wells must be at least 36" wide and project 36" from the foundation. Those deeper than 44" must have a means of escape, such as a tiered design that forms steps or an attached ladder. Drainage at the bottom of the well should extend down to the foundation footing drain, with pea gravel used as the drainage material.

Universal Design

Barrier-free living and universal design are intended for all people. While standard home and product design are based on the "average" person—that is, the average adult male—not everyone fits into that category. Some people are short, some tall; some have difficulty walking, while others walk ably but find bending difficult. And physical abilities change constantly, as do family situations. By incorporating the concepts of barrier-free living and universal design into your remodeling plans, you can create spaces that work better for everyone who lives in or visits your home, regardless of their size, age, or ability.

These "people-friendly" or "high-access" concepts are simply good design that improves everyday situations. For example, wide doorways make passage easier for a person carrying a load of laundry as well as for someone in a wheelchair or using a walker; windows that are easy to open enable people to better ventilate a room, even the entire home. More a way of thinking than a set of rules, barrier-free living and universal design can be applied to any area of your home—from room layouts to door hardware. In all cases, these design concepts encourage independent living by creating a safe, comfortable environment.

Replacing windows and doors can be one of your first steps toward accommodating changes in the household—before those changes become problems. Adapting ideas that promote barrier-free living and universal design will make your everyday life easier. And, it will also make your home more appealing to a wide range of potential buyers, if you choose to sell.

Much of the information provided here comes from universal design specialists, specialty builders, and product manufacturers.

For more help with planning for barrier-free living and universal design adaptations, contact a qualified professional. As always, be sure that all aspects of your project meet local building code requirements.

Universal design is about accessibility, and no house feature restricts access more than stairs. With some clever landscaping the owners of this home were able to regrade the front yard to eliminate entryway stairs.

Planning & Preparation

An important early step in your remodeling project is to carefully measure the windows and doors that you wish to replace. You will use these measurements to purchase the new unit, and you must be sure it will fit in the opening.

To finalize your project ideas and make sure they will really work, the next step is to put all the information down on paper. There are two basic types of construction drawings: floor plans and elevation drawings. These drawings may be required if your project needs a building permit.

Floor plans show a room as seen from above. These are useful for showing overall room dimensions, layouts, and the relationship between neighboring rooms. Elevation drawings show a side view of a room, usually with one wall per drawing. Elevations are made for both the interior and exterior of a house and generally show more architectural detail than floor plans.

Both floor plans and elevation drawings provide you with a method for planning and recording structural and mechanical systems for your project. They also help the local building department to ensure your project meets code requirements.

If you will be doing several projects in a short time, you may want to draw a plan of each complete floor of the home. If you're doing one isolated project, you may want to draw the plan of just that room.

To create floor plans, draw one story at a time. First, measure each room from wall to wall. Transfer the room's dimensions onto 1/4" grid paper, using a scale of 1/4" = 1 ft. Label each room for its use and note its overall dimensions. Include wall thicknesses, which you can determine by measuring the widths of window and door jambs—do not include the trim.

Next, add these elements to your drawings:

- Windows and doors; note which way the doors swing.
- Stairs and their direction as it relates to each story.
- Permanent features such as plumbing fixtures, major appliances, countertops, built-in furniture, and fireplaces.
- Overhead features such as exposed beams or wall cabinets—use dashed lines.
- Plumbing, electrical, and HVAC elements. You may want a separate set of drawings for these mechanical elements and service lines.
- Overall dimensions measured from outside the home. Use these to check the accuracy of interior dimensions.
- To create elevation drawings, use the same 1/4" = 1 ft. scale, and draw everything you see on one wall (each room has four elevations). Include:
- Ceiling heights and the heights of significant features such as soffits and exposed beams.
- Windows, including the height and width of the sills and tops of the openings.
- Doors, including the heights (from the floor to the top of the opening) and widths.
- Trim and other decorative elements.

When your initial floor plans and elevations are done, use them to sketch your remodeling layout options. Use tissue overlays to show hidden elements or proposed changes to a plan. Photographs of your home's interior and exterior may also be helpful. Think creatively, and draw many different sketches; the more design options you consider, the better your final plans will be.

When you have completed your remodeling plans, draft your final drawings and create a materials list for the project.

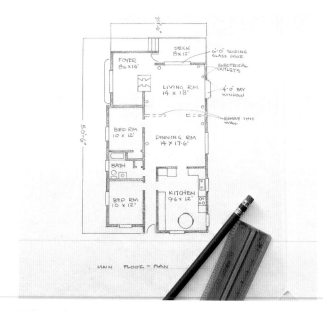

A floor plan can help you envision how a new door or window will impact the living space and traffic patterns.

Measuring Windows & Doors

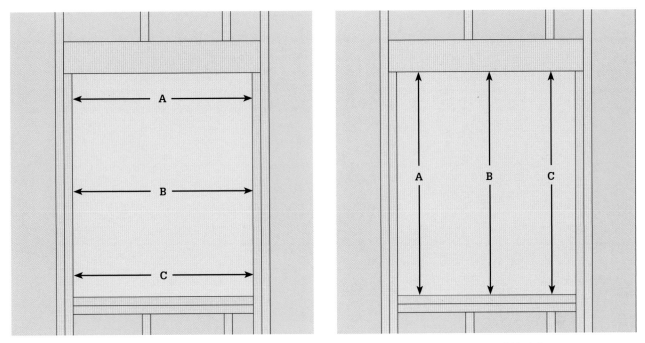

Determine the exact size of your new window or door by measuring the opening carefully. For the width (left), measure between the jack studs in three places: near the top, at the middle, and near the bottom of the opening. Use the same procedure for the height (right), measuring from the header to the sill near the left edge, at the middle, and near the right edge of the opening. Use the smallest measurement of each dimension for ordering the unit.

Working with Plans

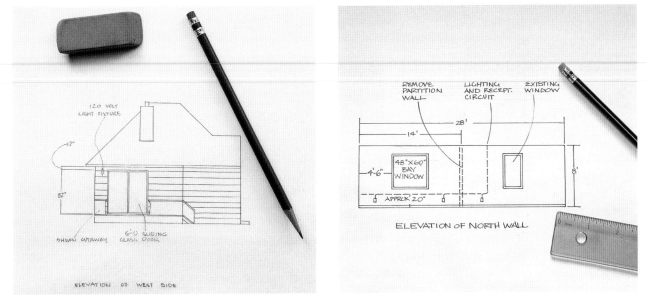

Create elevation drawings showing a side view layout of windows and doors, as viewed from both inside and outside the home. Indicate the size of windows and doors, ceiling heights, and the location of wiring and plumbing fixtures.

Window & Door Placement

One of the important considerations when deciding exactly where to install your new windows and doors is the environment. In some parts of the country, weather conditions change dramatically from season to season, as well as throughout the day and night.

Minimizing the number of windows and doors on the north side of a home may be important if you live with harsh winters. If you must deal with extreme heat or long hours of bright sunshine, you may consider fewer windows on the south and west sides of the home. No matter how energy-efficient your new windows and doors are, you will benefit from placing them to your best advantage.

Of course, prudent landscaping with trees, the use of eaves and overhangs, and controlling ventilation are other components to making your home comfortable year-round.

Changing the position of a door, or adding a second one, will definitely change the traffic pattern within a room. Be sure to consider whether that change will be positive or negative. Changing or adding windows may not change traffic movement through the room but it may well dramatically alter its focal point. More or larger windows can highlight a great view, but they can also reveal a poor view. Be sure to look outside the proposed window location to see what you might be bringing inside.

A unique type of interior design called feng shui has grown in popularity in recent years. It is an ancient Chinese method of constructing and optimizing residences to bring about happiness, abundance, and harmony. The goal of feng shui is to increase the amount of ch'i—or universal life force—in the home. It is believed that correctly placing windows and doors within a home encourages ch'i to circulate through the home, which has a positive influence on the residents.

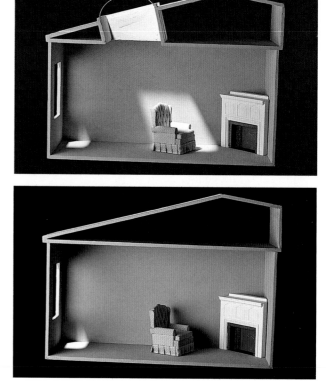

Traffic patterns through the home are determined by the placement of doors. Rooms with many doors seem smaller because traffic patterns consume much of the available space (top). When planning room layout, reserve plenty of space for doors to swing freely.

Consider the effect of sunlight when planning window positions. For example, when installing one skylight, choose a location and build the shaft to direct the light where you want it. A bank of several skylights can also dramatically change the ambience of the room.

Before You Begin

Be sure to check for hidden mechanicals in the work area before you begin the actual work on any project. You may need to shut off and reroute electrical wiring, plumbing pipes, and other utility lines. If you are not comfortable performing these tasks, hire a professional.

Then, to be absolutely sure of your drawings, you will want to physically plot out the locations for new windows and doors with masking tape. Always mark the full swinging arc of hinged doors. Use newspaper or cardboard to make full-sized cutouts of furniture, and use them to experiment with different room layouts. For barrier-free living and universal design, your floor plan should allow ample room around furniture: 22" around a bed; 36" around couches, chairs, and tables; 40" in front of dressers, chests, and closets.

Walk through the room along different paths to judge how the room elements will interact. Remember to allow a 40"-wide path for foot traffic across a room. Once you have found a pleasing layout, make final floor plan and elevation drawings (pages 38 and 39).

Physically plot out your project area with masking tape so you can plan for door swing as well as overall window or door sizing.

Checking the Room Layout

Careful planning can make your new windows and doors more accessible and easier to operate. Make sure they all have clear approach spaces and that windows are positioned at heights that accommodate small people and people in wheelchairs. See page 18 for tips on selecting new doors, windows, and their hardware when you're remodeling to incorporate universal design.

- Plan a clear approach space to each window, 30" deep × 48" wide.
- Position view windows at a maximum sill height of 30 to 36", so that children and seated people can see out. Lower sills may pose a safety risk to children; be sure to choose your window heights accordingly.
- Choose tempered glass for windows less than 18" from the floor or within 24" of a door, when required by local building codes.
- Position windows so that hardware is at a maximum height of 48" if the window is operable.

- Provide a clear, 48 × 48" approach space in front of each door. This includes an 18"- to 24"-wide space between the latch side of the door and an adjacent wall to allow users room to maneuver.
- Frame doorless openings at a minimum of 32" wide (36" preferred).
- Consider the swing direction when choosing doors that will open into the room.

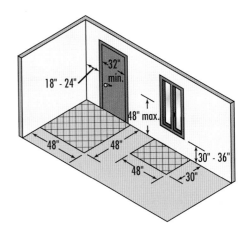

Tools Needed

Router

Random-orbit sander

Biscuit joiner

Circular saw

Compound power miter saw

Belt sander

Power planer

Finish sander

Jig saw

Reciprocating saw

Cordless drill

Table saw

Power Tools

Power tools allow you to work more quickly and accurately than with hand tools, and they make repetitive tasks like sawing, drilling, and sanding more enjoyable and efficient. Window and door projects will not require every power tool shown here, but you'll probably need at least a circular saw and drill/driver for most installation or renovation jobs. A reciprocating saw is handy for removing old windows and doors or for cutting through roofing and wall sheathing to create new openings. A miter saw or table saw is useful for highly accurate trim carpentry work such as installing window stools and aprons or door casings.

Purchase power tools as you need them, keeping in mind that while the cheapest tool is not always your best option, the most expensive and powerful is probably not necessary either. Cheaper tools generally sacrifice precision, while the most expensive tools are made for people who use them every day, not just occasionally. Mid-priced power tools offer good compromise between economy and quality for the do-it-yourselfer.

Layout Tools

A core group of layout tools is essential for window and door projects, particularly when you are creating new openings for windows and doors or installing framing. This collection will serve you equally well for most other do-it-yourself projects also. A tape measure, squares, graduated steel rule, and T-bevel will help you measure and reproduce angles accurately. Short and long levels and a plumb bob are important tools for establishing square and plumb reference surfaces or lines. A carpenter's pencil has thicker lead than a standard pencil, which provides bolder reference lines and stays sharp longer. For creating longer reference lines, snap a chalk line between two reference points instead; it creates a bright, straight, and smudge-proof layout line that's easy to follow with saws.

Construction Tools

Whether you are cutting through wall sheathing, pulling nails, tacking a window flange, or prying off doorstop moldings, you'll need a basic collection of construction tools to get these tasks done. You probably have many of them in your tool collection already. For the demolition stages of your window and door projects, a dust mask, gloves, pry bars, drywall saw, and chisels are invaluable. Construction phases will require a comfortable hammer and nail sets in various sizes, screwdrivers, a small handsaw, and possibly a block plane or files. For speedier and even simpler fastening, consider using a framing or brad nailer powered by a small air compressor. If you don't want to buy these tools, they're inexpensive to rent and widely available. Whatever stage of a project you're doing, be sure to wear appropriate protective gear. Safety glasses and hearing protection are just as important as a good hammer in the toolbox. Get in the habit of wearing safety gear whenever you're using hand and power tools.

Steel rule, 4-ft. level, Tape measure, Wallboard square, Carpenter's pencil, 2-ft. level, Plumb bob, Chalk line, T-bevel, Stud finder, Combination square

Block plane, Handsaw, Hammer, End nippers, Utility knife, Dust mask, File, Nail set, Screwdriver, Cold chisel, Aviation snips, Pry bar, Putty knife, Ear plugs, Wood rasp, Sheetrock saw, Safety glasses, Ear protection, Gloves, Staple gun, Pneumatic brad nailer

Framing Anatomy

Many remodeling projects, including adding new exterior doors or windows, require that you remove one or more studs in a load-bearing wall to create an opening. When planning your project, remember that new openings require a permanent support beam called a header above the removed studs to carry the structural load.

The required size for the header is set by local building codes and varies according to the width of the rough opening. For a window or door opening, a header can be built from two pieces of 2" dimensional lumber sandwiched around ½" plywood (chart, right). When a large portion of a load-bearing wall (or an entire wall) is removed, a laminated beam product can be used to make the new header.

If you will be removing more than one wall stud, make temporary supports to carry the structural load until the header is installed.

Recommended Header Sizes ▸

Rough Opening Width	Recommended Header Construction
Up to 3 ft.	½" plywood between two 2 × 4s
3 ft. to 5 ft.	½" plywood between two 2 × 6s
5 ft. to 7 ft.	½" plywood between two 2 × 8s
7 ft. to 8 ft.	½" plywood between two 2 × 10s

Recommended header sizes shown above are suitable for projects where a full story and roof are located above the rough opening. This chart is intended for rough estimates only. For actual requirements, contact an architect or your local building inspector.

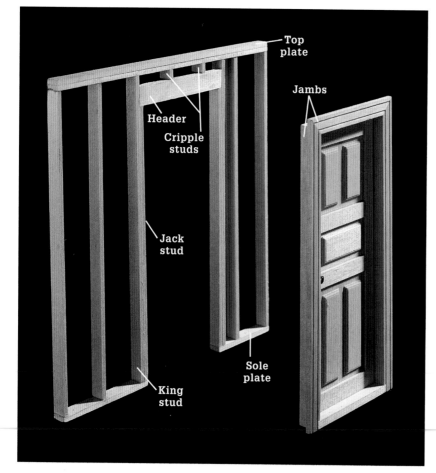

Top plate

Jambs

Header

Cripple studs

Jack stud

King stud

Sole plate

Door opening: The structural load above the door is carried by cripple studs that rest on a header. The ends of the header are supported by jack studs (also known as trimmer studs) and king studs that transfer the load to the sole plate and the foundation of the house. The rough opening for a door should be 1" wider and ½" taller than the dimensions of the door unit, including the jambs. This extra space lets you adjust the door unit during installation.

Framing Options for Window & Door Openings (new lumber shown in yellow) ▸

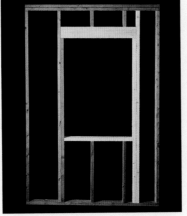

Using an existing opening avoids the need for new framing. This is a good option in homes with masonry exteriors, which are difficult to alter. Order a replacement unit that is 1" narrower and ½" shorter than the rough opening.

Enlarging an existing opening simplifies the framing. In many cases, you can use an existing king stud and jack stud to form one side of the new opening.

Framing a new opening is the only solution when you're installing a window or door where none existed or when you're replacing a unit with one that is much larger.

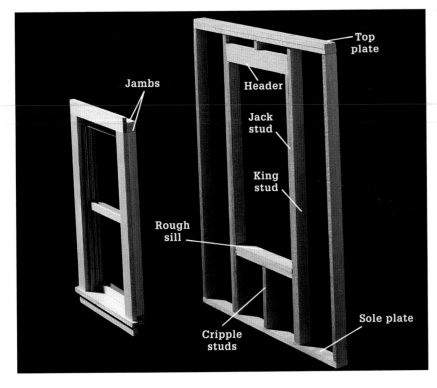

Jambs • Top plate • Header • Jack stud • King stud • Rough sill • Cripple studs • Sole plate

Window opening: The structural load above the window is carried by cripple studs resting on a header. The ends of the header are supported by jack studs and king studs, which transfer the load to the sole plate and the foundation of the house. The rough sill, which helps anchor the window unit but carries no structural weight, is supported by cripple studs. To provide room for adjustments during installation, the rough opening for a window should be 1" wider and ½" taller than the window unit, including the jambs.

Replacing Windows

This chapter will help guide you through the process of framing a wall opening for a window and then installing the window. You'll also learn how to retrofit an existing window with replacement sash. Before you begin any of these projects, plan carefully so you're confident about window placement and sizing issues. If you're unfamiliar with how to remove exterior siding, which may be a necessary step in your project, turn to page 280.

Be sure to read the installation manual that comes with your window for pertinent, additional information. Since those instructions will impact your product warranty, follow them carefully when they differ from the step-by-step instructions shown here.

This chapter includes:

- New Window Sash
- Framing & Installing Windows
- Garden Windows
- Bay Windows
- Glass Block Windows
- Skylights
- Tubular Lights
- Basement Egress Windows

New Window Sash

If you're looking to replace or improve old single- or double-hung windows, consider using sash-replacement kits. They can give you energy-efficient, maintenance-free windows without changing the outward appearance of your home or breaking your budget.

Unlike prime window replacement, which changes the entire window and frame, or pocket window replacement, in which a complete window unit is set into the existing frame, sash replacement uses the original window jambs, eliminating the need to alter exterior or interior walls or trim. Installing a sash-replacement kit involves little more than removing the old window stops and sashes and installing new vinyl jamb liners and wood or vinyl sash. And all of the work can be done from inside your home.

Most sash-replacement kits offer tilt features and other contemporary conveniences. Kits are available in vinyl, aluminum, or wood construction with various options for color and glazing, energy efficiency, security features, and noise reduction.

Nearly all major window manufacturers offer sash-replacement kits designed to fit their own windows. You can also order custom kits that are sized to your specific window dimensions. A good fit is essential to the performance of your new windows. Review the tips shown on the next page for measuring your existing windows, and follow the manufacturer's instructions for the best fit.

Tools & Materials ▶

- Sill-bevel gauge
- Flat pry bar
- Scissors
- Screwdriver
- Nail set
- Sash-replacement kit
- 1" galvanized roofing nails
- Fiberglass insulation
- Finish nails
- Wood-finishing materials
- Torpedo Level

Upgrade old, leaky windows with new, energy-efficient sash-replacement kits. Kits are available in a variety of styles to match your existing windows or to add a new decorative accent to your home. Most kits offer natural or painted interior surfaces and a choice of outdoor surface finishes.

How to Install a New Window Sash

Measure the width of the existing window at the top, middle, and bottom of the frame. Use the smallest measurement, then reduce the figure by ⅜". Measure the height of the existing window from the head jamb to the point where the outside edge of the bottom sash meets the sill. Reduce the figure by ⅜". *Note: Manufacturers' specifications for window sizing may vary.*

Check for a straight, level, and plumb sill, side, and head jambs using a torpedo level. Measure the frame diagonally to check for square (if the diagonal measurements are equal, the frame is square). If the frame is not square, check with the sash-kit manufacturer: Most window kits can accommodate some deviation in frame dimensions.

Carefully remove the interior stops from the side jambs, using a putty knife or pry bar. Save the stops for reinstallation.

With the bottom sash down, cut the cord holding the sash, balancing weight on each side of the sash. Let the weights and cords fall into the weight pockets.

(continued)

Lift out the bottom sash. Remove the parting stops from the head and side jambs. (The parting stops are the strips of wood that separate the top and bottom sash.) Cut the sash cords for the top sash, then lift out the top sash. Remove the sash-cord pulleys. If possible, pull the weights from the weight pockets at the bottom of the side jambs, then fill the weight pockets with fiberglass insulation. Repair any parts of the jambs that are rotted or damaged.

Position the jamb-liner brackets, and fasten them to the jambs with 1" galvanized roofing nails. Place one bracket approximately 4" from the head jamb and one 4" from the sill. Leave ¹⁄₁₆" clearance between the blind stop and the jamb-liner bracket. Install any remaining brackets, spacing them evenly along the jambs.

Position any gaskets or weatherstripping provided for the jamb liners. Carefully position each liner against its brackets and snap it into place. When both liners are installed, set the new parting stop into the groove of the existing head jamb, and fasten it with small finish nails. Install a vinyl sash stop in the interior track at the top of each liner to prevent the bottom sash from being opened too far.

Set the sash control mechanism, using a slotted screwdriver. Gripping the screwdriver firmly, slide down the mechanism until it is about 9" above the sill, then turn the screwdriver to lock the mechanism and prevent it from springing upward. The control mechanisms are spring-loaded—do not let them go until they are locked in place. Set the mechanism in each of the four sash channels.

Install the top sash into the jamb liners. Set the cam pivot on one side of the sash into the outside channel. Tilt the sash, and set the cam pivot on the other side of the sash. Make sure both pivots are set above the sash control mechanisms. Holding the sash level, tilt it up, depress the jamb liners on both sides, and set the sash in the vertical position in the jamb liners. Once the sash is in position, slide it down until the cam pivots contact the locking terminal assemblies.

Install the bottom sash into the jamb liners, setting it into the inside sash channels. When the bottom sash is set in the vertical position, slide it down until it engages the control mechanisms. Open and close both sash to make sure they operate properly.

Reinstall the stops that you removed in step 1. Fasten them with finish nails, using the old nail holes, or drill new pilot holes for the nails.

Check the tilt operation of the bottom sash to make sure the stops do not interfere. Remove the labels, and clean the windows. Paint or varnish the new sash as desired.

Framing & Installing Windows

Correct framing techniques will ensure ease of installation and keep your windows operating smoothly.

Many windows must be custom-ordered several weeks in advance. To save time, you can complete the interior framing before the window unit arrives, but be sure you have the exact dimensions of the window unit before building the frame. Do not remove the outside wall surface until you have the window and accessories and are ready to install them.

Follow the manufacturer's specifications for rough opening size when framing for a window. The listed opening is usually 1" wider and ½" taller than the actual dimensions of the window unit. The following pages show techniques for wood-frame houses with platform framing.

If your house has balloon framing where wall studs pass continuously from one floor to the next, use the method shown on page 271 to install a header. Consult a professional to install a window on the second story of a balloon-framed house.

If your house has masonry walls or if you are installing polymer-coated windows, you may want to attach your window using masonry clips instead of nails.

If your home's exterior has siding or is stucco, see pages 285 to 287 for tips on removing these surfaces and making the opening.

Tools & Materials ▸

Tape measure	10d common nails,
Pencil	1" galvanized roofing
Combination square	nails
Hammer	Shims
Level	2× lumber
Circular saw	⅛" plywood
Handsaw	Building paper
Pry bar	Drip edge
Nippers	10d galvanized casing
Drill	nails
Reciprocating saw	8d casing nails
Stapler	Fiberglass insulation
Nail set	Paintable silicone caulk
Caulk gun	

How to Frame a Window Opening

1

Prepare the project site and remove the interior wall surfaces (pages 266 and 271). Measure and mark the rough opening width on the sole plate. Mark the locations of the jack studs and king studs on the sole plate. Where practical, use the existing studs as king studs.

2

Measure and cut the king studs, as needed, to fit between the sole plate and the top plate. Position the king studs and toenail them to the sole plate with 10d nails.

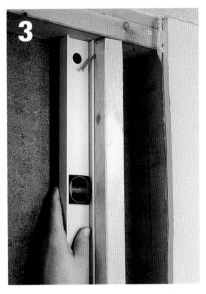

3

Check the king studs with a level to make sure they are plumb, then toenail them to the top plate with 10d nails.

4

Measuring from the floor, mark the top of the rough opening on one of the king studs. This line represents the bottom of the window header. For most windows, the recommended rough opening is ½" taller than the height of the window frame.

5

Measure and mark where the top of the window header will fit against the king studs. The header size depends on the distance between the king studs. Use a carpenter's level to extend the lines across the old studs to the opposite king stud.

6

Measure down from the header line and mark the double rough sill on the king stud. Use a carpenter's level to extend the lines across the old studs to the opposite king stud. Make temporary supports (pages 268 to 271) if removing more than one stud.

(continued)

7

Bottom
of sill

Set a circular saw to its maximum blade depth, then cut through the old studs along the lines marking the bottom of the rough sill and along the lines marking the top of the header. Do not cut the king studs. On each stud, make an additional cut about 3" above the sill cut. Finish the cuts with a handsaw.

8

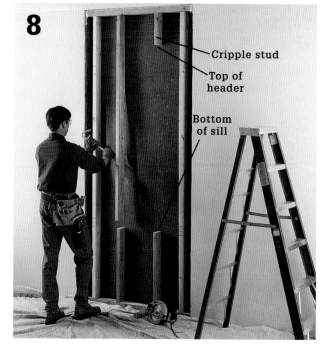

Cripple stud

Top of
header

Bottom
of sill

Knock out the 3" stud sections, then tear out the old studs inside the rough opening, using a pry bar. Clip away any exposed nails, using nippers. The remaining sections of the cut studs will serve as cripple studs for the window.

9

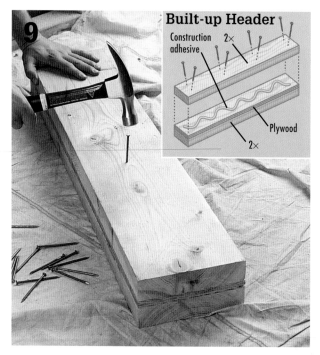

Built-up Header

Construction
adhesive

2×

Plywood

2×

Build a header to fit between the king studs on top of the jack studs, using two pieces of 2× lumber sandwiched around ½" plywood.

10

Cut two jack studs to reach from the top of the sole plate to the bottom header lines on the king studs. Nail the jack studs to the king studs with 10d nails driven every 12". *Note: On a balloon-framed house the jack studs will reach to the sill plate.*

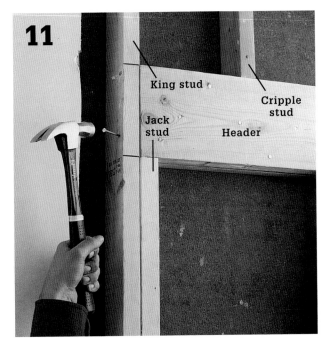

Position the header on the jack studs, using a hammer if necessary. Attach the header to the king studs, jack studs, and cripple studs, using 10d nails.

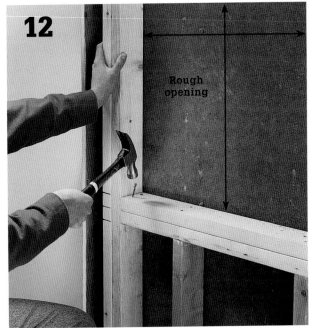

Build the rough sill to reach between the jack studs by nailing a pair of 2 × 4s together. Position the rough sill on the cripple studs, and nail it to the jack studs and cripple studs with 10d nails.

How to Install a Replacement Window with a Nailing Flange

Remove the existing window (see page 273), and set the new window into the rough opening. Center it left to right, and shim beneath the sill to level it. On the exterior side, measure out from the window on all sides, and mark the siding for the width of the brick molding you'll install around the new window. Extend layout lines to mark where you'll cut the siding.

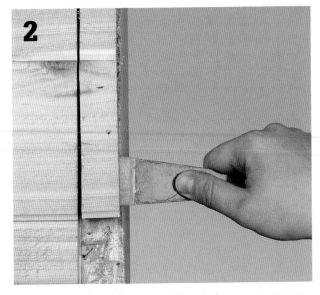

Remove exterior siding around the window area to expose the wall sheathing. Use a zip tool to separate vinyl siding for removal or use a pry bar and hammer to remove wood clapboard. For more on removing exterior surfaces, see pages 280 to 287.

(continued)

Cover the sill and rough opening framing members with self-adhesive, rolled flashing. Apply additional strips of flashing behind the siding and up the sill flashing. Finish flashing with a strip along the header. The flashing should cover the front edges and sides of the opening members.

Apply a bead of silicone caulk around the back face of the window flange, then set it into the rough opening, centering it side-to-side in the opening. Tack the window in place by driving one roofing nail partway through the top flange. On the interior side, level and plumb the window, using shims to make any necessary adjustments.

Tack the window to the header at one end of the nailing flange, using a 1" galvanized roofing nail. Drive a roofing nail through the other top corner of the flange to hold the window in place, then secure the flange all around the window with more roofing nails. Apply strips of rolled, self-adhesive flashing to cover the window flanges. Start with a strip that covers the bottom flange, then cover the side flanges, overlapping the bottom flashing and extending 8 to 10" above the window. Complete the flashing with a strip along the top, overlapping the side flashing.

Install a piece of metal drip edge behind the siding and above the window. Secure it with silicone caulk only.

Cut and attach brick molding around the window, leaving a slight gap between the brick molding and the window frame. Use 8d galvanized casing nails driven into pilot holes to secure the brick molding to the rough framing. Miter the corner joints. Reinstall the siding in the window installation area, trimming as needed.

Use high-quality caulk to fill the gap between the brick molding and the siding. On the interior side, fill gaps between the window frame and surrounding framing with foam backer rod, low-expansion foam, or fiberglass insulation. Install the interior casing.

Tip Installation Variation: Masonry Clips ▸

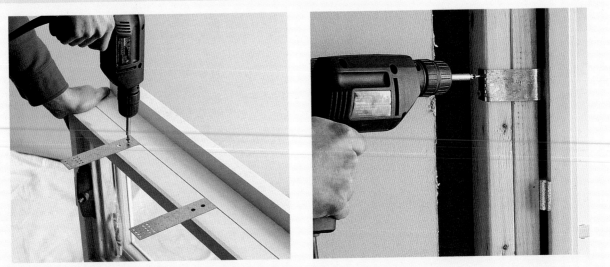

Use metal masonry clips when the brick molding on a window cannot be nailed because it rests against a masonry or brick surface. The masonry clips hook into precut grooves in the window jambs (above, left) and are attached to the jambs with screws. After the window unit is positioned in the rough opening, the masonry clips are bent around the framing members and anchored with screws (above, right). *Note: Masonry clips can also be used in ordinary lap siding installations if you want to avoid making nail holes in the smooth surface of the brick moldings. For example, windows that are precoated with polymer-based paint can be installed with masonry clips so that the brick moldings are not punctured with nails.*

How to Install a Round-Top Window

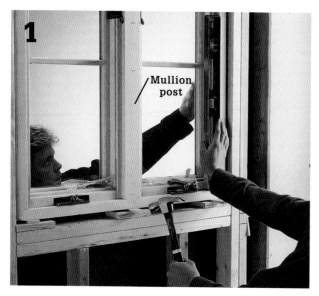

Remove the exterior wall surface as directed on pages 280 to 287, then test-fit the window, centering it in the rough opening. Support the window with wood blocks and shims placed under the side jambs and mullion post. Check to make sure the window is plumb and level, and adjust the shims, if necessary.

Trace the outline of the brick molding on the wood siding. Remove the window after finishing the outline. *Note: If you have vinyl or metal siding, you should have enlarged the outline to make room for the extra J-channel moldings required by these sidings.*

Tips for Framing a Round-top Window ▶

Create a template to help you mark the rough opening on the sheathing. Scribe the outline of the curved frame on cardboard, allowing an extra ½" for adjustments within the rough opening. A ¼ × 1¼" metal washer makes a good spacer for scribing the outline. Cut out the template along the scribed line.

Tape the template to the sheathing, with the top flush against the header. Use the template as a guide for attaching diagonal framing members across the top corners of the framed opening. The diagonal members should just touch the template. Outline the template on the sheathing as a guide for cutting the exterior wall surface.

Cut the siding along the outline just down to the sheathing. For a round-top window, use a reciprocating saw held at a low angle. For straight cuts, use a circular saw adjusted so the blade cuts through only the siding. Use a sharp chisel to complete the cuts at the corners.

Cut 8"-wide strips of building paper and slide them between the siding and sheathing around the entire window opening. Bend the paper around the framing members and staple it in place. Work from the bottom up, so each piece overlaps the piece below. *Note: You can also use adhesive-backed, rolled flashing instead of building paper.*

Cut a length of drip edge to fit over the top of the window, then slide it between the siding and building paper. For round-top windows, use flexible vinyl drip edge; for rectangular windows, use rigid metal drip edge (inset).

Insert the window in the opening, and push the brick molding tight against the sheathing. Nail through the brick molding, as usual, to secure the window in the opening.

How to Frame a Window in a Gable Wall

Although most windows in a home are located in load-bearing exterior walls, standard attic windows are commonly located in gable walls, which often are non-loadbearing. Installing a window in a non-loadbearing gable wall is fairly simple and doesn't require a temporary support for the framing. Some gable walls, however, are load-bearing: A common sign is a heavy structural ridge beam that supports the rafters from underneath, rather than merely at the rafter ends. Hire a contractor to build window frames in load-bearing gable walls. If you aren't certain what type of wall you have, consult a professional.

A common problem with framing in a gable wall is that the positions of the floor joists may make it difficult to attach new studs to the wall's sole plate. One solution is to install an extra-long header and sill between two existing studs, positioning them at the precise heights for the rough opening. You can then adjust the width of the rough opening by installing vertical studs between the header and sill.

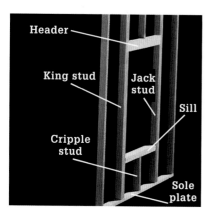

Window frames have full-length king studs, as well as jack studs that support the header. The sill defines the bottom of the rough opening.

Tools & Materials ▸

Circular saw
Handsaw
Plumb bob
T-bevel
4-ft. level
Combination square
Reciprocating saw

Framed window or door unit
2 × 4 lumber
16d, 10d, and 8d common nails
½"-thick plywood
Construction adhesive

Determine the rough opening width by measuring the window unit and adding 1". Add 3" to that dimension to get the distance between the king studs. Mark the locations of the king studs onto the sole plate of the gable wall.

Using a plumb bob, transfer the king-stud marks from the sole plate to the sloping top plates of the gable wall.

Cut the king studs to length, angle-cutting the top ends so they meet flush with the top plates. Fasten each king stud in place by toenailing the ends with three 8d nails.

Find the height of the rough opening by measuring the height of the window unit and adding ½". Measure up from where the finished floor height will be, and mark the top of the sill. Make a second mark for the bottom of the sill, 3" down from the top mark.

Measure up from the top sill mark, and mark the height of the rough opening (bottom of header). Make another mark 3½" up, to indicate the top of the header. Using a level, transfer all of these marks to the other king stud and to all intermediate studs.

Draw level cutting lines across the intermediate studs at the marks for the bottom of the sill and top of the header. Cut along the lines with a reciprocating saw, then remove the cutout portions. The remaining stud sections will serve as cripple studs.

Cut the jack studs to reach from the sole plate to the bottom header marks on the king studs. Nail the jack studs to the inside faces of the king studs using 10d common nails driven every 16".

Build a built-up header with 2 × 4s and plywood (page 54). Size it to fit snugly between king studs. Set header on top of jack studs. Nail through king studs into header with 16d nails, then toenail jack studs and cripple studs to header using 8d nails.

Build a sill to fit snugly between jack studs by nailing together two 2 × 4s. Position the sill at the top sill markings, and toenail it to the jack studs. Toenail the cripple studs to the sill. See pages 280 to 287 to remove the exterior wall surface and pages 55 to 57 to install the window.

Garden Windows

Although often found in kitchens, a garden window is an attractive option for nearly any room in your home. Projecting out from the wall 16 to 24", garden windows add space to a room, making it feel larger. The glass roof and box-like design make them ideal growing environments for plants or display areas for collectibles. Garden windows also typically include front- or side-opening windows. These allow for ventilation and are usually available in either awning or casement style.

Home stores often stock garden windows in several common sizes. However, it may be difficult to locate a stock window that will fit in your existing window rough opening. In cases like this you must rebuild the rough opening to the proper size. It may be worth the added expense to custom-order your garden window to fit into the existing rough opening.

The large amount of glass in a garden window has a direct effect on the window's energy efficiency. When purchasing a garden window, as a minimum, look for double-pane glass with low-emissivity (low-E) coatings. More expensive super-efficient types of glass are available for severely cold climates.

Installation methods for garden windows vary by manufacturer. Some units include a nailing flange that attaches to the framing and holds the window against the house. Other models hang on a separate mounting frame that attaches to the outside of the house. In this project, the garden window has a built-in mounting sleeve that slides into the rough opening and is attached directly to the rough framing.

Tools & Materials ▸

Tape measure	Shims
Hammer	Exterior trim
Level	Building paper
Framing square	3" screws
Circular saw	Drip edge
Wood chisel	Construction adhesive
Stapler	4d siding nails
Drill and bits	8d galvanized casing
Caulking gun	nails
Utility knife	Interior trim
Garden window kit	Paintable silicone caulk
Wood strips	
2 × 4s	

A garden window's glass roof makes it an ideal sun spot for houseplants, and it can also help a room feel larger.

How to Install a Garden Window

1

Prepare the project site and remove the interior and exterior trim, then remove the existing window (page 273).

2

Check the rough opening measurements to verify the correct window sizing. The rough opening should be about ½" larger than the window height and width. If necessary, attach wood strips to the rough framing as spacers to bring the opening to the required size.

3

Use a level to check that the sill of the rough opening is level and the side jambs are plumb. Use a framing square to make sure each corner is square. The rough framing must be in good condition in order to support the weight of the garden window. If the framing is severely deteriorated or out of plumb or square, you may need to reframe the rough opening (pages 53 to 55).

4

Insert the garden window into the opening, pressing it tight against the framing. Support the unit with notched 2 × 4s under the bottom edge of the window until it has been fastened securely to the framing.

(continued)

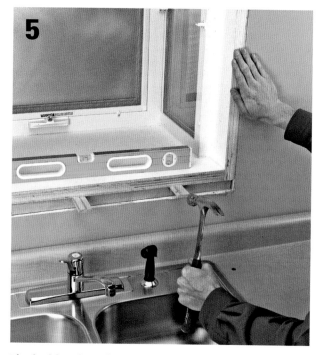

The inside edge of the window sleeve should be flush with the interior wall surface. Check the sill of the garden window for level. Shim beneath the lower side of the sill, if necessary, to make it level.

Once the garden window is in place and level, hold a piece of window trim in place along the exterior of the window and trace the outline onto the siding. Remove the window. Cut the siding down to the sheathing using a circular saw. See pages 280 to 287 for help with removing different types of siding.

Install strips of building paper between siding and sheathing. Wrap them around the framing and staple them in place. On the sides, work from the bottom up so each piece overlaps the piece below. Reposition the window and reshim. Make sure the space between the window and the siding is equal to the width of the trim on all sides.

Drill countersunk pilot holes every 12" to 16" through the window sleeve into the rough header, jack studs, and sill.

Insert shims between the window sleeve and rough frame at each hole location along the top and sides to prevent bowing of the window frame. Fasten the window to the framing using 3" screws. Continue checking for level, plumb, and square as the screws are tightened.

Locate and mark the studs nearest the edges of the window using a stud finder. Cut two pieces of siding to fit behind the brackets, and tack them in place over the marked studs with 4d siding nails. Position the support brackets with the shorter side against the siding and the longer side beneath the window. Fasten the brackets to the window and the studs using the included screws.

Cut a piece of drip edge to length, apply construction adhesive to its top flange, and slide it under the siding above the window. Cut each trim piece to size. Position the trim and attach it using 8d galvanized casing nails driven through pilot holes. Seal the edges of the trim with a bead of paintable silicone caulk, approximately ⅜" wide.

Cut all protruding shims flush with the framing using a utility knife or handsaw. Insulate or caulk gaps between the window sleeve and the wall. Finish the installation by reinstalling the existing interior trim or installing new trim.

Bay Windows

Modern bay windows are preassembled for easy installation, but it will still take several days to complete an installation. Bay windows are large and heavy, and installing them requires special techniques.

Have at least one helper to assist you, and try to schedule the work when there's little chance of rain. Using prebuilt bay window accessories will speed your work (see next page).

A large bay window can weigh several hundred pounds, so it must be anchored securely to framing members in the wall and supported by braces attached to framing members below the window. Some window manufacturers include cable-support hardware that can be used instead of metal support braces.

Before purchasing a bay window unit, check with the local building department regarding the code requirements. Many local codes require large windows and low bay windows with window seats to be glazed with tempered glass for safety.

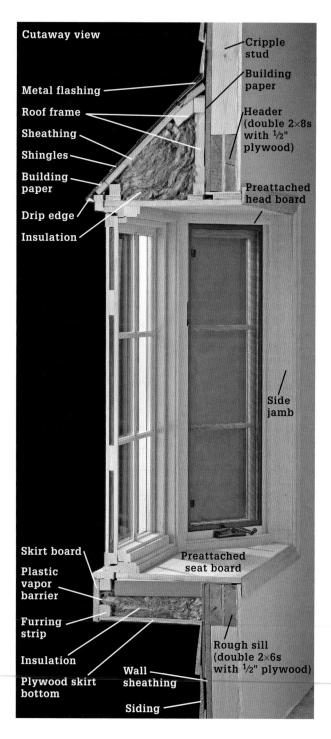

Cutaway view

- Metal flashing
- Roof frame
- Sheathing
- Shingles
- Building paper
- Drip edge
- Insulation
- Cripple stud
- Building paper
- Header (double 2×8s with ½" plywood)
- Preattached head board
- Side jamb
- Skirt board
- Plastic vapor barrier
- Furring strip
- Insulation
- Plywood skirt bottom
- Preattached seat board
- Rough sill (double 2×6s with ½" plywood)
- Wall sheathing
- Siding

Tools & Materials ▸

Straightedge
Circular saw
Wood chisel
Pry bar
Drill
Level
Nail set
Stapler
Aviation snips
Roofing knife
Caulk gun
Utility knife
T-bevel
Bay window unit
Prebuilt roof frame kit
Metal support brackets
2× lumber
16d galvanized common nails
16d and 8d galvanized casing nails

3" and 2" galvanized utility screws
16d casing nails
Tapered wood shims
Building paper
Fiberglass insulation
6-mil polyethylene sheeting
Drip edge
1" roofing nails
Step flashing
Shingles
Top flashing
Roofing cement
2 × 2 lumber
5½" skirt boards
¾" exterior-grade plywood
Paintable silicone caulk

Tips for Installing a Bay Window ▸

Use prebuilt accessories to ease installation of a bay window. Roof frames (A) come complete with sheathing (B), metal top flashing (C), and step flashing (D) and can be special-ordered at most home centers. You will have to specify the exact size of your window unit and the angle (pitch) you want for the roof. You can cover the roof inexpensively with building paper and shingles or order a copper or aluminum shell. Metal support braces (E) and skirt boards (F) can be ordered at your home center if not included with the window unit. Use two braces for bay windows up to 5 ft. wide and three braces for larger windows. Skirt boards are clad with aluminum or vinyl and can be cut to fit with a circular saw or miter saw.

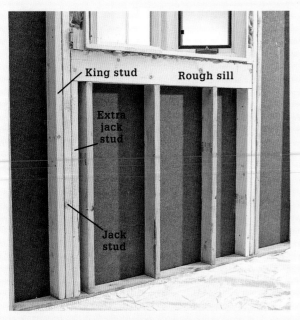

Construct a bay window frame similar to that for a standard window (see pages 53 to 55) but use a built-up sill made from two 2 × 6s sandwiched around ½" plywood. Install extra jack studs under the sill ends to help carry the window's weight.

Build an enclosure above the bay window if the roof soffit overhangs the window. Build a 2 × 2 frame (top) to match the angles of the bay window, and attach the frame securely to the wall and overhanging soffit. Install a vapor barrier and insulation (page 74), then finish the enclosure so it matches the siding (bottom).

How to Install a Bay Window

Prepare the project site and remove interior wall surfaces (pages 276 to 279), then frame the rough opening. Remove the exterior wall surfaces as directed on pages 280 to 287. Mark for removal a section of siding directly below the rough opening. The width of the marked area should equal that of the window unit and the height should equal that of the skirt board.

Set the blade on a circular saw just deep enough to cut through the siding, then cut along the outline. Stop just short of the corners to avoid damaging the siding outside the outline. Use a sharp chisel to complete the corner cuts. Remove the cut siding inside the outline.

Position the support braces along the rough sill within the widest part of the bay window and above the cripple stud locations. Add cripple studs to match the support brace locations, if necessary. Draw outlines of the braces on the top of the sill. Use a chisel or circular saw to notch the sill to a depth equal to the thickness of the top arm of the support braces.

Slide the support braces down between the siding and the sheathing. Pry the siding material away from the sheathing slightly to make room for the braces, if necessary. *Note: On stucco, you will need to chisel notches in the masonry surface to fit the support braces.*

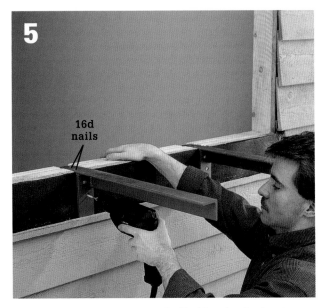

Attach the braces to the rough sill with galvanized 16d common nails. Drive 3" utility screws through the front of the braces and into the rough sill to prevent twisting.

Lift the bay window onto the support braces and slide it into the rough opening. Center the unit within the opening.

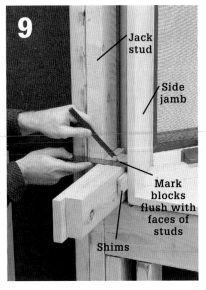

Check the window unit to make sure it is level. If necessary, drive shims under the low side to level the window. Temporarily brace the outside bottom edge of the unit with 2 × 4s to keep it from moving on the braces.

Set the roof frame on top of the window, with the sheathing loosely tacked in place. Trace the outline of the window and roof unit onto the siding. Leave a gap of about ½" around the roof unit to allow room for flashing and shingles.

If the gap between the side jambs and jack studs is more than 1" wide, mark and cut wood blocks to bridge the gap (smaller gaps require no blocks). Leave a small space for inserting wood shims. Remove the window, then attach blocks every 12" along studs.

(continued)

10

Cut the siding just down to the sheathing along the outline using a circular saw. Stop just short of the corners, then use a wood chisel to complete the corner cuts. Remove the cut siding. Pry the remaining siding slightly away from the sheathing around the roof outline to allow for easy installation of the metal flashing. Cover the exposed sheathing with 8"-wide strips of building paper (step 4, page 59).

11

Shim

Brace

Set the bay window unit back on the braces, and slide it back into the rough opening until the brick moldings are tight against the sheathing. Insert wood shims between the outside end of the metal braces and the seat board (inset). Check the unit to make sure it is level, and adjust the shims, if necessary.

12

Anchor the window by drilling pilot holes and driving 16d casing nails through the brick molding and into the framing members. Space nails every 12", and use a nail set to drive the nail heads below the surface of the wood.

13

Blocking

Shim

Jack stud

Drive wood shims into the spaces between the side jambs and the blocking or jack studs and between the headboard and header, spacing the shims every 12". Fill the spaces around the window with loosely packed fiberglass insulation. At each shim location, drive 16d casing nails through the jambs and shims and into the framing members. Cut off the shims flush with the framing members using a handsaw or utility knife. Use a nail set to drive the nail heads below the surface. If necessary, drill pilot holes to prevent splitting the wood.

Staple sheet plastic over the top of the window unit to serve as a vapor barrier. Trim the edges of the plastic around the top of the window using a utility knife.

Remove the sheathing pieces from the roof frame, then position the frame on top of the window unit. Attach the roof frame to the window and to the wall at stud locations using 3" utility screws.

Fill the empty space inside the roof frame with loosely packed fiberglass insulation. Screw the sheathing back onto the roof frame using 2" utility screws.

Staple asphalt building paper over the roof sheathing. Make sure each piece of building paper overlaps the one below by at least 5".

Cut drip edges with aviation snips, then attach them around the edge of the roof sheathing using roofing nails.

(continued)

19

Step flashing

Cut and fit a piece of step flashing on each side of the roof frame. Adjust the flashing so it overhangs the drip edge by ¼". Flashings help guard against moisture damage.

20

Trim the end of the flashing to the same angle as the drip edge. Nail the flashing to the sheathing with roofing nails.

21

Cut 6"-wide strips of shingles for the starter row. Use roofing nails to attach the starter row shingles so they overhang the drip edge by about ½". Cut the shingles along the roof hips with a straightedge and a roofing knife.

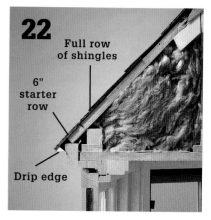

22

Full row of shingles

6" starter row

Drip edge

Nail a full row of shingles over the starter row, aligning the bottom edges with the bottom edge of the starter row. Make sure shingle notches are not aligned.

23

Second step flashing

Install another piece of step flashing on each side of the roof, overlapping the first piece of flashing by about 5".

24

Cut and install another row of full shingles. The bottom edges should overlap the tops of the notches on the previous row by ½". Attach the shingles with roofing nails driven just above the notches.

25

Continue installing alternate rows of step flashing and shingles to the top of the roof. Bend the last pieces of step flashing to fit over the roof hips.

26

When the roof sheathing is covered with shingles, install the top flashing. Cut and bend the ends over the roof hips, and attach it with roofing nails. Attach the remaining rows of shingles over the top flashing.

27

Find the height of the final row of shingles by measuring from the top of the roof to a point ½" below the top of the notches on the last installed shingle. Trim the shingles to fit.

28

Attach the final row of shingles with a thick bead of roofing cement—not nails. Press firmly to ensure a good bond.

29

Make ridge caps by cutting shingles into 1-ft.-long sections. Use a roofing knife to trim off the top corners of each piece, so the ridge caps will be narrower at the top than at the bottom.

30

Install the ridge caps over the roof hips, beginning at the bottom of the roof. Trim the bottom ridge caps to match the edges of the roof. Keep the same amount of overlap with each layer.

(continued)

31

At the top of the roof hips, use a roofing knife to cut the shingles to fit flush with the wall. Attach the shingles with roofing cement—do not use any nails.

32

Staple sheet plastic over the bottom of the window unit to serve as a vapor barrier. Trim the plastic around the bottom of the window.

33

Cut and attach a 2 × 2 skirt frame around the bottom of the bay window using 3" galvanized utility screws. Set the skirt frame back about 1" from the edges of the window.

34

Cut skirt boards to match the shape of the bay window bottom, mitering the ends to ensure a tight fit. Test-fit the skirt board pieces to make sure they match the bay window bottom.

Cut a 2 × 2 furring strip for each skirt board. Miter the ends to the same angles as the skirt boards. Attach the furring strips to the back of the skirt boards, 1" from the bottom edges, using 2" galvanized utility screws.

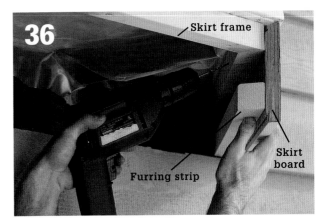

Attach the skirt board pieces to the skirt frame. Drill ⅛" pilot holes every 6" through the back of the skirt frame and into the skirt boards, then attach the skirt boards with 2" galvanized utility screws.

Measure the space inside the skirt boards using a T-bevel to duplicate the angles. Cut a skirt bottom from ¾" exterior-grade plywood to fit this space.

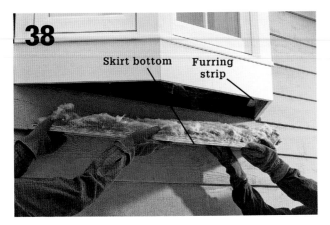

Lay fiberglass insulation on the skirt bottom. Position the skirt bottom against the furring strips and attach it by driving 2" galvanized utility screws every 6" through the bottom and into the furring strips.

Install any additional trim pieces (inset) specified by your window manufacturer using 8d galvanized casing nails. Seal the roof edges with roofing cement, and seal around the rest of the window with paintable silicone caulk. See pages 288 and 289 to finish the walls, and pages 144 to 155 to trim the interior of the window.

Glass Block Windows

Glass block is a durable material that transmits light while reducing visibility, making it a perfect material for creating unique windows. Glass block windows are energy-efficient and work particularly well as accent windows or in rooms where privacy is desired, such as bathrooms.

Glass block is available in a wide variety of sizes, shapes, and patterns. It can be found, along with other necessary installation products, at specialty distributors or home centers.

Building with glass block is much like building with mortared brick, with two important differences. First, glass block must be supported by another structure and cannot function in a load-bearing capacity. Second, glass block cannot be cut, so take extra time to make sure the layout is accurate.

When installing a glass block window, the size of the rough opening is based on the size and number of blocks you are using. It is much easier to make an existing opening smaller to accommodate the glass block rather than make it larger, which requires reframing the rough opening. To determine the rough opening width, multiply the nominal width of the glass block by the number of blocks horizontally and add ¼". For the height, multiply the nominal height by the number of blocks vertically and add ¼".

Because of its weight, a glass block window requires a solid base. The framing members of the rough opening will need to be reinforced. Contact your local building department for requirements in your area.

Use ¼" plastic T-spacers between blocks to ensure consistent mortar joints and to support the weight of the block to prevent mortar from squeezing out before it sets. (T-spacers can be modified into L or flat shapes for use at corners and along the channel.) For best results, use premixed glass block mortar. This high-strength mortar is a little drier than regular brick mortar, because glass doesn't wick water out of the mortar as brick does.

Because there are many applications for glass block and installation techniques may vary, ask a glass block retailer or manufacturer about the best products and methods for your specific project.

Glass block windows provide exceptional durability, light transmission, and privacy. New installation products are also making these windows easier for the do-it-yourselfer to install.

Tools & Materials ▸

Tape measure	Caulk gun
Circular saw	2 × 4 lumber
Hammer	16d common nails
Utility knife	Glass block perimeter
Tin snips	channels
Drill	1" galvanized flat-head
Mixing box	screws
Trowel	Glass block mortar
4-ft. level	Glass blocks
Rubber mallet	¼" T-spacers
Jointing tool	Expansion strips
Sponge	Silicone caulk
Nail set	Construction adhesive
Paintbrush	Mortar sealant

How to Install a Glass Block Window

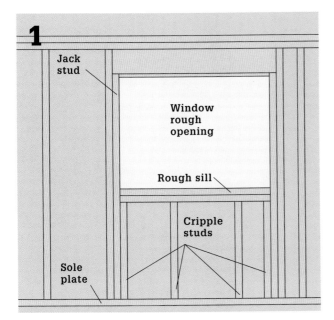

1

Jack stud

Window rough opening

Rough sill

Cripple studs

Sole plate

Measure the size of the rough opening and determine the size of the glass block window you will install (opposite page). Reinforce the rough opening framing by doubling the rough sill and installing additional cripple studs. Cut all pieces to size and fasten with 16d common nails.

2

Cut the perimeter channel to length for the sill and side jambs, mitering the ends at 45°. Align the front edge of the channel flush with the front edge of the exterior wall sheathing. Drill pilot holes every 12" through the channels (if not provided), and fasten the channels in place with 1" galvanized flat-head screws. *Note: Paint screw heads white to help conceal them.*

3

For the header, cut a channel to length, mitering the ends at 45°, then cut it in half lengthwise, using a utility knife. Align one-half of the channel flush with the exterior face of the sheathing, and fasten in place with 1" galvanized flat-head screws.

4

Set two blocks into the sill channel, one against each jamb—do not place mortar between blocks and channels. Place a ¼" flat spacer against the first block. Mix glass block mortar and liberally butter the leading edge of another block, then push it tight against the first block. Make sure the joint is filled with mortar.

(continued)

Lay the remainder of the first course, building from both jambs toward the center. Use flat spacers between blocks to maintain proper spacing. Plumb and level each block as you work, then also check the entire course for level. Tap blocks into place using the rubber handle of the trowel—do not use metal tools with glass block. Butter both sides of the final block in the course to install it.

At the top of the course, fill any depression at the top of each mortar joint with mortar and insert a ¼" T-spacer, then lay a ⅜" bed of mortar for the next course. Lay the blocks for each course, using T-spacers to maintain proper spacing. Check each block for level and plumb as you work.

Test the mortar as you work. When it can resist light finger pressure, remove the T-spacers (inset) and pack mortar into the voids, then tool the joints with a jointing tool. Remove excess mortar with a damp sponge or a bristle brush.

To ease block placement in the final course, trim the outer tabs off one side of the T-spacers using tin snips. Install the blocks of the final course. After the final block is installed, work in any mortar that has been forced out of the joints.

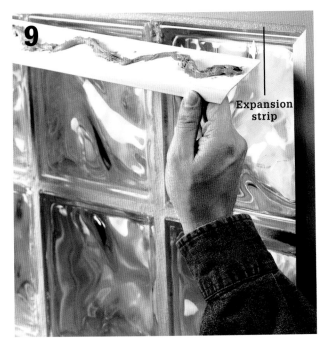

Cut an expansion strip for the header 1½" wide and to length. Slide it between the top course of block and the header of the rough opening. Apply a bead of construction adhesive to the top edge of the remaining half of the header channel, and slide it between the expansion strip and header.

Clean the glass block thoroughly with a wet sponge, rinsing often. Allow the surface to dry, then remove cloudy residue with a clean, dry cloth. Caulk between glass block and channels and between channels and framing members before installing exterior trim. After brick molding is installed, allow the mortar to cure for two weeks. Apply sealant.

Variation: Glass Block Window Kits ▶

Some glass block window kits do not require mortar. Instead, the blocks are set into the perimeter channels and the joints are created using plastic spacer strips. Silicone caulk is then used to seal the joints.

Preassembled glass block windows are simple to install. These vinyl-clad units have a nailing flange around the frame, which allows them to be hung using the same installation techniques as for standard windows with a nailing flange (pages 55 to 57).

Skylights

Since skylights let in so much light, their sizing and placement are important considerations. A skylight that's too big can quickly overheat a space, especially in an attic. The same is true of using too many skylights in any one room. For that reason it's often best to position a skylight away from the day's brightest sun. You may want an operable skylight that opens and closes to vent warm air.

When a skylight is installed above an unfinished attic space, a special skylight shaft must be constructed to channel light directly to the room below.

Installing a skylight above finished space involves other considerations. First, the ceiling surface must be removed to expose the rafters. To remove wall and ceiling surfaces, see pages 86 to 89.

A skylight frame is similar to a standard window frame. It has a header and sill, like a window frame, but it has king rafters rather than king studs. Skylight frames also have trimmers that define the sides of the rough opening. Refer to the manufacturer's instructions to determine what size to make the opening for the skylight you select.

With standard rafter-frame roof construction, you can safely cut into one or two rafters as long as you permanently support the cut rafters, as shown in the following steps. If your skylight requires alteration of more than two rafters or if your roofing is made with unusually heavy material, such as clay tile or slate, consult an architect or engineer before starting the project.

Today's good-quality skylight units are unlikely to leak, but a skylight is only as leakproof as its installation. Follow the manufacturer's instructions, and install the flashing meticulously, as it will last a lot longer than any sealant.

Skylights can offer warmth in the winter, cooling ventilation in the summer, and a view of the sky or the treetops around your house during any season. And, of course, skylights provide natural light.

Tools & Materials ▸

4-ft. level	1 × 4
Circular saw	Building paper
Drill	Roofing cement
Combination square	Skylight flashing
Reciprocating saw	2", 1¼", and ¾"
Pry bar	roofing nails
Chalk line	Finish nails
Stapler	Fiberglass insulation
Caulk gun	½" wallboard
Utility knife	Twine
Aviation snips	Wallboard screws
Plumb bob	6-mil polyethylene
Jig saw	sheeting
Wallboard tools	Finishing materials
2× lumber	
16d and 10d	
common nails	

How to Install a Skylight

Use the first rafter on each side of the planned rough opening as a king rafter. Measure and mark where the double header and sill will fit against the king rafters. Then, use a level as a straightedge to extend the marks across the intermediate rafter.

Brace the intermediate rafter by installing two 2 × 4s between the rafter and the attic floor. Position the braces just above the header marks and just below the sill marks. Secure them temporarily to the rafter and subfloor (or joists) with screws.

Reinforce each king rafter by attaching a full-length "sister" rafter against its outside face. Cut sister rafters from the same size of lumber as existing rafters, matching lengths and end cuts exactly. Work each one into position, flush against the outside face of the king rafters, then nail the sisters to the kings with pairs of 10d common nails spaced 12" apart.

Use a combination square to transfer the sill and header marks across the face of the intermediate rafter, then cut along the outermost lines with a reciprocating saw. Do not cut into the roof sheathing. Carefully remove the cutout section with a pry bar. The remaining rafter portions will serve as cripple rafters.

(continued)

5

Build a double header and double sill to fit snugly between the king rafters, using 2× lumber that is the same size as the rafters. Nail the header pieces together using pairs of 10d nails spaced 6" apart.

6

Cripple rafter

Install the header and sill, anchoring them to the king rafters and cripple rafters with 16d common nails. Make sure the ends of the header and sill are aligned with the appropriate marks on the king rafters.

7

Trimmers

If your skylight unit is narrower than the opening between the king studs, measure and make marks for the trimmers: They should be centered in the opening and spaced according to the manufacturer's specifications. Cut the trimmers from the same 2× lumber used for the rest of the frame, and nail them in place with 10d common nails. Remove the 2 × 4 braces.

8

Mark the opening for the roof cutout by driving a screw through the sheathing at each corner of the frame. Then, tack a couple of scrap boards across the opening to prevent the roof cutout from falling and causing damage below.

Replacing Doors

This chapter will guide you through the process of framing walls and installing interior or exterior doors. You'll learn how to retrofit a new door in an existing jamb in this chapter as well. Before you begin any of these projects, review the planning information (pages 30 to 37) so you're confident about door placement and sizing issues. If you're unfamiliar with how to remove wallboard or exterior siding, turn to page 280.

Be sure to read the installation manual that comes with your door for pertinent, additional information. Since those instructions will impact your product warranty, follow them carefully when they differ from the instructions shown here.

This chapter includes:

- Framing Doors
- Prehung Interior Doors
- Pocket Doors
- Bifold Doors
- French Doors
- Hanging a New Door in an Old Jamb
- Entry Doors
- Storm Doors
- Patio Doors
- Attic Access Ladders

Framing Doors

Creating an opening for a door in a wall involves building a framework about 1" wider and ½" taller than the door's jamb frame. This oversized opening, called a rough opening, will enable you to position the door easily and shim it plumb and level. Before framing a door, it's always a good idea to buy the door and refer to the manufacturer's recommendations for rough opening size.

Door frames consist of a pair of full-length king studs and two shorter jack studs that support the header above the door. A header provides an attachment point for wallboard and door casings. On load-bearing walls, it also helps to transfer the building's structural loads from above down into the wall framework and eventually the foundation.

Door framing requires flat, straight, and dry framing lumber, so choose your king, jack, and header pieces carefully. Sight down the edges and ends to look for warpage, and cut off the ends of pieces with splits.

Tools & Materials ▸

Tape measure
Framing square
Hammer or nail gun
Handsaw or
  reciprocating saw
Framing lumber

10d or pneumatic
  framing nails
⅜" plywood (for
  structural headers)
Construction adhesive

Creating a square, properly sized opening for a door is the most important element of a successful door installation project.

How to Frame an Exterior Door

1

Prepare the project site and remove the interior wall surfaces (pages 266 to 276).

2

Measure and mark the rough opening width on the sole plate. Mark the locations of the jack studs and king studs on the sole plate. (Where practical, use existing studs as king studs.)

3

If king studs need to be added, measure and cut them to fit between the sole plate and top plate. Position the king studs and toenail them to the sole plate with 10d nails.

(continued)

4

Check the king studs with a level to make sure they are plumb, then toenail them to the top plate with 10d nails.

5

Measuring from the floor, mark the rough opening height on one king stud. For most doors, the recommended rough opening is ½" taller than the height of the door unit. This line marks the bottom of the door header.

6

Determine the size of the header needed (page 44), and measure and mark where the top of it will fit against a king stud. Use a level to extend the lines across the intermediate studs to the opposite king stud.

7

Cut two jack studs to reach from the top of the sole plate to the rough opening marks on the king studs. Nail the jack studs to the king studs with 10d nails driven every 12". Make temporary supports (pages 268 to 271) if you are removing more than one stud.

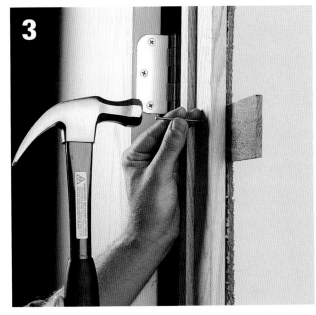

3

Anchor the hinge-side jamb with 8d casing nails driven through the jamb and shims and into the jack stud. You may want to predrill the nail holes to prevent splitting the shims.

4

Insert pairs of shims in the gap between the framing members and the latch-side jamb and top jamb, spaced every 12". With the door closed, adjust the shims so the gap between the door edge and jamb is ⅛" wide. Drive 8d casing nails through the jambs and shims into the framing members.

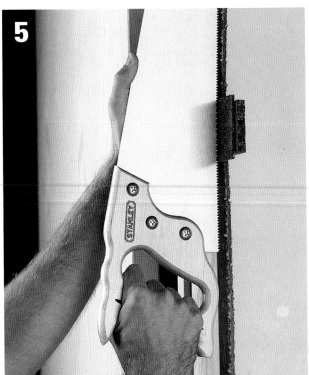

5

Cut the shims flush with the wall surface using a handsaw. Hold the saw vertically to prevent damage to the door jamb or wall. Finish the door and install the lockset as directed by the manufacturer. See page 151 to install trim around the door.

Tip ▶

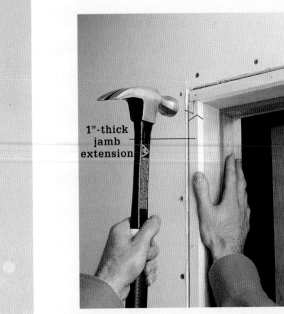

1"-thick jamb extension

If your walls are built with 2 × 6 studs, you'll need to extend the jambs by attaching 1"-thick wood strips to the edges of the jamb after the door is installed. Use glue and 4d casing nails when attaching jamb extensions. Make the strips from the same wood as the jamb.

Pocket Doors

Pocket doors are a space-saving alternative to traditional hinged interior doors. Swinging doors can monopolize up to 16 square feet of floor space in a room, which is why pocket doors are a perfect choice for tight spaces, like small bathrooms. Installed in pairs, pocket doors can divide large rooms into more intimate spaces and can still be opened to use the entire area.

Pocket door hardware kits generally are universal and can be adapted for almost any interior door. In this project, the frame kit includes an adjustable track, steel-clad split studs, and all the required hanging hardware. The latch hardware, jambs, and the door itself are all sold separately. Pocket door frames can also be purchased as preassembled units that can be easily installed into a rough opening.

Framing and installing a pocket door is not difficult in new construction or a major remodel. But retrofitting a pocket door in place of a standard door or installing one in a wall without an existing door, is a major project that involves removing the wall material, framing the new opening, installing and hanging the door, and refinishing the wall. Hidden utilities, such as wiring, plumbing, and heating ducts, must be rerouted if encountered.

The rough opening for a pocket door is at least twice the width of a standard door opening. If you are installing the pocket door in a non-loadbearing wall, see page 102 to learn how to frame the opening. If the wall is load bearing, you will need to install an appropriately sized header (page 103).

Because pocket doors are easy to open and close and require no threshold, they offer increased accessibility for wheelchair or walker users, provided the handles are easy to use (page 115). If you are installing a pocket door for this purpose, be aware that standard latch hardware may be difficult to use for some individuals.

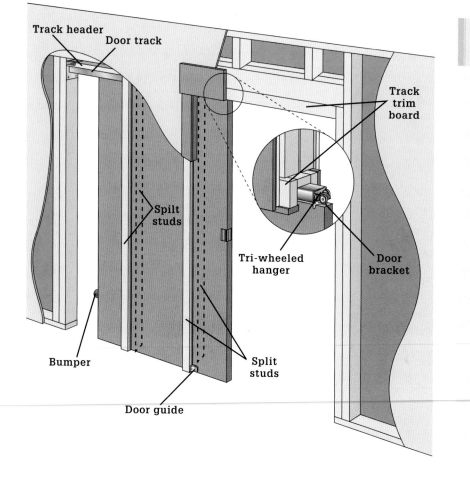

Track header
Door track
Track trim board
Spilt studs
Tri-wheeled hanger
Door bracket
Bumper
Split studs
Door guide

Tools & Materials ▸

Tape measure
Circular saw
Hammer, nail set
Screwdriver
Level
Drill
Handsaw
Hacksaw
Wallboard tools
2 × 4 lumber
16d, 8d & 6d common nails
Pocket door frame kit
Door
1¼" wallboard screws
Wallboard materials
Manufactured pocket door jambs (or build jambs from 1× material)
8d & 6d finish nails
1½" wood screws
Door casing

How to Install a Pocket Door

Prepare the project area and frame the rough opening to the manufacturer's recommended dimensions. Measuring from the floor, mark each jack stud at the height of the door plus ¾ to 1½" (depending on the door clearance above the floor) for the overhead door track. Drive a nail into each jack stud, centered on the mark. Leave about ⅛" of the nail protruding.

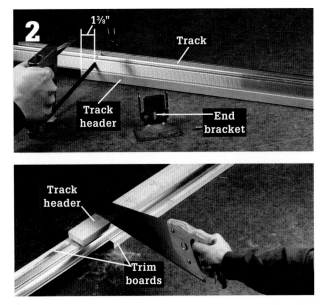

Remove the adjustable end bracket from the overhead door track. Cut the wooden track header at the mark that matches your door size. Turn the track over and cut the metal track 1⅜" shorter than the wooden track header using a hacksaw (top). Replace the end bracket. Cut the side trim boards along the marks corresponding to your door size, being careful not to cut the metal track (bottom).

Set end brackets of the track on the nails in the jack studs. Adjust the track to level and set the nails. Then drive 8d common nails through the remaining holes in the end brackets.

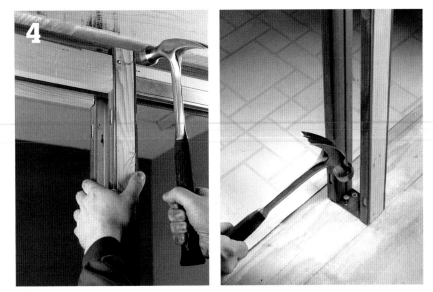

Snap chalk lines on the floor across the opening, even with the sides of the rough opening. Tap the floor plate spacers into the bottom ends of the pairs of steel-clad split studs. Butt one split stud pair against the door track trim board, check it for plumb, and fasten it to the track header using 6d common nails (left). Center the other split stud pair in the "pocket" and fasten it to the track header. Plumb the split studs again and attach them to the floor with 8d common nails or 2" screws driven through spacer plates (right).

(continued)

Tri-wheeled hanger

Lock arm

Cover the open framing with wallboard to the edge of the opening. You may want to leave the wallboard off one side of the wall to allow for door adjustment. Use 1¼" wallboard screws, which will not protrude into the pocket.

Paint or stain the door as desired. When the door has dried, attach two door brackets to the top of the door, using included screws driven through pilot holes. Install the rubber bumper to the rear edge of the door with its included screw.

Slide two tri-wheeled hangers into the overhead door track. Set the door in the frame, aligning the hangers with the door brackets. Then raise the door and press each hanger into the door bracket until it snaps into place. Close the lock arm over the hanger.

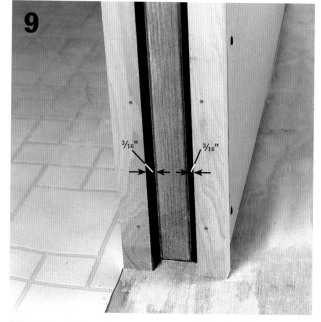

3/16" **3/16"**

Cut the strike-side jamb to length and width. Fasten it to the jack stud using 8d finish nails, shimming the jamb to plumb as necessary. Close the door and adjust the hanger nuts to fine-tune the door height so the door is parallel with the jamb from top to bottom.

Measure and cut the split jambs to size. Fasten each split jamb to the front edge of the split stud using 8d finish nails. Maintain 3/16" clearance on both sides of the door. If necessary, shim between the bumper and door until the door is flush with the jambs when open.

Measure and cut the split head jambs to size. Use 1½" wood screws driven through countersunk pilot holes to attach the head jamb on the side that has access to the lock arm of the hangers to allow for easy removal of the door. Attach the other head jamb using 6d finish nails. Maintain ³⁄₁₆" clearance on each side of the door.

Install the included door guides on both sides of the door near the floor at the mouth of the pocket. Install the latch hardware according to the manufacturer's directions. Finish the wallboard and install casing around the door. Fill all nail holes, then paint or stain the jambs and casing as desired.

Improving Pocket Door Accessibility ▶

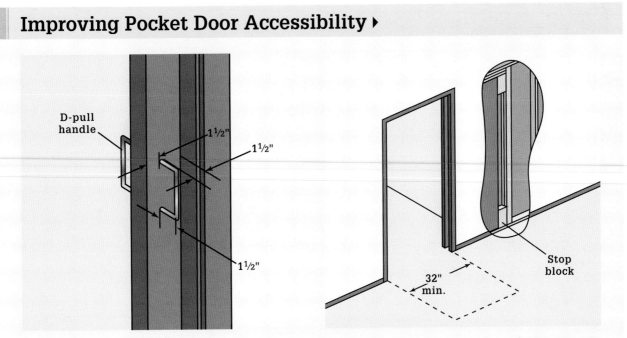

D-pull handles are easier to use than standard recessed hardware. Choose pulls that project at least 1½" from the door. Mount the pulls 1½" from the edge of the door to provide room for fingers when the door is closed (left). Install a stop block at the back of the frame (right), so the door stops 1½" short of the D-pull to provide room for fingers when the door is open. Because this design reduces the width of the door opening by 3", you must use a 36"-wide door to maintain the recommended doorway width of 32".

Bifold Doors

Bifold doors provide easy access to a closet without requiring much clearance for opening. Most home centers stock kits that include two pairs of prehinged doors, a head track, and all the necessary hardware and fasteners. Typically, the doors in these kits have predrilled holes for the pivot and guide posts. Hardware kits are also sold separately for custom projects. There are many types of bifold door styles, so be sure to read and follow the manufacturer's instructions for the product you use.

Tools & Materials ›

Tape measure
Level
Circular saw
Straightedge
    (optional)
Drill
Plane
Screwdriver

Hacksaw
Prehinged bifold
    doors
Head track
Mounting hardware
Panhead screws
Flathead screws

A variety of designer bifold doors are available for installation between rooms and closets. They provide the same attractive appearance as French doors but require much less floor space.

How to Install Bifold Doors

1

Cut the head track to the width of the opening using a hacksaw. Insert the roller mounts into the track, then position the track in the opening. Fasten it to the header using panhead screws.

2

Measure and mark each side jamb at the floor for the anchor bracket so the center of the bracket aligns exactly with the center of the head track. Fasten the brackets in place with flathead screws.

3

Check the height of the doors in the opening, and trim if necessary. Insert pivot posts into predrilled holes at the bottoms and tops of the doors. Insert guide posts at the tops of the leading doors. Make sure all posts fit snugly.

4

Fold one pair of doors closed and lift into position, inserting the pivot and guide posts into the head track. Slip the bottom pivot post into the anchor bracket. Repeat for the other pair of doors. Close the doors and check alignment along the side jambs and down the center. If necessary, adjust the top and bottom pivots following the manufacturer's instructions.

French Doors

French doors are made up of two separate doors, hinged on opposing jambs of a doorway. The doors swing out from the center of the doorway and into or out from a room. Like most doors, French doors are typically sold in prehung units, but are also available separately. They are generally available only in wood with a variety of designs and styles to choose from.

Before purchasing a prehung French door unit, determine the size of doors you will need. If you are planning to install the doors in an existing doorway, measure the dimensions of the rough opening from the unfinished framing members, then order the unit to size—the manufacturer or distributor will help you select the proper unit.

You can also pick the prehung unit first, then alter an existing opening to accommodate it (as shown in this project). In this case, build the rough opening a little larger than the actual dimensions of the doors to accommodate the jambs. Prehung units typically require adding 1" to the width and ½" to the height.

If the doorway will be in a load-bearing wall, you will need to make temporary supports (pages 268 to 271) and install an appropriately sized header. Sizing the header (depth) is critical: it's based on the length of the header, the material it's made from, and the weight of the load it must support. For actual requirements, consult your local building department.

When installing French doors, it is important to have consistent reveals between the two doors and between the top of the doors and the head jamb. This allows the doors to close properly and prevents the hinges from binding.

Tools & Materials ›

Tape measure	Prehung French door
Circular saw	unit
4-ft. level	2 × 4 and 2 × 6 lumber
Hammer	½" plywood
Handsaw	10d & 16d common
Drill	nails
Utility knife	Wood shims
Nail set	8d finish nails

Traditionally, French doors open onto the patio or lush garden of a backyard. But you can create stylish entrances inside your home by bringing French doors to formal dining rooms, sitting rooms, dens, and master suites.

How to Install French Doors

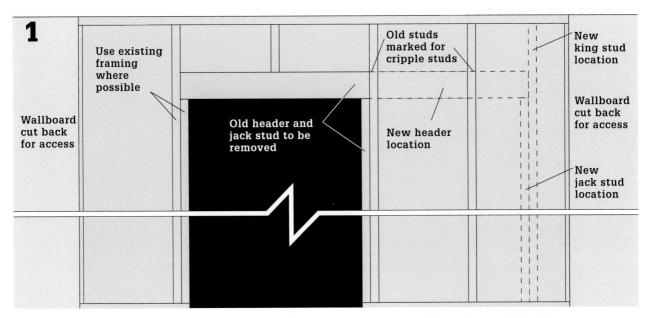

Shut off power and water to the area. Remove the wall surfaces from both sides of the wall (pages 276 to 279), leaving one stud bay open on each side of the new rough opening. Also remove or reroute any wiring, plumbing, or ductwork. Lay out the new rough opening, marking the locations of all new jack and king studs on both the top and bottom plates. Where practical, use existing framing members. To install a new king stud, cut a stud to size and align with the layout marks; toenail to the bottom plate with 10d common nails, check for plumb, then toenail to the top plate to secure. Finally, mark both the bottom and top of the new header on one king stud, then use a level to extend the lines across the intermediate studs to the opposite king stud. If using existing framing, measure and mark from the existing jack stud.

Cut the intermediate studs at the reference marks for the top of the header using a reciprocating saw. Pry the studs away from the sole plates and remove—the remaining top pieces will be used as cripple studs.

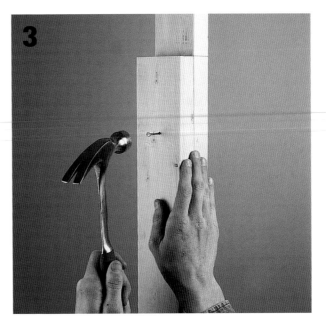

To install a jack stud, cut the stud to fit between the sole plate and the bottom of the header, as marked on the king stud. Align it at the mark against the king stud, then fasten it in place with 10d common nails driven every 12".

(continued)

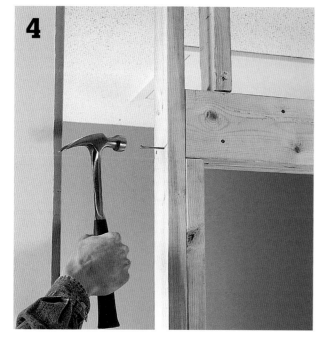

4

Build the header to size (page 44, and page 54, step 9) and install, fastening it to the jack studs, king studs, and cripple studs using 16d common nails. Use a handsaw to cut through the bottom plate so it's flush with the inside faces of the jack studs. Remove the cutout portion.

5

Finish the walls (for wallboard installation, see pages 288 to 289) before installing the doors, then set the prehung door unit into the framed opening so the jamb edges are flush with the finished wall surfaces and the unit is centered from side to side.

6

Using a level, adjust the unit to plumb one of the side jambs. Starting near the top of the door; insert pairs of shims driven from opposite directions into the gap between the framing and the jamb, sliding the shims until they are snug. Check the jamb to make sure it remains plumb and does not bow inward.

7

Working down along the jamb, install shims near each hinge and near the floor. Make sure the jamb is plumb, then anchor it with 8d finish nails driven through the jamb and shims and into the framing. Leave the nail heads partially protruding so the jamb can be readjusted later if necessary.

8

Install shims at the other side jamb, aligning them roughly with the shims of the first jamb. With the doors closed, adjust the shims so the reveal between the doors is even and the tops of the doors are aligned.

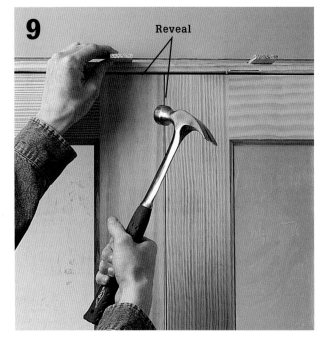

9

Reveal

Shim the gap between the header and the head jamb to create a consistent reveal along the top when the doors are closed. Insert pairs of shims every 12". Drive 8d finish nails through the jambs and shims and into the framing members.

10

Drive all the nails fully, then set them below the surface of the wood with a nail set. Cut off the shims flush with the wall surface using a handsaw or utility knife. Hold the saw vertically to prevent damage to the door jamb or wall. Install the door casing.

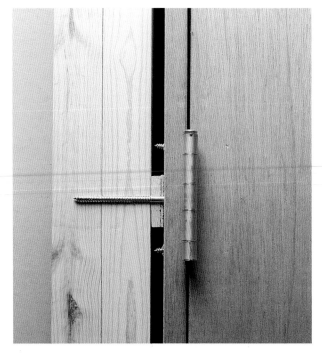

Option: Replace the center mounting screw on each hinge with a 3" wood screw to provide extra support for door hinges and jambs. These long screws extend through the side jambs and deep into the framing members. Be careful not to overtighten screws, which will cause the jambs to bow.

Hanging a New Door in an Old Jamb

If you've got an unsightly or damaged door to replace but the jamb and trimwork are in good condition, there's no need to remove the jambs. Instead, buy a slab door and hang it in the existing jamb. It's an excellent way to preserve existing moldings and trim, especially if you live in an old home, and you won't have to color-match a new jamb to its surroundings.

If the hinges are also in good condition, you can reuse them as well. This may be particularly desirable in a historic home with ornate hinges. Most home centers stock six-panel slab doors, or you can order them in a variety of styles and wood types. For aesthetic and practical reasons, choose a door size as close to the original door as possible.

The process for hanging the door involves shimming the door into position in the jamb, scribing the ends and edges, and trimming or planing it to fit the opening. You'll also need to chisel hinge mortises in the door edge to accommodate the jamb hinge positions.

This is a project where patience and careful scribing will pay dividends in the end. Have a helper on hand to hold the door in position as you scribe and fit the door in place.

Tools & Materials ▸

Door shims	Power plane or
Tape measure	hand plane
Compass	Hammer
Combination square	Chisel
Utility knife	Drill/driver
Circular saw	Hole saw
C-clamps	Spade bit
Self-centering	Slab door
drill bit	Hinge screws

Before **After**

Installing a new door in an old jamb dramatically updates the curb appeal of your home.

How to Hang a New Door in an Old Jamb

Have a helper hold the new door in place against the jamb from inside the room. Slide a pair of thick shims under the door to raise it up slightly off the floor or threshold. Move the shims in or out until the door's top and side rails are roughly even with the jamb so it looks balanced in the opening, then make a mark along the top edge of the the door.

Use pieces of colored masking tape to mark the outside of the door along the hinge edge. This will help keep the door's orientation clear throughout the installation process.

Use a pencil compass, set to an opening of ³⁄₁₆", to scribe layout lines along both long edges of the door and across the top. These lines will create a clear space for the hinges and door swing. If the bottom of the door will close over carpet, set the dividers for ½" and scribe the bottom edge. Remove the door and transfer these scribe lines to the other door face.

Lay the door on a sturdy bench or across a pair of sawhorses with the tape side facing up. Score the top and bottom scribe lines with a utility knife to keep the wood fibers from splintering when you cut across the ends.

(continued)

Trim the door ends with a circular saw equipped with a fine-cutting blade. Run the saw base along a clamped straightedge with the blade cutting 1/16" on the waste side of the layout lines. Check to make sure the blade is set square to the saw base before cutting. Use a power planer or hand plane to plane the door ends to the layout lines.

Stand the door on edge and use a power planer or hand plane to plane down to the edge of the scribe lines. Set the tool for a fine cut; use a 1/16" cutting depth for power planing and a shallower cutting depth for a hand plane. Try to make each planing pass in long strokes from one end of the door to the other.

Shim the door back into position in the jamb with a helper supporting it from behind. Set the door slightly out from the doorstop moldings so you can mark the hinge locations on the door face.

Use a combination square or one of the hinge leaves to draw hinge mortise layout lines on the door edge. Score the layout lines with a utility knife.

Cut shallow hinge leaf mortises in the door edge with a sharp chisel and hammer. First score the mortise shape with a straightedge and utility knife or a chisel, then make a series of shallow chisel cuts inside the hinge leaf area. Pare away this waste so the mortise depth is slightly deeper than the hinge leaf thickness.

Set the hinges in the door mortises, and drill pilot holes for the hinge screws. Attach the hinges to the door.

Hang the door in the jamb by tipping it into place so the top hinge leaf rests in the top mortise of the jamb. Drive one screw into this mortise. Then set the other leaves into their mortises and install the remaining hinge screws.

Bore holes for the lockset and bolt using a hole saw and spade bit. If you're reusing the original hardware, measure the old door hole sizes and cut matching holes in the new door, starting with the large lockset hole. For new locksets, use the manufacturer's template and hole sizing recommendations to bore the holes. Install the hardware.

Entry Doors

Few parts of a house have a more dramatic effect on the way your home is perceived than the main entry door. A lovely, well-maintained entryway that is tastefully matched architecturally to the house can utterly transform a home's appearance. In fact, industry studies have suggested that upgrading a plain entry door to a higher-end entry door system can pay back multiple times in the resale of your house. But perhaps more importantly, depending on your priorities, it makes a great improvement in how you feel about your home. Plus, it usually pays benefits in home security and energy efficiency as well.

If you are replacing a single entry door with a double door or a door with a sidelight or sidelights, you will need to enlarge the door opening (see pages 104 to 109). Be sure to file your plans with your local building department and obtain a permit. You'll need to provide temporary support from the time you remove the wall studs in the new opening until you've installed and secured a new door header that's approved for the new span distance (see pages 268 to 271).

The American Craftsman style door with sidelights (see Resources, page 296) installed in this project has the look and texture of a classic wood door, but it is actually created from fiber-glass. Today's fiberglass doors are quite convincing in their ability to replicate wood grain, while still offering the durability and low-maintenance of fiberglass.

Tools & Materials ▸

Tape measure	Shims
Level	Framing nails
Reciprocating saw	Finish nails
Caulk & caulk gun	Nail set
Hammer	Finishing materials

After

Before

Replacing an ordinary entry door with a beautiful new upgrade has an exceptionally high payback in increased curb appeal and in perceived home value, according to industry studies.

How to Replace an Entry Door

Remove the old entry door by cutting through the fasteners driven into the jamb with a reciprocating saw (see pages 272 and 273). If the new door or door system is wider, mark the edges of the larger rough opening onto the wall surface. If possible, try to locate the new opening so one edge will be against an existing wall stud. Be sure to include the thickness of the new framing you'll need to add when removing the wall coverings.

Frame in the new rough opening for the replacement door (see pages 104 to 109). The instructions that come with the door will recommend a rough opening size, which is usually sized to create a ½" gap between the door and the studs and header. Patch the wall surfaces (see pages 288 to 293).

Cut metal door dripcap molding to fit the width of the opening and tuck the back edge up behind the wallcovering at the top of the door opening. Attach the dripcap with caulk only–do not use nails or screws.

Unpack the door unit and set it in the rough opening to make sure it fits correctly. Remove it. Make sure the subfloor is clean and in good repair, and then apply heavy beads of caulk to the underside of the door sill and to the subfloor in the sill installation area. Use plenty of caulk.

(continued)

5

Set the door sill in the threshold and raise the unit up so it fits cleanly in the opening, with the exterior trim flush against the wall sheathing. Press down on the sill to seat it in the caulk and wipe up any squeeze-out with a damp rag

6

Use a 6-ft. level to make sure the unit is plumb and then tack it to the rough opening stud on the hinge side, using pairs of 10d nails driven partway through the casing on the weatherstripped side of the door (or the sidelight). On single, hinged doors, drive the nails just above the hinge locations. *Note: Many door installers prefer deck screws over nails when attaching the jambs. Screws offer more gripping strength and are easier to adjust, but covering the screw heads is more difficult than filling nail holes.*

7

Drive wood shims between the jamb and the wall studs to create an even gap. Locate the shims directly above the pairs of nails you drove. Doublecheck the door with the level to make sure it is still plumb.

8

Drive shims between the jamb on the latch side of the unit and into the wall stud. Only drive the nails part way. Test for plumb again and then add shims at nail locations (you may need to double-up the shims, as this gap is often wider than the one on the hinge side). Check to make sure the door jamb is not bowed.

9

Drive finish nails at all remaining locations, following the nailing schedule in the manufacturer's installation instructions.

10

Use a nail set to drive the nail heads below the wood surface. Fill the nail holes with wood putty (you'll get the best match if you apply putty that's tinted to match the stained wood after the finish is applied). The presence of the wood shims at the nail locations should prevent the jamb from bowing as you nail.

11

Install the lockset, strikeplates, deadbolts or multipoint locks, and any other door hardware. If the door finish has not been applied, you may want to do so first, but generally it makes more sense to install the hardware right away so the door can be operated and locked. Attach the door sill to the threshold and adjust it as needed, normally using the adjustment screws (inset).

12

Apply your door finish if it has not yet been applied. Read the manufacturer's suggestions for finishing very closely and follow the suggested sequences. Some manufacturers offer finish kits that are designed to be perfectly compatible with their doors. Install interior case molding and caulk all the exterior gaps after the finish dries.

Storm Doors

Storm doors protect the entry door from driving rain or snow. They create a dead air buffer between the two doors that acts like insulation. When the screen panels are in place, the door provides great ventilation on a hot day. And, they deliver added security, especially when outfitted with a lockset and a deadbolt lock.

If you want to install a new storm door or replace an old one that's seen better days, your first job is to go shopping. Storm doors come in many different styles to suit just about anyone's design needs. And they come in different materials, including aluminum, vinyl, and even fiberglass. (Wood storm doors are still available but not in preassembled form.) All these units feature a prehung door in a frame that is mounted on the entry door casing boards. Depending on the model you buy, installation instructions can vary. Be sure to check the directions that come with your door before starting the job.

Tools & Materials ▸

Drill/driver
Tape measure
Finish nails
Screwdriver
Paintbrush

Masking tape
Hacksaw
Level
Primer
Paint

A quality storm door helps seal out cold drafts, keeps rain and snow off your entry door, and lets a bug-free breeze into your home when you want one.

How to Install a Storm Door

1

Test-fit the door in the opening. If it is loose, add a shim to the hinge side of the door. Cut the piece with a circular saw and nail it to the side of the jamb, flush with the front of the casing.

2

Install the drip edge molding at the top of the door opening. The directions for the door you have will explain exactly how to do this. Sometimes it's the first step, like we show here; otherwise it's installed after the door is in place.

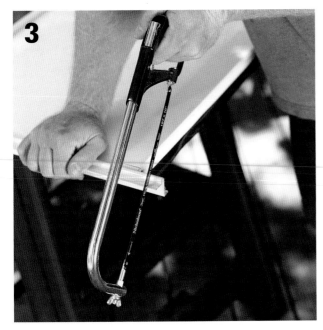

3

Measure the height of the opening and cut the hinge flange to match this measurement. Use a hacksaw and work slowly so the saw won't hop out of the cut and scratch a visible area of the hinge.

4

Lift the door and push it tightly into the opening. Partially drive one mounting screw near the bottom and another near the top. Check the door for plumb, and when satisfied, drive all the mounting screws tight to the flange.

(continued)

5

Measure from the doorway sill to the rain cap to establish the length of the latch-side mounting flange.

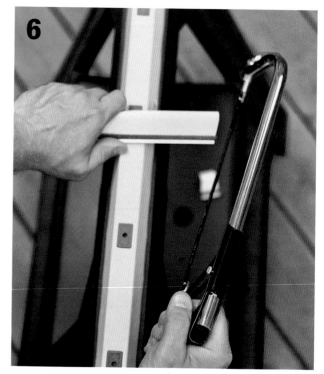

6

Cut the latch-side flange with a hacksaw. Work carefully so you don't pull out the weatherstripping from the flange channel as you cut. Install the flange with screws.

7

To install the door sweep, slide it over the bottom of the door and install its mounting screws loosely. Make sure the sweep forms a tight seal with the sill, then tighten the screws.

8

Mount the lockset on the door. Tape can help hold the outside hardware in place while you position the inner latch and tighten the screws.

Install the strike plates for both the lockset (shown here) and the deadbolt locks. These plates are just screwed to the door jamb where the lock bolt and deadbolt fall. Install the deadbolt.

Begin installing the door closer by screwing the jamb bracket in place. Most of these brackets have slotted screw holes so you can make minor adjustments without taking off the bracket.

Install the door closer bracket on the inside of the door. Then mount the closer on the jamb bracket and the door bracket. Usually the closer is attached to these with some form of short locking pin.

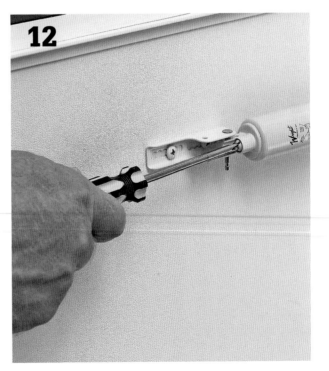

Adjust the automatic door closer so it closes the door completely without slamming it. The adjustment is usually made by turning a set screw in and out with a screwdriver.

Patio Doors

For easy installation, buy a patio door with the door panels already mounted in a preassembled frame. Try to avoid patio doors sold with frame kits that require complicated assembly.

Because patio doors have very long bottom sills and top jambs, they are susceptible to bowing and warping. To avoid these problems, be very careful to install the patio door so it is level and plumb and to anchor the unit securely to framing members. Yearly caulking and touch-up painting helps prevent moisture from warping the jambs.

Tools & Materials ▸

Pencil	Drill and bits
Hammer	Nail set
Circular saw	Shims
Handsaw	Drip edge
Wood chisel	Building paper
Stapler	Silicone and latex caulk
Caulk gun	10d casing nails
Level	3" wood screws
Pry bar	Sill nosing
Cordless screwdriver	Fiberglass insulation
	Patio door kit

Patio doors offer the best qualities of both windows and doors—plenty of natural light, a great view, wide room access, and reasonable security.

If not included with the unit, screen doors can be ordered from most patio door manufacturers. Screen doors have spring-mounted rollers that fit into a narrow track on the outside of the patio door threshold.

Tips for Installing Sliding Patio Doors ▸

Remove heavy glass panels if you must install the door without help. Reinstall the panels after the frame has been placed in the rough opening and nailed at opposite corners. To remove and install the panels, remove the stop rail found on the top jamb of the door unit.

Adjust the bottom rollers after installation is complete. Remove the coverplate on the adjusting screw, found on the inside edge of the bottom rail. Turn the screw in small increments until the door rolls smoothly along the track without binding when it is opened and closed.

Tips for Installing Hinged Patio Doors ▸

Provide extra support for door hinges by replacing the center mounting screw on each hinge with a 3" wood screw. These long screws extend through the side jambs and deep into the framing members.

Keep a uniform ⅛" gap between the door, side jambs, and top jamb to ensure that the door will swing freely without binding. Check this gap frequently as you shim around the door unit.

How to Install a Patio Door

1

Prepare the work area and remove the interior wall surfaces (pages 276 to 279), then frame the rough opening for the patio door (pages 100 to 109). Remove the exterior surfaces inside the framed opening (pages 280 to 287).

2

Test-fit the door unit, centering it in the rough opening. Check to make sure the door is plumb. If necessary, shim under the lower side jamb until the door is plumb and level. Have a helper hold the door in place while you adjust it.

3

Trace the outline of the brick molding onto the siding, then remove the door unit. *Note: If you have vinyl or metal siding, see page 282 for advice on removing the siding.*

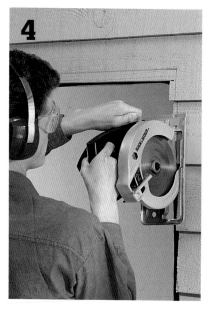

4

Cut the siding along the outline, just down to the sheathing using a circular saw. Stop just short of the corners to prevent damage to the remaining siding. Finish the cuts at the corners with a sharp wood chisel.

5 Drip edge

To provide an added moisture barrier, cut a piece of drip edge to fit the width of the rough opening, then slide it between the siding and the existing building paper at the top of the opening. Do not nail the drip edge.

Cut 8"-wide strips of building paper and slide them between the siding and sheathing. Bend the paper around the framing members and staple it in place. Each piece overlaps the piece below it.

Apply several thick beads of silicone caulk to the subfloor at the bottom of the door opening.

Apply silicone caulk around the front edge of the framing members where the siding meets the building paper.

Use a pry bar to center the door in the rough opening so the brick molding is tight against the sheathing. Have a helper hold the door unit from outside.

Check the door threshold to make sure it is level. If necessary, shim under the lower side jamb until the patio door unit is level.

(continued)

11

12

If there are gaps between the threshold and subfloor, insert shims coated with caulk into the gaps, spaced every 6". Shims should be snug, but not so tight that they cause the threshold to bow. Clear off excess caulk immediately.

Place pairs of hardwood wedge shims together to form flat shims. Insert the shims every 12" into the gaps between the side jambs and the jack studs. For sliding doors, shim behind the strike plate for the door latch.

13

14

15

Insert shims every 12" into the gap between the top jamb and the header.

From outside, drive 10d casing nails, spaced every 12", through the brick molding and into the framing members. Use a nail set to drive the nail heads below the surface of the wood.

From inside, drive 10d casing nails through the door jambs and into the framing members at each shim location. Use a nail set to drive the nail heads below the surface of the wood.

Remove one of the screws and cut the shims flush with the stop block found in the center of the threshold. Replace the screw with a 3" wood screw driven into the subfloor as an anchor.

Cut off the shims flush with the face of the framing members using a handsaw. Fill gaps around the door jambs and beneath the threshold with loosely packed fiberglass insulation.

Reinforce and seal the edge of the threshold by installing sill nosing under the threshold and against the wall. Drill pilot holes and attach the sill nosing with 10d casing nails.

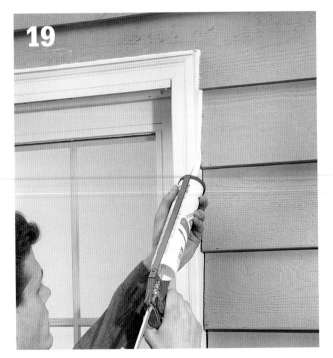

Make sure the drip edge is tight against the top brick molding, then apply paintable silicone caulk along the top of the drip edge and along the outside edge of the side brick moldings. Fill all exterior nail holes with caulk.

Caulk completely around the sill nosing, using your finger to press the caulk into any cracks. As soon as the caulk is dry, paint the sill nosing. Finish the door and install the lockset as directed by the manufacturer. See page 150 to trim the interior of the door.

Attic Access Ladders

Pull-down attic ladders provide instant access to your attic space, making it easy to store and retrieve items without squeezing through a tight access panel. You can replace an existing access panel with a ladder kit or install the ladder in a more convenient location.

When purchasing an access ladder, consider the amount of use it will get. A basic wooden ladder system may be sufficient for occasional use a few times a year. More frequent use may call for a more sturdy model, such as an aluminum ladder, or a disappearing staircase.

It's important that the ladder you install is the proper size for your ceiling height. Never install one that is shorter than your ceiling height. Compare units for weight load, incline angle, and quality of materials when choosing the right ladder for your home. Although most attic ladders are installed the same way, always follow the manufacturer's directions.

Tools & Materials ›

Tape measure
Framing square
Pencil
Wallboard saw
Reciprocating saw
Drill and bits
Hammer
Hacksaw
Attic access ladder
   kit
Stiff wire

2× lumber (for
   framing and
   temporary
   supports)
3" deck screws
2" and 1¼"
   wallboard screws
Casing
1 × 4 lumber
   (for temporary
   ledgers)

An attic access ladder can turn an otherwise useless space into a handy storage area or roof access.

How to Install an Attic Access Ladder

Mark the approximate location for the attic access door on the room ceiling. Drill a hole at one of the corners and push the end of a stiff wire up into the attic. In the attic, locate the wire and clear away insulation in the area. Using dimensions provided by the manufacturer, mark the rough opening across the framing members, using one of the existing joists as one side of the frame. Add 3" to the rough opening length dimension to allow for the headers.

If the width of your ladder unit requires that you cut a joist, build temporary supports in the room below to support each end of the cut joist to prevent damage to your ceiling (pages 268 to 271). Use a reciprocating saw to cut through the joist at both end marks, then remove the cut piece. *Caution: Do not stand on the cut joist.*

Cut two headers to fit between the joists using 2× lumber the same size as your ceiling joists. Position the headers perpendicular to the joists, butting them against the cut joists. Make sure the corners are square, and attach the headers with three 3" deck screws into each joist.

Cut a piece of 2× lumber to the length of the rough opening to form the other side of the frame. Square the corners, and attach the side piece to each header with three 3" deck screws.

(continued)

5

Cut the rough opening in the ceiling using a wallboard saw. Use the rough opening frame to guide your saw blade.

6

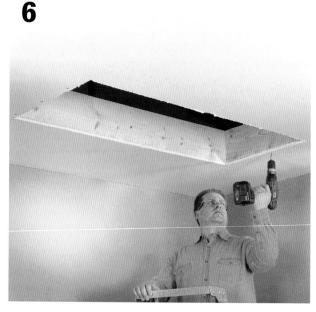

Fasten the edges of the wallboard to the rough opening frame using 1¼" wallboard screws spaced every 8". Prepare the ladder's temporary support clips according to the manufacturer's directions.

7

If your ladder does not include support clips, attach 1 × 4 boards at both ends of the opening, slightly overlapping the edges, to act as ledgers to support the unit while fastening.

8

With a helper, lift the unit through the opening and rest it on the ledgers. Make sure the unit is square in the frame and the door is flush with the ceiling surface. Shim the unit as needed. *Note: Do not stand on the unit until it is firmly attached to the framing.*

9

Attach the ladder unit to the rough framing with 10d nails or 2" screws driven through the holes in the corner brackets and hinge plates. Continue fastening the unit to the frame, driving screws or nails through each side of the ladder frame into the rough frame. Remove the temporary ledgers or support clips when complete.

10

Open the ladder, keeping the lower section folded back. With the tape measure along the top of the rail, measure the distance from the end of the middle section to the floor on each rail. Subtract 3" and mark the distances on the right and left rails of the third section. Use a square to mark a cutting line across the rails. Place a support under the lower section and trim along the cutting line with a hacksaw. (For wooden ladders, see manufacturer's directions.)

11

Fully extend the ladder and test-fit the adjustable feet on the rails. Adjust the feet so there are no gaps in the hinges and the feet are flush with the floor. Drill through the rails, using a recommended size bit, and attach the adjustable feet with included nuts, washers, and bolts.

12

Install casing around the edges to cover the gap between the ceiling wallboard and the ladder frame. Leave a 3⁄8" clearance between the door panel and the casing.

Finishing Techniques

In order to give your window and door projects the quality finish they deserve, you'll want the surrounding moldings to look professionally installed. When properly applied, moldings should create a smooth transition to the walls or exterior siding with miter or butt joints closing tightly. You'll learn trim design options and the correct techniques for installing it in the pages that follow.

This chapter also explains the process for installing locksets, deadbolts, and other necessary hardware items.

This chapter includes:

- Window & Door Casings
- Stool & Apron Window Trim
- Decorative Door Headers
- Basement Window Trim
- Shutters
- Locksets & Deadbolts
- Keyless Entry Deadbolts
- Door Closers
- Securing Windows & Doors

Window & Door Casings

Case Moldings

Window and door casings are the one of the most defining elements of trim in every home. Casing and base trim are commonly the foundation on which all other elements of trim are based. This means they play a crucial role in defining the style of your home.

Take your time deciding on a particular style of casing. When you have made your decision, follow that style throughout your home for a balanced appearance. The following pages will help you choose a casing style. Window casings are covered first, followed by door treatments. Some of the styles shown are projects in this book. The other styles use similar installation techniques with different combinations of trim.

A built-up Victorian window casing consists of two pieces of stock molding with a solid 1" band around the perimeter. The two stock moldings are stacked together and capped with the square stock. Built-up casings such as these are easier to install when they are preassembled on a work surface and installed as one piece because all three moldings can be mitered at the same time. This treatment would be mitered at the top corners and butt into a stool at the base of the window. The stool treatment is plain square stock so it will not draw attention away from the more elaborate casing.

Arts & Crafts casings have many different variations that all have one thing in common: straight clean lines with emphasis on wood grain. In the example shown, a solid 1 × 4 piece is used with butt joints as casing. It is then capped with a back band molding that is mitered at the corners. The apron treatment maintains the back band edge as a continuation of the lines from the casing, interrupted only by a plain piece of flat 1× stock used as a stool. Top corner joints of this treatment are commonly joined with a biscuit to aid in alignment and strength of the joint, but use of a biscuit is not mandatory. Quartersawn white or red oak is frequently used for this style to show off grain pattern, but painted moldings are also acceptable.

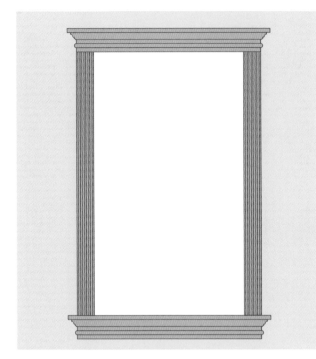

A common Neoclassical window treatment is fluted casings with a decorative head cap. The fluted casings are butted into an ordinary stool and apron at the sill and finished off with a built-up cap similar to the one on page 156. This style is very similar to Victorian fluted casings, but uses a decorative cap rather than rosette blocks at the upper corners.

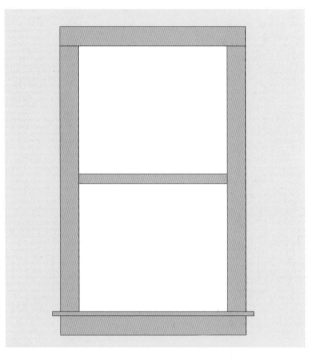

Modern casings may sound dull compared to the curvy style of Victorian casings; however, similar to Arts & Crafts, Modern trim emphasizes smooth straight lines. In the example shown, $3\frac{1}{2}$" birch plywood strips are clear-coated to show off the end grain of the product. The casings are butted together at the top corners with the head capping the legs, and the stool and apron are made entirely of plywood, with no effort made to conceal the plies of the product. Other examples of Modern window treatments include clamshell moldings and plain wallboard without casing.

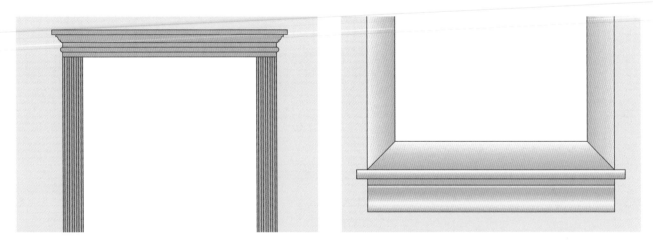

Traditional style casings are also frequently installed to add visual variety to windows or doors in rooms with mixed styles. The example shown, a stock molding with a mix of curves and straight angles, helps to blend together different styles. A standard stool of square stock is finished off with an apron built up from base molding and base cap stacked together.

Door Casing Styles

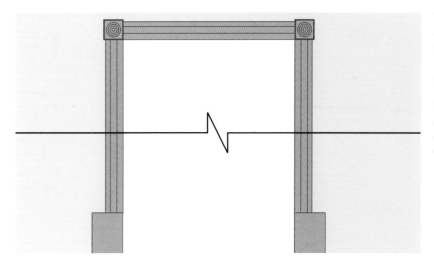

Victorian door treatments include a distinctive style made up of fluted casings with plinth blocks at the floor and rosette blocks at the top corners. This is a classic Victorian trademark that holds many advantages for the do-it-yourselfer. Most notably, this style eliminates mitering and uses style treatments with butt joints at each corner, making installation easy and quick.

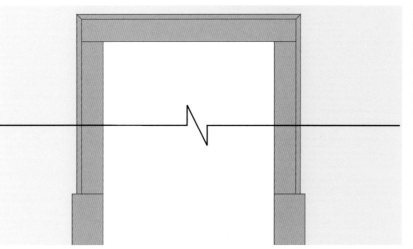

A thicker head casing in an Arts & Crafts installation creates a reveal across the bottom edge of the header, making it easier to deal with irregular walls. A slight miter to the ends of the head casing creates visual appeal. $\frac{5}{4}$ milled stock for the head casing is available at most lumberyards or hardwood suppliers.

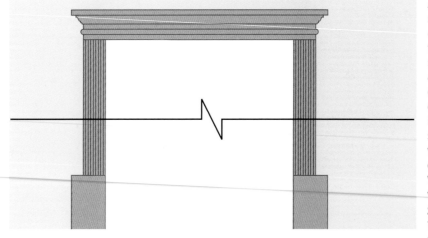

A crossette corner is a Neoclassical style with Georgian roots. Crossette corners, or "shoulders," can be built up to any size. The corner shown is made of standard 1× material with a 1" wide, 6- to 10"-long extension placed at the top of each leg. The head casing caps the tops of the legs and a thicker piece of molding is applied as a back band. In the image shown, exterior brick molding is cut down with a table saw and butted to the edges of the casings, mitered in the corners. Winged casings are easier to build on a work surface prior to installation. Paint-grade material is recommended to hide the seam between the casing and the casing extension.

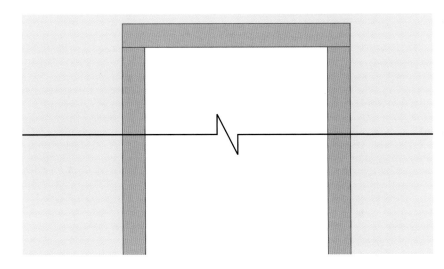

A basic installation of clamshell or ranch-style casing is a good example of Modern style. These casings are generally made of soft woods and painted to blend in with their surroundings. While basic clamshell moldings don't give you a lot to look at visually, if the room has busy faux painted walls or other features you want to highlight, clamshell casings are a simple and inexpensive alternative.

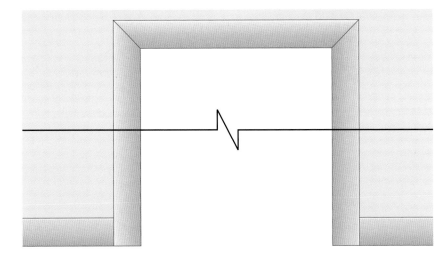

Traditional-style door casings mix well with many different styles and include extensive built-up casings as well as off-the-shelf moldings with little adaptation. In this example, a solid 1 × 4 is installed with butt joints. A stop molding is installed over the perimeter face of the 1 × 4 with mitered joints. Finally, a cove molding is applied to the outer edge of the 1 × 4 to cover the seam along the perimeter. This style of molding may be stained or painted.

How to Make Mitered Casings

1

On each jamb, mark a reveal line 1/8" from the inside edge. The casings will be installed flush with these lines.

2

Place a length of casing along one side jamb, flush with the reveal line. At the top and bottom of the molding, mark the points where horizontal and vertical reveal lines meet. (When working with doors, mark the molding at the top only.)

3

Make 45° miter cuts on the ends of the moldings. Measure and cut the other vertical molding piece, using the same method.

4

Drill pilot holes spaced every 12" to prevent splitting, and attach the vertical casings with 4d finish nails driven through the casings and into the jambs. Drive 6d finish nails into the framing members near the outside edge of the casings.

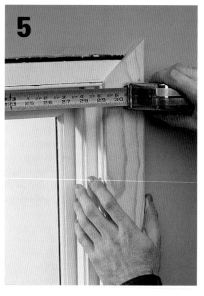

5

Measure the distance between the side casings, and cut top and bottom casings to fit, with ends mitered at 45°. If the window or door unit is not perfectly square, make test cuts on scrap pieces to find the correct angle of the joints. Drill pilot holes and attach with 4d and 6d finish nails.

6

Locknail the corner joints by drilling pilot holes and driving 4d finish nails through each corner, as shown. Drive all nail heads below the wood surface using a nail set, then fill the nail holes with wood putty.

How to Make Butted Door Casings

On each jamb, mark a reveal line ⅛" from the inside edge. The casings will be installed flush with these lines.

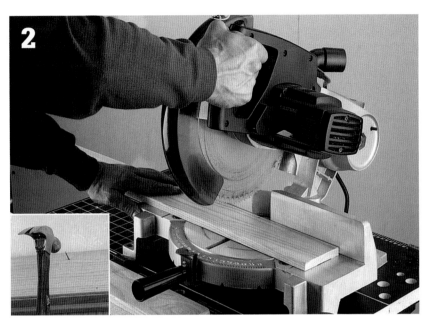

Cut the head casing to length. Mark the centerpoint of the head casing and the centerpoint of the head jamb. Align the casing with the head jamb reveal line, matching the centerpoints so that the head casing extends evenly beyond both side jambs. Nail the casing to the wall at stud locations and at the jamb (inset).

Hold the side casings against the head casing and mark them for cutting, then cut the side casings to fit.

Align the side casings with the side jamb reveal lines, then nail the casings to the jambs and framing members. Set the nails using a nail set. Fill the nail holes with wood putty.

Stool & Apron Window Trim

Stool and apron trim brings a traditional look to a window, and it is most commonly used with double-hung styles. The stool serves as an interior sill; the apron (or the bottom casing) conceals the gap between the stool and the finished wall.

In many cases, such as with 2 × 6 walls, jamb extensions made from 1× finish-grade lumber need to be installed to bring the window jambs flush with the finished wall. Many window manufacturers also sell jamb extensions for their windows.

The stool is usually made from 1× finish-grade lumber, cut to fit the rough opening, with "horns" at each end extending along the wall for the side casings to butt against. The horns extend beyond the outer edge of the casing by the same amount that the front edge of the stool extends past the face of the casing, usually under 1".

If the edge of the stool is rounded, beveled, or otherwise decoratively routed, you can create a more finished appearance by returning the ends of the stool to hide the end grain. A pair of miter cuts at the rough horn will create the perfect cap piece for wrapping the grain of the front edge of the stool around the horn. The same can be done for an apron cut from a molded casing.

When installing these trim components, use a pneumatic nailer—you don't want to spend all that time shimming the jambs perfectly only to knock them out of position with one bad swing of a hammer.

As with any trim project, tight joints are the secret to a successful stool and apron trim job. Take your time to ensure all the pieces fit tightly.

Tip ▸

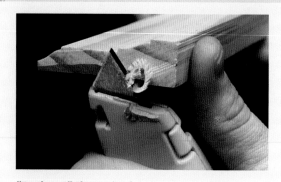

"Back cut" the ends of casing pieces where needed to help create tight joints using a sharp utility knife.

Tools & Materials ▸

Tape measure
Straightedge
Circular saw or
  jigsaw
Handsaw
Plane or rasp
Drill
Hammer
Pneumatic nailer
  (optional)

1× finish lumber
Casing
Wood shims
4d, 6d, and 8d finish
  nails

How to Install Stool & Apron Window Trim

Cut the stool to length, with several inches at each end for creating the horn returns. With the stool centered at the window and tight against the wallboard, shim it to its finished height. At each corner, measure the distance between the window frame and the stool, then mark that dimension on the stool.

Open a compass so it touches the wall and the tip of the rough opening mark on the stool, then scribe the plane of the wall onto the stool to complete the cutting line for the horn.

Cut out the notches for the horn using a jigsaw or a sharp handsaw. Test-fit the stool, making any minor adjustments with a plane or a rasp to fit it tightly to the window and the walls.

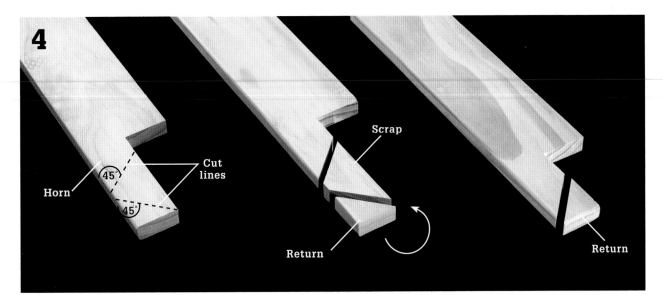

To create a return at the horn of the stool, miter-cut the return pieces at 45° angles. Mark the stool at its overall length and cut it to size with 45° miter cuts. Glue the return to the mitered end of the horn so the grain wraps around the corner. *Note: Use this technique to create the returns on the apron (step 13, page 155), but make the cuts with the apron held on-edge, rather than flat.*

(continued)

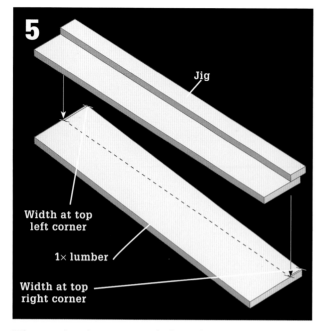

5

Jig

Width at top
left corner

1× lumber

Width at top
right corner

Where extensions are needed, cut the head extension to its finished length—the distance between the window side jambs plus the thickness of both side extensions (typically 1× stock). For the width, measure the distance between the window jamb and the finished wall at each corner, then mark the measurements on the ends of the extension. Use a straightedge to draw a reference line connecting the points. Build a simple cutting jig, as shown.

6

Clamp the jig on the reference line, then rip the extension to width using a circular saw; keep the baseplate tight against the jig and move the saw smoothly through the board. Reposition the clamp when you near the end of the cut. Cut both side extensions to length and width, using the same technique as for the head extension (step 5).

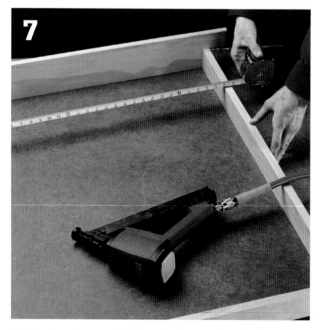

7

Build a box frame with the extensions and stool using 6d finish nails and a pneumatic nailer. Measure to make sure the box has the same dimensions as the window jambs. Drive nails through the top of the head extension into the side extensions and through the bottom of the stool into the side extensions.

8

Apply wood glue to the back edge of the frame, then position it against the front edge of the window jambs. Use wood shims to adjust the frame, making sure the pieces are flush with the window jambs. Fasten the frame at each shim location using 8d finish nails driven through pilot holes. Loosely pack insulation between the framing members and extensions.

On the edge of each extension, mark a ¼" reveal at the corners, the middle, and the stool. Place a length of casing along the head extension, aligned with the reveal marks at the corners. Mark where the reveal marks intersect, then make 45° miter cuts at each point. Reposition the casing at the head extension and attach using 4d finish nails at the extensions and 6d finish nails at the framing members.

Cut the side casings to rough length, leaving the ends slightly long for final trimming. Miter one end at 45°. With the pointed end on the stool, mark the height of the side casing at the top edge of the head casing.

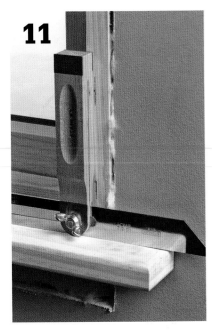

To get a tight fit for the side casings, align one side of a T-bevel with the reveal, mark the side extension, and position the other side flush against the horn. Transfer the angle from the T-bevel to the end of the casing, and cut the casing to length.

Test-fit the casings, making any final adjustments with a plane or rasp. Fasten the casing with 4d finish nails at the extensions and 6d finish nails at the framing members.

Cut apron to length, leaving a few inches at each end for creating the returns (step 4, page 153). Position the apron tight against the bottom edge of the stool, then attach it using 6d finish nails driven every 12".

Decorative Door Headers

Replacing plain head casing on a door or window with a decorative built-up version is a quick and easy way to add some sophistication to any ordinary feature of your home.

Adding a decorative head casing to a door is a simple way to dress up your existing trim. Although head treatments are more common over doors, this project will work for window trim as well. Designing your own decorative molding can be creative and fun, but try not to overwhelm the room with an elaborate piece, as it may detract from the décor.

Standard stock door casings have an outer-edge thickness of approximately $^{11}/_{16}$". Build your custom header around this thickness. Use it to create a reveal line to a thinner piece of trim, or build out from the edge for a bolder, more substantial appearance. In the project shown, a bed molding or a smaller piece of crown molding is used to build the header away from the wall. The ends of the molding are returned to the wall, and the entire piece is capped with a piece of

lattice molding. Installing a decorative header of this style on an interior door may require the installation of additional blocking. For installation over an exterior door or a window, nail the pieces in place directly to the load-bearing framing in the wall above the opening.

Tools & Materials ▸

Pencil
Tape measure
Power miter saw
Finish nail gun
Brad nail gun

Moldings
Wood glue

How to Install a Decorative Door Header

1

Measure the width of your door casing and rough-cut a piece of bed or crown molding 6" longer. Use the casing width dimension to lay out cut marks on the bottom edge of the molding. Start the marks 2" from the end to allow space for cutting the mitered ends.

2

With the molding upside down and against the fence, cut a 45° outside corner miter angle at each end on the casing reference marks from step 1.

3

Cut mitered returns for the molding using the leftover piece. Set the angle of the power miter saw to the opposing 45° angle and cut the returns with the molding upside down and against the fence. Dry-fit the pieces, recutting them if necessary. Apply glue to the return pieces and nail them to the ends of the head molding with 1" brad nails.

4

Nail the new header in place with 2½" finish nails driven at an angle through the bed molding and into the framing members of the wall.

5

Cut lattice molding 1" longer than the length of the bed molding and nail it in place with ⅝" brad nails so that it has a uniform overhang of ½". Fill all nail holes with spackle and sand them with fine-grit sandpaper. Apply the final coat of finish.

Basement Window Trim

Basement windows bring much-needed sunlight into dark areas, but even in finished basements they often get ignored on the trim front. This is partly because most basement foundation walls are at least 8" thick, and often a lot thicker. Add a furred-out wall and the window starts to look more like a tunnel with a pane of glass at the end. But with some well-designed and well-executed trim carpentry, you can turn the depth disadvantage into a positive.

A basement window opening may be finished with wallboard, but the easiest way to trim one is by making extra-wide custom jambs that extend from the inside face of the window frame to the interior wall surface. Because of the extra width, plywood stock is a good choice for the custom jambs. The project shown here is created with veneer-core plywood with oak veneer surface. The jamb members are fastened together into a nice square frame using rabbet joints at the corner. The frame is scribed and installed as a single unit and then trimmed out with oak casing. The casing is applied flush with the inside edges of the frame opening. If you prefer to have a reveal edge around the interior edge of the casing, you will need to add a solid hardwood strip to the edge of the frame so the plies of the plywood are not visible.

Tools & Materials ▸

Pencil
Tape measure
Table saw, drill with bits
2-ft level
Framing square
Utility knife
Straightedge

Finish-grade ¾" oak plywood
Spray-foam insulation
1¼" composite or cedar wood shims
2" finish nails
1⅝" drywall screws
Carpenter's glue

Because they are set into thick foundation walls, basement windows present a bit of a trimming challenge. But the thickness of the foundation wall also lets you create a handy ledge that's deep enough to hold potted plants or even sunning cats.

How to Trim a Basement Window

Check to make sure the window frame and surrounding area are dry and free of rot, mold, or damage. At all four corners of the basement window, measure from the inside edges of the window frame to the wall surface. Add 1" to the longest of these measurements.

Set your table saw to make a rip cut to the width arrived at in step 1. If you don't have a table saw, set up a circular saw and straightedge cutting guide to cut strips to this length. With a fine-tooth panel-cutting blade, rip enough plywood strips to make the four jamb frame components.

Miter gauge

$3/8 \times 3/4$" rabbet

Cross-cut the plywood strips to correct lengths. In our case, we designed the jamb frame to be the exact same outside dimensions as the window frame, since there was some space between the jamb frame and the rough opening.

Cut $3/8$"-deep × $3/4$"-wide rabbets at each end of the head jamb and the sill jamb. A router table is the best tool for this job, but you may use a table saw or handsaws and chisels. Inspect the jambs first and cut the rabbets in whichever face is in better condition. To ensure uniformity, we ganged the two jambs together (they're the same length). It's also a good idea to include backer boards to prevent tear-out.

(continued)

Glue and clamp the frame parts together, making sure to clamp near each end from both directions. Set a carpenter's square inside the frame and check it to make sure it's square.

Before the glue sets, carefully drill three perpendicular pilot holes, countersunk, through the rabbeted workpieces and into the side jambs at each corner. Space the pilot holes evenly, keeping the end ones at least ¾" in from the end. Drive a 1⅝" drywall screw into each pilot hole, taking care not to overdrive. Double-check each corner for square as you work, adjusting the clamps if needed.

Let the glue dry for at least one hour (overnight is better), then remove the clamps and set the frame in the window opening. Adjust the frame so it is centered and level in the opening and the exterior-side edges fit flush against the window frame.

Taking care not to disturb the frame's position (rest a heavy tool on the sill to hold it in place if you wish), press a steel rule against the wall surface and mark trimming points at the point where the rule meets the jambs at each side of all four frame corners using a sharp pencil.

Remove the frame and clamp it on a flat work surface. Use a straightedge to connect the scribe marks at the ends of each jamb frame side. Set the cutting depth of your circular saw to just a small fraction over ¾". Clamp a straightedge guide to the frame so the saw blade will follow the cutting line and trim each frame side in succession. (The advantage of using a circular saw here is that any tear-out from the blade will be on the nonvisible faces of the frame.)

Replace the frame in the window opening in the same orientation as when you scribed it and install shims until it is level and centered in the opening. Drive a few finish nails through the side jambs into the rough frame. Also drive a few nails through the sill jamb. Most trim carpenters do not drive nails into the head jamb.

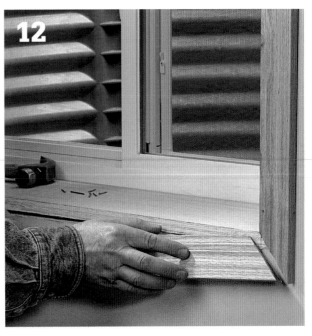

Insulate between the jamb frame and the rough frame with spray-in polyurethane foam. Look for minimal-expanding foam labeled "window and door" and don't spray in too much. Let the foam dry for a half hour or so and then trim off the excess with a utility knife. *Tip: Protect the wood surfaces near the edges with wide strips of masking tape.*

Remove the masking tape and clean up the mess from the foam (there is always some). Install case molding. We used picture-frame techniques to install fairly simple oak casing.

Shutters

Wooden shutters have long been a popular window treatment, adding charm to any window setting. Accordion-fold shutters may be used on almost any window. They offer privacy and open neatly to expose the full width of the window. Shutters with louvers offer greater light control than many other window treatments.

If the exact size of ready-made shutters isn't available, select a pair that is slightly larger than your measurements. Half-shutters on a double-hung window usually reach (but do not extend past) the top of the lower sash.

You can trim the shutters to the correct height with a miter saw, radial arm saw, or table saw. If you're removing ³⁄₄" or less, take it all off the bottom of the shutters. If you need to remove more, take half off the top and half off the bottom.

Make sure the window frame is square before installing the shutters. Tape two shutters together and stand them in the window opening with the left-hand shutter touching the left jamb. Be sure the bottoms of the shutters are flat on the window stool. If there's no gap between the jamb and the shutter, that side is square. Tape the other two shutters together and check the right side the same way.

If there is a gap, the window is out of square and you must taper the shutters to accommodate the variance before installing them (see step 1, next page).

Interior shutters serve many purposes. They're attractive window features, they help control sunlight as well as heat, and they allow you to easily choose between visibility or privacy.

Tools & Materials ▸

Miter saw	Shutters, tape
Radial arm saw or table saw	¹⁄₈"-wide shims
	120-grit sandpaper
Jointer, belt sander, or hand plane	2¹⁄₂" non-mortising hinges
Screwdriver	Screws
Paintbrush	Paint or varnish
Tape measure	Latch
Pencil compass	

How to Install Interior Shutters

Adjust a pencil compass to the widest part of the gap. Hold the pivot point against the jamb and slide the compass down from top to bottom, marking a corresponding line. Use a jointer, belt sander, or hand plane to trim the shutter to the pencil line. Repeat for the other side, and test-fit both sides in the window.

Stand all four shutters in position, adding ⅛"-thick shims beneath them and along both sides. Check for uniform spaces. If necessary, trim the shutters to fit. Remove from the window and lightly sand each shutter with 120-grit sandpaper. Paint, stain, or varnish using a narrow brush to reach between the louvers.

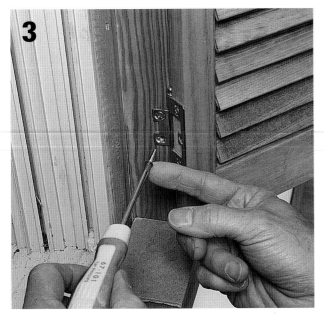

Join each pair of shutters with two 2½" non-mortising hinges so that they fold outward and swing away from the sash. Attach two hinges to each shutter edge that abuts the side jamb. If the middle gap is not uniform when the shutters are closed, shim behind the jamb hinge to adjust it. Attach a small latch to hold the shutters closed.

Tip ▶

Nonfunctional shutters serve as decorative side panels. They are simply mounted on the wall. They can be painted or "pickled" with a colored stain (as shown here). Instead of matching the window frame, the shutters may be finished to match one of the fabrics in the room.

Building Custom Exterior Storm Shutters

Working exterior shutters are a permanent alternative to the frenzied rush of installing plywood over your windows in the hours before an approaching storm, only to have to remove it again once the danger has passed. For those of you far from the threat of coastal storms, working shutters provide a quick and easy way to protect the windows on summer cabins or cottages while you are away.

These easy-to-construct shutters are built from exterior-grade tongue-and-groove boards. Their simple, rustic design is offset with stylish beveled cleat-and-fan battens. A customized decorative trim, visible when open, can turn these utilitarian shutters into a fashionable complement to your home's exterior.

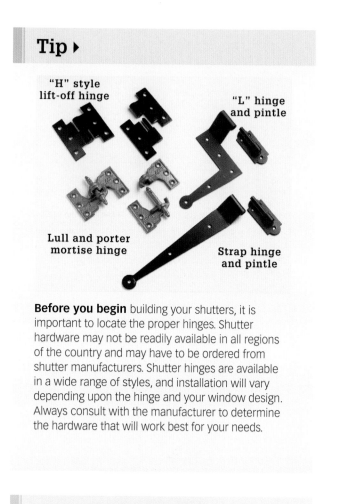

Tip ▶

"H" style lift-off hinge

"L" hinge and pintle

Lull and porter mortise hinge

Strap hinge and pintle

Before you begin building your shutters, it is important to locate the proper hinges. Shutter hardware may not be readily available in all regions of the country and may have to be ordered from shutter manufacturers. Shutter hinges are available in a wide range of styles, and installation will vary depending upon the hinge and your window design. Always consult with the manufacturer to determine the hardware that will work best for your needs.

Tools & Materials ▶

Tape measure	1 × 8 tongue-and-
Pipe clamps	groove lumber
Straightedge	1 × 4 dimensional
Circular saw	lumber, wood glue
Router with chamfer	1¼ and 3" galvanized
bit	deck screws
Paintbrush	Paint
Drill	Shutter hardware

These customized shutters are designed to protect your windows from the high winds and flying debris of severe storms.

How to Build Custom Exterior Storm Shutters

To determine dimensions for your shutters, first measure the height of the window opening. Because windows may not be square, it's best to take both a right- and left-side measurement. Subtract ½" from the actual height to allow for clearance. To find the width of each shutter, measure the width between the inside edges of the window jamb, divide by two, and subtract ⅜" to allow for hinge clearance.

Assemble two to four tongue-and-groove 1 × 8s so that each shutter is slightly larger than its determined width. Hold the 1 × 8s together with pipe clamps, then use a straightedge to mark the dimensions on the face of each shutter. Cut the shutters to length using a circular saw.

Remove the clamps. Use a circular saw to rip the shutters to width, removing the grooved edge from one side of each shutter and the tongue edge from the other. Reattach the clamps.

Cleat

End piece

Cut four cleats 3" shorter than the shutter width from 1 × 4 exterior-grade lumber. Also cut four end pieces, mitering the ends at 45°. Bevel all edges that will not butt another piece using a router and chamfer bit.

(continued)

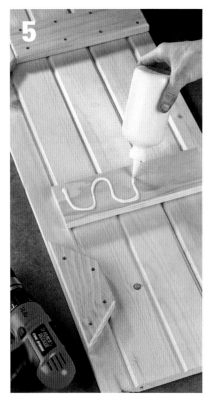

Attach the cleats and end pieces using waterproof wood glue and countersunk 1¼" galvanized screws. Allow glue to fully dry before installing the shutters.

Variation: To spruce up the simple design and construction of these shutters, consider a customized decorative trim design for the side that is visible when open. Ideas for trim include a sawtooth design or a traditional X- or Z-style (as shown above) barn door. Each design can be cut from 1 × 4 material and attached with wood glue and screws.

Paint or stain the shutters as desired and allow to dry. Drill pilot holes and attach the shutter hinges to the cleats with included fasteners or 1¼" galvanized screws.

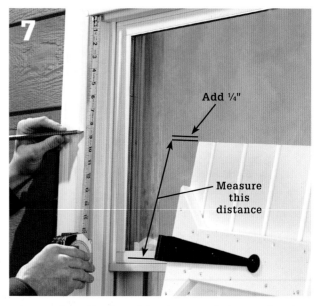

Add ¼"

Measure this distance

Measure from the top of the shutter to the lower edge of the upper hinge and add ¼". Measure down this distance from the edge of the top jamb and make a mark. Align the bottom of the pintle's pin with the mark. Attach the pintle to the window molding using 3" galvanized screws.

8

9

Set the top hinge on the pintle. Support the shutter until both hinges are attached. Align the lower pintle with the lower hinge and attach it with 3" galvanized screws. Repeat steps 7 and 8 for the other shutter. *Note: Hinge installation may vary due to hinge style and window design. Always follow manufacturer's directions.*

Install decorative holdbacks (also called shutter dogs) to hold the shutters in the open position. A slide latch can be installed inside or outside the shutters. An inexpensive alternative to latches is to install a pair of bar holders on the outside of the shutters and secure them with a 2 × 4 during the storm.

Variation: Manufactured Storm Shutters ▸

Manufactured storm shutters are available in many traditional styles, including louvered, raised panel, and board-and-batten.

Rolling shutters adjust to any position to provide storm protection or light control. They can be controlled manually or automatically.

Bahama-style shutters function as sun awnings when open and provide wind and impact protection when closed.

Locksets & Deadbolts

Home security is not so much a matter of tenacious crime prevention as it is a question of peace of mind. If you have been burglarized, you're bound to feel vulnerable. So we all have an interest in keeping what's outside, outside. There are many different approaches to accomplishing this; some cost a lot of money, some don't cost much at all. The first (and most expensive) is having a whole-house security system installed that notifies the police if there's any trouble. But not everyone needs or wants something so involved. A more passive approach serves their needs. This generally means a combination of motion-activated floodlights and quality door locks. When someone carefully approaches a back door at night, there are few things as alarming as having a bright light suddenly flash in their eyes. And there's nothing quite as discouraging as trying to break through a door with a deadbolt lock when you want to go unnoticed.

If you only care to do one of these security building jobs, pick installing better locks. They're on the job every day, all day and all night, whether the power is on or off.

Tools & Materials ▶

Holesaw	Keys
Putty knife	Strike plates
Drill	Collar
Utility knife	Strike bolts
Allen wrenches	Deadbolt
Screwdriver	Thumb latch
Wood chisel	Cutout pattern
New lockset	Bolt plates

You never know when you'll need to replace a door lockset or deadbolt, but there are many situations when you'll be glad you know how to do it.

How to Install a Lockset

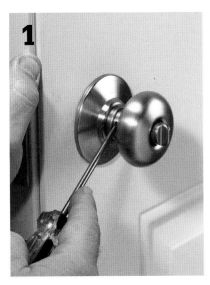

1

Remove the old lockset. The knob on the inside of the door is usually held in place with a small clip. This is located on the side of the sleeve that extends from the knob to the flange on the door surface. To release this clip, just push it into the flange with a screwdriver or an awl. Then pull off the knob.

2

Remove the flange next. These are usually snapped in place over the lock mechanism underneath. To remove one, just pry it off with a screwdriver pushed into a slot designed for it. Other flanges are held by small spring clips. By pushing down on the clip with a screwdriver, the flange can easily be pulled off with your fingers.

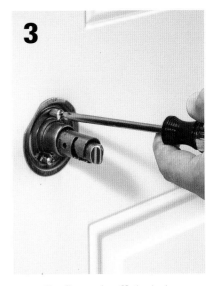

3

Once the flange is off, the lock mechanism will be accessible. The two sides of the lock are joined together by two screws. Remove these screws and take the lock components out of the lockset hole in the door.

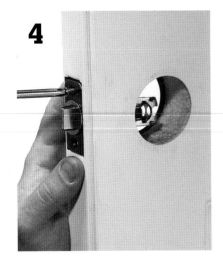

4

With both sides of the lock removed, the lock bolt can be taken out. Remove the screws that hold the bolt plate to the edge of the door. Then pull out the bolt mechanism.

5

Install the new bolt assembly and make sure that the screws in the bolt plate are driven tightly into the door. Separate the lock halves and slide them together with the door and bolt assembly sandwiched between.

6

While holding one side of the lock against the door, maneuver the other side of the lock so the screws fall in the slots made for them. Once the screw heads have cleared the slots, tighten the screws so both halves of the lock are tight against the door. Install the new knobs and new strike plate.

How to Install a Deadbolt

Template Tip ▸

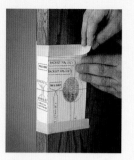

Many doors sold today come with holes for the lockset predrilled. Some also are predrilled for a deadbolt, but very often you'll need to drill holes for the actual deadbolt you purchase. To assist in this, manufacturers provide a template that you tape to the door for reference. Following the manufacturer's instructions, tape the hole template to the door (make sure you've oriented the template to correspond to the actual thickness of your door) and mark the center point of each hole, including the bolt hole in the edge of the door. The deadbolt is usually located 7 or 8" above the lockset.

Determine the size of holesaw you need by checking the installation instructions that came with the lock. Then chuck this tool into a drill and bore the hole. Stop boring when the tip of the drill bit, at the center of the holesaw, breaks through the other side.

Go to the other side of the door and slide the pilot bit of the hole saw into the hole and cut out the rest of the waste material. If you try to cut through the door in a single pass, you risk tearing the steel covering (on steel-clad doors) as the holesaw teeth break through the surface.

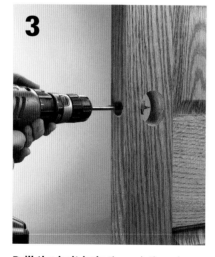

Drill the bolt hole through the edge of the door using a spade bit or forstner bit. Make sure to keep the bit level so the bolt hole will enter the lock hole at the proper point.

Push the bolt assembly into the bolt hole so the bolt plate is flat on the edge of the door. Trace around the plate with a utility knife. Remove the mechanism and cut a ⅛"-deep mortise in the edge of the door with a sharp chisel (see next page).

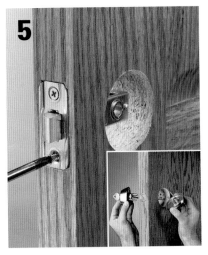

5

Once you're satisfied with the fit, press the bolt plate into its mortise and attach it by driving in the two plate screws. Slide both sides of the lock into the bolt mechanism and attach them by driving the screws that hold the two parts together. Make sure these screws are tight (inset).

Mortising Technique ▸

Installing hardware plates requires using a wood chisel to create a mortise for the hardware.

1

Deepen the outline for the mortise to ⅛" with a wood chisel (try to find a chisel the same width as the mortise). With the beveled face of the chisel blade facing into the mortise, rap the handle with a mallet.

2

Chisel a series of ⅛"-deep parallel cuts about ¼" apart.

3

Position the chisel bevel-side down at about a 45° angle. Strike with a mallet to chisel out the waste. Smooth the mortise bottom.

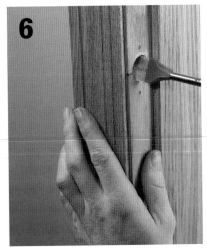

6

Extend the lock bolt and color its end with lipstick, a grease pencil, or a crayon. Then retract the bolt, close the door, and extend the bolt so its end hits the jamb. This will yield the precise location of the bolt hole that's needed on the jamb. Drill a hole (usually 1½" deep) for the bolt with a spade bit (see installation instructions for actual hole size requirements).

7

Close the door and test the deadbolt to make sure the bolt fits into the bolt hole in the jamb. If not, enlarge the hole slightly. Once the bolt fits, center the strike plate over the bolt hole and trace it with a utility knife. Cut a mortise for the strike plate using a sharp chisel.

8

Finish up by installing the strike plate on the jamb. Some of these plates are oversized like the one above. But most look more like standard lockset strike plates. Both types, however, feature long screws that are driven through the jamb and deep into the wall studs behind.

Keyless Entry Deadbolts

Keyless entry provides home security with the push of a button. These systems generally work with either a small keychain remote or a programmable keypad. It is a great addition if you have children who must come home to an empty house after school. After you teach your children the keypad code, you won't have to worry about lost or stolen keys.

If you are replacing an old deadbolt with a keyless entry system, don't assume that the new lock will fit the existing holes. If the door and jamb holes are slightly misaligned, the lock will not work properly. Consult the manufacturer's directions for measurement requirements, and make sure the holes in the door and jamb are properly sized and aligned.

Tools & Materials ›

Awl, drill with ⅛" bit
Hole saw
Spade bits
Utility knife
Hammer
Chisel

Flat-head and Phillips
  screwdrivers
Keyless entry deadbolt
  kit
Nail
3" wood screws

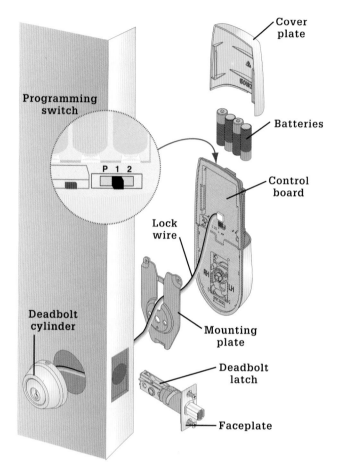

Programming switch

Cover plate

Batteries

Control board

Lock wire

Deadbolt cylinder

Mounting plate

Deadbolt latch

Faceplate

How to Install a Keyless Entry Deadbolt

Tape the template supplied with your lock to the door in the desired location, usually about 5½" above the existing lockset. Mark the center positions for the cylinder and deadbolt holes with an awl (inset). Then, drill pilot holes at the marked points entirely through the door face and 2" deep into the door edge.

Use a drill and hole saw of the recommended size to bore the cylinder hole. To avoid splintering the wood, drill through one side until the pilot bit comes through, then finish drilling the hole from the other side.

3

Mark the center of the strike box onto the door jamb by closing the door and pressing a nail from inside the cylinder hole through the pilot hole in the door edge until it marks the door jamb (inset). Use the recommended spade bit to bore a 1"-deep hole into the jamb. Bore the deadbolt latch hole through the door edge and into the cylinder hole using the recommended spade bit.

4

Insert the deadbolt latch into the edge hole and hold it in place temporarily with the included screws. Score around the faceplate with a utility knife (inset). Then, remove the latch and use a hammer and chisel to carefully remove material until the faceplate fits flush with the door. Attach the faceplate to the door with the included screws.

5

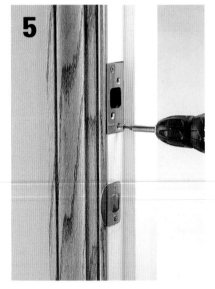

Insert the strike box into the door jamb, and make sure the deadbolt is precisely aligned with the strike plate. Mark and chisel out a recess so the strike plate is flush with the jamb. Drill pilot holes and install the strike plate with 3" wood screws.

6

Fit the exterior portion of the lock into the cylinder hole, sliding the cylinder tailpiece through the proper hole on the deadbolt. Route the lock wire underneath the deadbolt, making sure it is free of any moving parts. Fit the wire through the proper hole on the interior mounting plate and attach the plate to the deadbolt with the included screws.

7

Follow the manufacturer's instructions to align your lock control for a left- or right-hand door. Plug the lock wire into the receiving wire on the interior control board. With the bolt extended and the knob in the vertical position, slide the board into place and attach it with the included screws. Install the batteries and follow the manufacturer's instructions to program the remote and entry codes.

Door Closers

The basic function of a door closer is to close and latch the door with a smooth, controlled motion after the door has been released. Many local building codes require door closers on fire doors between the garage and the residence. Closers can also help protect children from the dangers of basements, laundry rooms, or workshops.

Most door closers have adjustment screws for door speed and closing power, which allow you to adjust the closing action to your needs. Some applications call for the door to close quickly and then slow down to avoid slamming. For other doors, you may want the door to close slowly, then speed up at the end to ensure that it latches.

Tools & Materials ▶

Tape measure
Pencil
Screwdriver
Drill and bits
Door closer

A door closer can bring both convenience and safety to some doors, especially with a curious toddler at home.

How to Install a Door Closer

Assemble the arm and closer according to manufacturer's directions. Mark and drill pilot holes into the pull side of the door and frame using the template or dimensions provided by manufacturer.

Position the closer on the door, making sure the closing-speed adjustment valves are facing the hinges. Attach the closer to the door with included screws. Then attach the shoe to the door frame.

Adjust the length of the forearm so it forms a right angle with the door. Connect the arm to the shoe with its included screw. Adjust the door speed and closing power according to the manufacturer's directions.

Installation Variations ▸

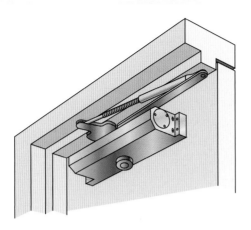

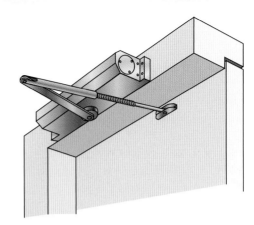

Parallel arm method: This method allows the closer arm to tuck against the jamb and out of the room space. Install the closer on the push side of the door using the included optional mounting bracket. Consult the manufacturer's directions for parallel arm installation methods. *Note: Adjustment screws should face away from the hinges when using this method.*

Top jamb method: Mount the closer to the frame above the door on the push side of the door and attach the shoe to the door. Consult the manufacturer's directions for top jamb installation methods.

Door Closer Options ▸

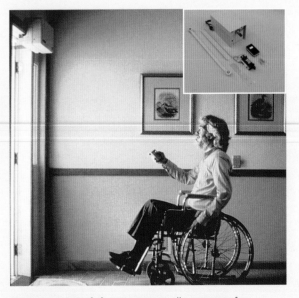

Hinge-pin closers use an adjustable spring to pull doors shut. To install, simply replace the pin in the existing door hinge with the hinge-pin closer. Check the hinge-pin closer for door weight ratings—heavy doors may require more than one closer.

Remote control door openers allow access for wheelchair users or those who lack the strength to open heavy doors. Some of these remote systems are quite complex and should be installed by a professional.

Securing Windows & Doors

Securing windows and doors is often simply a matter of having the right hardware pieces. But skimping on strength or quality with any of them will undermine the security of the whole system.

Glass is both the strength and weakness of windows, in terms of security. An intruder can easily break the glass, but may not, since the noise it would make is likely to draw attention. Aside from installing metal bars, there's no way to secure the glass. Make sure your windows can't be opened from the outside.

Entry doors should be metal or solid wood—at least 1¾" thick—and each one in the home should have a deadbolt lock, as doorknob locks provide little security. Lock quality varies widely; just make sure to choose one that has a bolt (or bolt core) of hardened steel and a minimum 1" throw—the distance the bolt protrudes from the door when engaged.

Door hinges are easy to secure. Manufacturers offer a variety of inexpensive devices that hold a door in place even when the hinge pins are removed.

Garage doors are structurally secure, but their locking devices can make them easy targets. When you're away from home, place a padlock in the roller track. If you have an automatic door opener, make sure the remote transmitter uses a rolling code system, which prevents thieves from copying your signal. An electronic keypad can make your garage door as secure and easy to use as your front door.

Tools & Materials ▶

Hammer	Plywood
Drill	Casing nails
Hole saw	Board
Spade bit	Eye bolts
Awl	Hinge
Screwdriver	Screws
Chisel	Dowel
Utility knife	Security devices

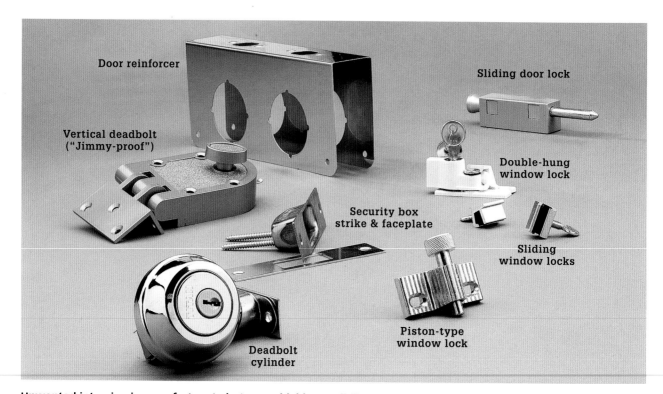

Door reinforcer

Sliding door lock

Vertical deadbolt ("Jimmy-proof")

Double-hung window lock

Security box strike & faceplate

Sliding window locks

Deadbolt cylinder

Piston-type window lock

Unwanted intrusion is an unfortunate but unavoidable possibility for every homeowner—regardless of where you live. Securing windows and doors with appropriate hardware can bring peace of mind as well as property protection.

Plywood shim

Original shim

Install plywood shims in the gaps between the door frame and wall studs to prevent pry-bar attacks. Remove the casing molding on the inside of the frame and inspect the gap; if it's wider than ¼", install new plywood shims in the spaces between the original shims. Be sure to shim directly above, below, and behind the strike plate. Drill pilot holes, and secure the shims with 10d casing nails.

Replace short hinge screws with longer screws (3 or 4") that extend through the door jamb and into the wall studs. This helps resist door kick-ins. Tighten the screws snug, but avoid overtightening them, which can pull the frame out of square.

Add metal door reinforcers to strengthen the areas around locks and prevent kick-ins. Remove the lockset (page 169) and slip the reinforcer over the door's edge. Be sure to get a reinforcer that is the correct thickness for your door.

Add a heavy-duty latch guard to reinforce the door jamb around the strike plate. For added protection, choose a guard with a flange that resists pry-bar attacks. Install the guard with long screws that reach the wall studs.

(continued)

Tips for Securing Sliding Glass Doors ▶

Make a custom lock for your door track using a thick board and a hinge. Cut the board to fit behind the closed door, then cut it again a few inches from one end. Install a hinge so you can flip up the end and keep the door secure while it's ajar. Attach knobs to facilitate use.

Drive screws into the upper track to keep the sliding panel from being pried up and out of the lower track. Use sturdy panhead screws spaced about every 8", and drive them so their heads just clear the top of the door. For metal door frames, use self-tapping screws and a low drill speed.

Attach a sliding-door lock to the frame of the sliding panel. Drill a hole for the deadbolt into the upper track. Then drill an additional hole a few inches away so you can lock the door in an open position.

Tips for Securing Windows ▶

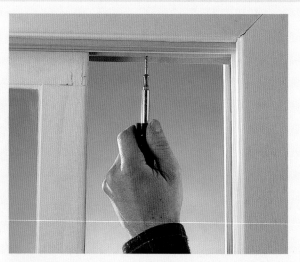

Pin together sashes of single- and double-hung windows with ¼ × 3" eye bolts. With the window closed, drill a ¼"-dia. hole, at a slight downward angle, through the top rail of the bottom sash and into the bottom rail of the top sash. Avoid hitting the glass, and stop the hole about three quarters of the way through the top sash. To lock the window in open positions, drill holes along the sash stiles (vertical pieces) instead.

Drive screws into the top channel of sliding windows to prevent intruders from lifting the window sash out of the lower channel. The screws should just clear the top of the window and not interfere with its operation. Use sturdy screws, and space them about 6" apart.

Block sash channels on sliding windows with a narrow board or a thick dowel.

Use auxiliary locks on sliding windows when a dowel or board won't work. Most types can be installed on the upper or lower window track.

Replace old sash locks on double-hung windows with keyed devices. Traditional sash locks can be highly vulnerable—especially on old windows. Be sure to store a key nearby for emergency exits.

Removing the handles from casement and awning windows keeps intruders from cranking the window open after breaking the glass.

Security bars or gates can be installed in ground-floor windows to prevent intruders from gaining entry to your home.

Entryway Additions

Enhancing your home's entry isn't limited to just installing a new front door or replacing a nearby window. With some ingenuity and a little courage, you can stretch your do-it-yourself skills by undertaking some light masonry. Just imagine the "facelift" possibilities that could be had by adding tile or brickwork where only concrete had once been. Masonry adds shadow lines, dashes of earthy color, and even striking new geometric patterns to your entryway, not to mention an added degree of durability against foot traffic and the elements. Laying a bed of mortar or setting new tile isn't complicated work, but it does take some careful planning, a good shovel and trowel, and, of course, a strong back.

Each project in this chapter includes a complete Tools & Materials list of what you'll need and step-by-step photos to help you through the construction process. Here's a chance to give your entryway that crowning touch it deserves. So, roll up your sleeves and give masonry a try. You'll surely be impressed with the results.

This chapter includes:

- Tiled Entryway Steps
- Brick Pillars
- Paved Landing with Planters

Tiled Entryway Steps

In addition to the traditional tricks for improving your home's curb appeal—landscaping, fresh paint, pretty windows—a tiled entry makes a wonderful, positive impression. To be suitable for tiling, stair treads must be deep enough to walk on safely. Check local building codes for specifics, but most require that treads be at least 11" deep (from front to back) after the tile is added.

Before you start laying any tiles, the concrete must be free of curing agents, clean, and in good shape. Make necessary repairs and give them time to cure. An isolation membrane can be applied before the tile. This membrane can be a fiberglass sheet or it can be brushed on as a liquid to dry. In either case, it separates the tile from the concrete, which allows the two to move independently and protects the tile from potential settling or shifting of the concrete.

Choose exterior-rated, unglazed floor tile with a skid-resistant surface. Tile for the walking surfaces should be at least ½" thick. Use bullnose tiles at the front edges of the treads (as you would on a counter-top) and use cove tiles as the bottom course on risers.

Tools & Materials ▸

Pressure washer
Masonry trowel
4-foot level
Carpenter's square
Straightedge
Tape measure
Chalk line
Tile cutter or wet saw
Tile nippers
Square-notched trowel
Needle-nose plier
Rubber mallet
Grout float
Grout sponge
Caulk gun
Latex or epoxy patching compound
Isolation membrane
Tile spacers
Buckets
Paintbrush and roller
Plastic sheeting
Paper towels
Dry-set mortar
Field tile
Bullnose tile
Grout
Grout additive
Latex tile caulk
Grout sealer
Tile sealer
2 × 4
Carpet scrap
Cold chisel or flathead screwdriver
Wire brush
Broom

The geometric pattern and rich color of tile adds a custom touch to the steps of your entryway.

How to Tile Concrete Steps

Use a pressure washer to clean the surface of the concrete. (Use a washer with at least 4,000 psi and follow the manufacturer's instructions carefully to avoid damaging the concrete with the pressurized spray.)

Dig out rubble in large cracks and chips using a small cold chisel or flathead screwdriver. Use a wire brush to loosen dirt and debris in small cracks. Sweep the area or use a wet/dry vacuum to remove all debris.

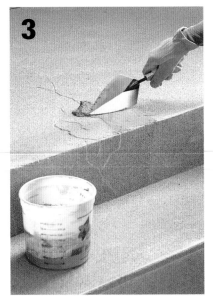

Fill small cracks and chips with masonry patching compound using a masonry trowel. Allow the patching compound to cure according to manufacturer's directions.

If damage is located at a front edge, clean it as described above. Place a board in front and block the board in place with bricks or concrete blocks. Wet the damaged area and fill it with patching compound. Use a masonry trowel to smooth the patch and then allow it to cure thoroughly.

Test the surface of the steps and stoop for low spots using a 4-ft. level or other straightedge. Fill any low spots with patching compound and allow the compound to cure thoroughly.

(continued)

Spread a layer of isolation membrane over the concrete using a notched trowel. Smooth the surface of the membrane using the flat edge of a trowel. Allow the membrane to cure according to manufacturer's directions.

The sequence is important when tiling a stairway with a landing. The primary objective is to install the tile in such a way that the fewest possible cut edges are visible from the main viewing position. If you are tiling the sides of concrete steps, start laying tile there first. Begin by extending horizontal lines from the tops of the stair treads back to the house on the sides of the steps. Use a 4-ft. level.

Mix a batch of thinset mortar with latex bonding adhesive and trowel it onto the sides of the steps, trying to retain visibility of the layout lines. Because the top steps are likely more visible than the bottom steps, start on top and work your way down.

Begin setting tiles into the thinset mortar on the sides of the steps. Start at the top and work your way downward. Try to lay out tile so the vertical gaps between tiles align. Use spacers if you need to.

Wrap a 2 × 4 in old carpet and drag it back and forth across the tile surfaces to set them evenly. Don't get too aggressive here—you don't want to dislodge all of the thinset mortar.

Measure the width of a riser, including the thickness of the tiles you've laid on the step sides. Calculate the centerpoint and mark it clearly with chalk or a marker.

Next, install the tiles on the stair risers. Because the location of the tops of the riser tiles affects the positioning of the tread and landing tiles, you'll get the most accurate layout if the riser tiles are laid first. Start by stacking tiles vertically against the riser. (In some cases, you'll only need one tile to reach from tread to tread.) Add spacers. Trace the location of the tread across the back of the top tile to mark it for cutting.

Cut enough tiles to size to lay tiles for all the stair risers. Be sure to allow enough space for grout joints if you are stacking tiles.

Trowel thinset mortar mixed with bonding adhesive onto the faces of the risers. In most cases, you should be able to tile each riser all at once.

Lay tiles on the risers. The bottom tile edges can rest on the tread, and the tops of the top tiles should be flush with or slightly lower than the plane of the tread above.

(continued)

Dry-lay tile in both directions on the stair landing. You'll want to maintain the same grout lines that are established by the riser tiles, but you'll want to evaluate the front-to-back layout to make sure you don't end up with a row of tiles that is less than 2" or so in width.

Cut tiles as indicated by your dry run, and then begin installing them by troweling thinset adhesive for the bullnose tiles at the front edge of the landing. The tiles should overlap the top edges of the riser tiles, but not extend past their faces.

Set the first row of field tiles, maintaining an even gap between the field tiles and the bullnose tiles.

Add the last row of tiles next to the house and threshold, cutting them as needed so they are between ¼ and ½" away from the house.

Install tiles on the stair treads, starting at the top tread and working your way downward. Set a bullnose tile on each side of the centerline and work your way toward the sides, making sure to conceal the step-side tiles with the tread tiles.

Fill in the field tiles on the stair treads, being sure to leave a gap between the back tiles and the riser tiles that's the same thickness as the other tile gaps.

Let the thinset mortar cure for a few days, and then apply grout in the gaps between tiles using a grout float. Wipe away the grout after it clouds over. Cover with plastic, in the event of rain.

After a few weeks, seal the grout lines with an exterior-rated grout sealer.

Select (or have prepared) a pretinted caulk that's the same color as your grout. Fill the gap between the back row of tiles and the house with caulk. Smooth with a wet finger if needed.

Brick Pillars

Nothing gives a landscape a greater sense of permanence and substance than well-planned and well-executed masonry work. It makes the impression that the structures will be there for decades, not just a few summers. And masonry doesn't have to mean just simple projects like walking paths or borders around your plantings. If you're feeling ambitious, you can tackle a bit of bricklaying.

As masonry projects go, this one is fairly simple. Even if you're a beginner, you can build these elegant, professional-looking pillars if you proceed slowly and follow the instructions carefully. Of course, if you have a friend or relative who knows his (or her) way around brick and mortar, it can't hurt to have an experienced eye check out your progress.

Your adventure in bricklaying begins with choosing a site for the pillars and pouring footings to support them. These below-grade columns of concrete provide a stable foundation that will protect your pillars when freezes and thaws cause the soil to shift.

The finished pillars can serve many functions. They can support a gate, frame a flower bed of which you're particularly proud, or support meandering vines.

Whatever their primary purpose, you'll enjoy them for years, perhaps decades, as they weather and gain character. And you'll be proud to tell everyone that you built them.

Tools & Materials ▶

Mason's string	Concrete mix
Shovel	Standard modular
Wheelbarrow	bricks (4 × 2⅔ × 8")
Pencil	Type N mortar mix
Masonry trowel	Small dowel
Level	Vegetable oil
Jointer	½" wire mesh
Tape measure	2 capstones
Circular saw	⅜" plywood scraps
Hand maul	2½" deck or wallboard
Rope	screws
Stakes	⅜"-thick wood scraps
2 × 4s, 2 × 2, 1 × 2	

Brick pillars are a substantial and attractive addition to any landscape. Using these plans, it's possible to create garden pillars with different decorative or functional qualities. The columns are ideal for framing stairs or fences, but there are many possibilities. Build three or four pillars in graduated sizes to create a terraced effect. Use pillars as pedestals around the garden to highlight large pots full of cascading blooms or favorite outdoor statuary. Build short pillars that act as the base of an arbor or outdoor bench.

How to Build Brick Columns

Mark the pillar locations. Make an outline of each footing. Then lay out a 16 × 20" footing for each pillar with mason's string. Strip away sod. Dig a hole for each footing to code-mandated depth using the mason's strings as guides. Following the layout, build 16 × 20" forms (interior dimensions) using 2 × 4s and screws. Sink the forms into the ground slightly so the visible portions of the footings will look neat and provide a flat, even surface for laying bricks. Drive stakes outside the 2 × 4s to support the form. Adjust the forms until they're level and square.

Mix the dry concrete with water following the manufacturer's instructions. Pour the concrete into one footing hole, filling it to the top of the form. Screed away any excess concrete with a 2 × 4. The surface of the footing should be smooth and even. Repeat the process for the other footing. Let the concrete cure for at least two days before removing the forms and building on top of the footings. Waiting a week is even better.

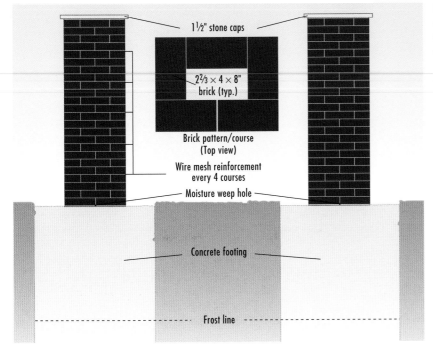

1½" stone caps

2⅔ × 4 × 8" brick (typ.)

Brick pattern/course (Top view)

Wire mesh reinforcement every 4 courses

Moisture weep hole

Concrete footing

Frost line

Brick columns are built on wide concrete footings. Wire mesh placed every four courses reinforces the columns, while weep holes at the bottoms allow moisture to drain. Stone caps can be custom ordered from a stone supplier. Have them cut so they overlap the columns by 1½".

(continued)

A story pole allows you to check the positions of the courses of brick and the thickness of the mortar joints. Build a story pole by cutting spacers from ⅜" plywood. On a worksurface, lay out 10 or more courses of brick. With the bricks on their sides, insert spacers between each pair, spacing them ⅜" apart. Place a straight 1 × 2 alongside the bricks; then mark the space between each pair of bricks, indicating location and thickness of each layer of mortar.

After the footings have cured, arrange five of the bricks to form a rectangle on one of the footings. Insert spacers between the bricks to establish the thickness of the vertical mortar joints. Take care that the bricks are correctly centered on each footing and square in relation to each other. With a grease pencil or carpenter's pencil, draw reference lines on the footing around the bricks.

Trowel mortar within the reference lines to a thickness of ⅜". Apply ⅜" of mortar to the sides of alternating bricks so that mortar fills the spaces between them, and set the bricks on the mortar bed, tapping each gently with the trowel handle. On one side of the pillar, use a pencil coated with vegetable oil to make a weep hole in the wet mortar between two bricks. When all five bricks in the first course are laid, check for square and level, and adjust bricks by tapping them with the trowel handle.

Apply mortar to the top of the first course of bricks, ⅜" thick. Lay the second course of brick in the mortar, but rotate the pattern 180º. Check the pillar with a level, making sure your work is both level and plumb. Adjust bricks as necessary. Then, use the story pole as a guide to make sure the two courses on all sides are correctly spaced. Small errors made low on the pillar will be exaggerated with each successive course. Check your work after every two courses of brick.

Proceed with the next two courses and apply mortar to the top of the fourth course. Then cut a piece of ¼" wire mesh slightly smaller than the dimensions of a course of bricks and lay it into the mortar for lateral reinforcement. Apply more mortar to the top of the wire mesh, and lay the fifth course of brick. Add wire-mesh reinforcement after every fourth course.

After the fifth course, use a jointer to tool the mortar joints. Continue to lay bricks until the next-to-last course. Apply mortar to the next-to-last course, and add wire mesh. Apply mortar to the entire surface of the wire mesh. Lay the side of the last course formed by two bricks. Then add an extra brick in the center, over the mortar-covered wire mesh. Lay the remaining bricks so they fit snugly around the center brick. Tool any remaining joints as they become firm.

Create the second column by laying the first course of brick, following the instructions in steps 5 and 6 on page 190. Measure the distance between the pillars with a tape measure. Make a measuring rod by cutting a 2 × 2 or other straight board to match the distance between the bases of the two pillars. Use the rod every few courses to check that the second pillar is aligned with (parallel to) the first. Also, consult the story pole after every two courses. Complete the second pillar, following the instructions in steps 4 through 8.

Draw diagonal reference lines from corner to corner on the bottoms of the capstones. Then, using the dimensions of the pillar and the diagonal lines, draw a rectangle centered on the bottom of each capstone. Apply a ½"-thick bed of mortar to the pillar and place the capstone. Tool the mortar flush with the brick. *Note: If mortar squeezes out, press ⅜"-thick shims into the mortar on each side to support the cap. After 24 hours, tap out the wood scraps and fill in the spaces with fresh mortar.*

Paved Landing with Planters

The entry area is the first detail that visitors to your home will notice. Create a memorable impression by building a brick-paver step landing that gives any house a more formal appearance. Add a special touch to the landing by building a permanent planter next to it (page 195) using matching brick.

In many cases, a paver landing like the one shown here can be built directly over an existing sidewalk. Make sure the sidewalk is structurally sound and free from major cracks. If you're adding an adjoining structure, like a planter, create a separate building base and be sure to include isolation joints so the structure is not connected to the landing area or to the house.

Using the same techniques, you can turn an old concrete walkway into a dramatic mortared brick path. The mortar applied over the old concrete provides a level foundation for the new brick surface.

Tools & Materials ▶

Drill	Mason's trowel
Level	Isolation board
Masonry hoe	Type S mortar
Rubber mallet	Pavers
Mortar bag	Plastic sheeting
Jointing tool	

Brick or concrete pavers can be set into sand or mortared to a concrete footing or, in some cases, a sidewalk or driveway. Because of freeze/thaw issues, the success rate for mortared paver projects is significantly higher in more temperate climates.

How to Build a Paved Landing with Planters

Dry-lay the pavers onto the concrete surface and experiment with the arrangement to create a layout that uses whole bricks, if possible. Mark outlines for the layout onto the concrete. Attach an isolation board to prevent the mortar from bonding with the foundation. Mix a batch of mortar, and dampen the concrete slightly.

Lay a bed of mortar for three or four border pavers, starting at one end or corner. Level off the bed to about ½" in depth with the trowel.

Begin laying the border pavers, buttering an end of each paver with mortar as you would a brick. Set pavers into the mortar bed, pressing them down so the bed is ⅜" thick. Cut off excess mortar from the tops and sides of the pavers. Use a level to make sure the pavers are even across the tops, and check mortar joints to confirm that they are uniform in thickness.

Finish the border section next to the foundation, checking with a level to make sure the row is even in height. Trim off any excess mortar, then fill in the third border section, leaving the front edge of the project open to provide easier access for laying the interior field pavers.

(continued)

Apply a ½"-thick bed of mortar between the border pavers in the work area closest to the foundation. Because mortar is easier to work with when fresh, mix and apply the mortar in small sections (no more than 4 sq. ft.).

Begin setting pavers in the field area without buttering the edges. Check the alignment with a straightedge. Adjust paver height as needed, making sure joints are uniform in width. *Note: Pavers often are cast with spacing flanges on the sides, but these are for sand-set projects. Use a spacing guide, like a dowel, when setting pavers in mortar.*

Fill in the rest of the pavers to complete the pattern in the field area, applying mortar beds in small sections. Add the final border section. Every 30 minutes, add mortar to joints between pavers until it is even with the tops. Tip: To minimize mess when adding mortar, use a mortar bag to deliver the mortar into the joints.

Smooth and shape the mortar joints with a jointing tool. Tool the full-width "running" joints first, then tool the joints at the ends of the pavers. Let the mortar dry for a few hours, then remove any residue by scrubbing the pavers with a coarse rag and water. Cover the walkway with plastic and let the mortar cure for at least two days. Remove plastic, but do not walk on the pavers for at least one week.

Lay one section of the first course for the planter, checking the bricks frequently with a level to make sure the tops are level and even. Lay two corner return bricks perpendicular to the end bricks in the first section, and use a level to make sure they are even across the tops.

Install weep holes for drainage in the first course of bricks on the sides farthest away from permanent structures. Cut ⅜"-dia. copper or PVC tubing about ¼" longer than the width of one brick, and set the pieces into the mortar joints between bricks, pressing them into the mortar bed so they touch the footing. Make sure mortar doesn't block the openings.

Finish building all sides of the first course. Lay the second course of bricks, reversing the directions of the corner bricks to create staggered vertical joints if using a running-bond pattern. Fill in the brick courses to full height, building up one course at a time. Check frequently to make sure the tops of the bricks are level and sides are plumb.

Install cap bricks to keep water from entering the cores of the brick and to enhance the visual effect. Set the cap bricks into a ⅜"-thick mortar bed, buttering one end of each cap brick. Let the mortar cure for one week. Before adding soil, pour a 4" to 6"-thick layer of gravel into the bottom of the planter for drainage, then line the bottom and sides of the planter with landscape fabric to prevent dirt from running into and clogging the drainage tubes.

Garage Doors & Openers

Given their size and weight, garage doors may seem like perilous items for a do-it-yourselfer to replace. However, the process of removing an old garage door and installing a new one is no more hazardous or complex than other door and window replacements, if you work carefully and exercise good judgment. You may be surprised to learn that, start to finish, you can easily replace a garage door in a day's time with a modest collection of tools. You'll also need a helper or two to assist you with lifting or stabilizing the large parts.

Replacing a garage door opener is a reasonably easy DIY project, and this chapter will show you how.

Both projects featured here include a list of tools and materials you'll need and detailed, step-by-step instructions. However, garage doors and openers have many different designs, and the installation process varies from manufacturer to manufacturer. Be sure to read the installation manual that comes with your door or opener. Since those instructions will impact your product warranty, follow them carefully when they differ from what you see here.

This chapter includes:

- Garage Door Openers
- Sectional Garage Doors

Garage Door Openers

This illustration indicates all the components of a garage door opener. If your opener style differs, refer to your owner's manual for clarification.

Hanging bracket

Opener

Wall console

Screw terminals

Braces

Rail

Pulley bracket

Header bracket

Trolley

Door arm

Structural support

Door bracket

Sensor eye

Sensor mounting bracket

Those cold dashes from your car to the garage door and back can be a thing of the past with the convenience of a garage door opener. Add to this the benefit of secured access and you have all the reasons you need to install an automatic garage door opener. Garage door openers come in three basic models, each with its own benefits and drawbacks, but this project shows the basic steps for installing a chain-drive system—the most common and least expensive type— on a sectional door in a garage with exposed joists. If you have a one-piece door, a lightweight metal or glass-paneled door, or a garage with a finished ceiling, consult the manufacturer's directions for alternative installation procedures.

Before you begin, read all the manufacturer's instructions and the list of safety tips on the next page. Then, make sure your garage door is properly balanced and moves smoothly. Open and close the door to see if it sticks or binds at any point. Release the door in the half-open position. It should stay in place, supported by its own springs. If your door is not balanced or sticks at any point, call a garage door service professional before installing the opener.

Most garage door openers plug into a standard grounded receptacle located near the unit. Some local codes may require openers to be hard-wired into circuits. Consult the manufacturer's directions for hard-wiring procedures.

Tools & Materials ▸

Stepladder	Adjustable wrench
Tape measure	½ and ⁷⁄₁₆" sockets and
Screwdriver	ratchet wrench
Pliers	Drill and bits
Wire cutters	Garage door opener kit
Pencil	2× lumber (for door
Hammer	header, if necessary)

Garage Door Safety Tips ▸

Whether you're adding an opener to a new or old garage door, these tips will help make it a safe part of your home. (Also see pages 248 to 253 for information on repairing garage doors.)

- Before beginning the installation, be sure the garage door manually opens and closes properly.
- If you have a one-piece door, with or without a track, read all additional manufacturer's installation information.
- The gap between the bottom of the garage door and the floor must not exceed ¼". If it does, the safety reversal system may not work properly.
- If the garage has a finished ceiling, attach a sturdy metal bracket to the structural supports before installing the opener. This bracket and hardware are not usually provided with the garage door opener kit.
- Install the wall-mounted garage door control within sight of the garage door, out of reach of children (at a minimum height of 5 ft.), and away from all moving parts of the door.

- Never use an extension cord or two-wire adapter to power the opener. Do not change the opener plug in any way to make it fit an outlet. Be sure the opener is grounded.
- When an obstruction breaks the light beam while the door is closing, most door models stop and reverse to full open position, and the opener lights flash 10 times. If no bulbs are installed, you will hear 10 clicks.
- To avoid any damage to vehicles entering or leaving the garage, be sure the door provides adequate clearance when open fully.
- Garage doors may include tempered glass, laminate glass, or clear-plastic panels—all safe window options.

Make sure your garage door opener is securely supported to trusses or ceiling framing with sturdy metal hanging brackets.

Use the emergency release handle to disengage the trolley only when the garage door is closed. Never use the handle to pull the door open or closed.

How to Install a Garage Door Opener

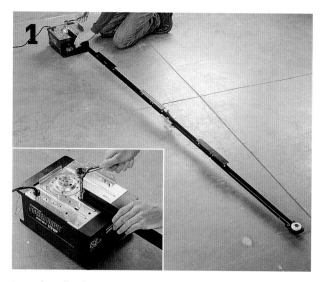

Start by aligning the rail pieces in proper order and securing them with the included braces and bolts. Screw the pulley bracket to the door end of the rail and slide the trolley onto the rail. Make sure the pulley and all rail pieces are properly aligned and that the trolley runs smoothly without hitting any hardware along the rail. Remove the two screws from the top of the opener, then attach the rail to the opener using these screws (inset).

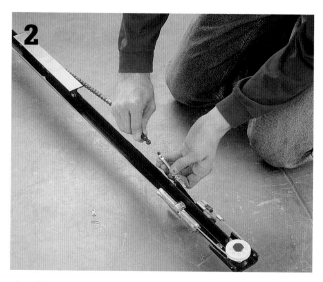

The drive chain/cable should be packaged in its own dispensing carton. Attach the cable loop to the front of the trolley using the included linking hardware. Wrap the cable around the pulley, then wrap the remaining chain around the drive sprocket on the opener. Finally, attach it to the other side of the trolley with linking hardware. Make sure the chain is not twisted, then attach the cover over the drive sprocket. Tighten the chain by adjusting the nuts on the trolley until the chain is ½" above the base of the rail.

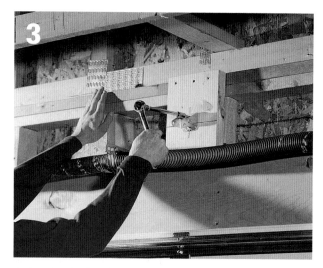

To locate the header bracket, first extend a vertical line from the center of the door onto the wall above. Raise the door and note the highest point the door reaches. Measure from the floor to this point. Add 2" to this distance and mark a horizontal line on the front wall where it intersects the centerline. If there is no structural support behind the cross point, fasten 2× lumber across the framing. Then fasten the header bracket to the structural support with the included screws.

Support the opener on the floor with a board or box to prevent stress and twisting to the rail. Attach the rail pulley bracket to the header bracket above the door with the included clevis pin. Then place the opener on a stepladder so it is above the door tracks. Open the door and shim beneath the opener until the rail is 2" above the door.

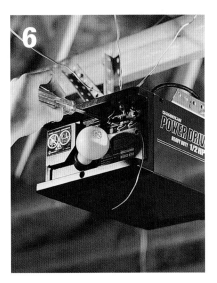

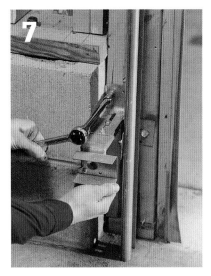

Hang the opener from the ceiling joists with the included hanging brackets and screws. Angle at least one of the hanging brackets to increase the stability of the unit while in operation. Attach the manual release cord and handle to the release arm of the trolley.

Strip ¼" of sheathing from the wall-console bell wire. Connect the wire to the screw terminals on the console, then attach it to the inside wall of the garage with included screws. Run the wires up the wall and connect them to the proper terminals on the opener. Secure the wire to the wall with insulated staples, being careful not to pierce the wire. Install the lightbulbs and lenses.

Install the sensor-eye mounting brackets at each side of the garage door, parallel to each other, about 4 to 6" from the floor. The sensor brackets can be attached to the door track, the wall, or the floor, depending upon your garage layout. See the manufacturer's directions for the best configuration for your garage.

Attach the sensor eyes to the brackets with the included wing nuts, but do not tighten the nuts completely. Make sure the path of the eyes is unobstructed by the door tracks. Run wires from both sensors to the opener unit and connect the wires to the proper terminals. Plug the opener into a grounded receptacle and adjust the sensors until the indicator light shows the correct eye alignment (inset), then tighten the wing nuts. Unplug the unit and attach the sensor wires to the walls with insulated staples.

Center the door bracket 2 to 4" below the top of the door. Drill holes and attach the bracket with the included carriage bolts. Connect the straight and curved arm sections with the included bolts. Attach the arm to the trolley and door bracket with the included latch pins. Plug the opener into a grounded receptacle and test the unit. See the manufacturer's directions for adjustment procedures.

Sectional Garage Doors

Garage doors bear the brunt of everything Mother Nature and an active household throw at them— seasonal temperature swings, moisture, buffeting winds, blistering sunlight, or a badly misfired half-court jump shot. Plus, a garage door cycles up and down at least four times per day on the average home, which adds up to nearly 1,500 or more uses every year. Eventually, garage doors simply wear out.

Aside from age and use, there are other reasons to replace your garage door. For one, a new garage door contributes to your home's curb appeal. These days, you don't have to settle for a drab, flat-panel door. Door manufacturers provide many options for cladding colors, panel layout and texture, exterior hardware and window styles. New garage doors such as the fiberglass and steel model shown here (see Resources, page 296) also benefit from improved material construction, more sophisticated safety features, and enhanced energy efficiency.

Replacing a garage door is surprisingly straight-forward and safe. If you have moderate tool skills and a helper or two, you should have little difficulty removing an old door and replacing it with a new one in a single day. Garage door kits come with all the necessary hardware and detailed instructions. Generally, you won't have to modify the door opening once the old door is removed in order to install a new one. And, most garage door openers can be retrofitted to a new door with a few minor adjustments.

Tools & Materials ▶

Masking tape
Tape measure
4-ft. level
Pencil
Screwdriver
Sockets and ratchet
Locking and regular pliers

Drill and bits
Gloves
Hammer
Stepladder
Garage door kit
2× lumber (for door header, if necessary)

After

Before

A failing garage door not only detracts from the appearance of your home, it can be a real headache. If only one section of the door is damaged, you may be able to get by replacing that section only, but it's easier and not that much more costly to replace the whole door.

How to Remove a Garage Door

With the garage door lowered, remove the clevis pin or bolt and nut that connects the garage door opener trolley arm to the garage door. Then activate the garage door opener to move the trolley to the rear of the track.

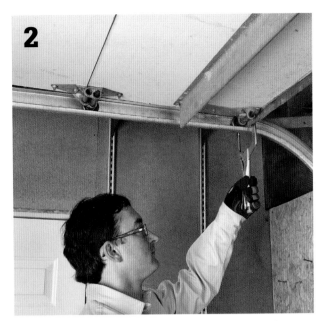

With the door fully raised, attach locking pliers or a clamp on the door track underneath the door's bottom rollers. Do this on both door tracks. The pliers or clamp will prevent the door from falling when you remove the extension springs.

Release the tension in the door spring or springs. If your opener has an extension spring in each channel, you simply need to unhook and remove them with the door open. If your opener operates with torsion springs, like the one shown here, you'll need a special tool called a winding bar to unwind the spring. But be aware that this is a very dangerous job (see tip box, right) and it is recommended that you hire a professional garage door installer to do it.

Warning: Beware of Torsion Springs ▸

Winding and unwinding torsion springs is a very risky task for do-it-yourselfers and it is recommended that you hire a garage door installer for this part of the job. These heavy coils are installed parallel to the door header instead of in the track channels, like lighter-weight extension springs. Torsion springs hold massive amounts of energy and can easily throw a tool if they slip during the winding or unwinding process. When installed, the spring is wound with a winding bar that fits into lugs that are attached to the loose ends of the springs. The installer counts a prescribed number of turns to get the correct spring tension and then affixes the plug to the cylinder with a set screw or bolt. The manual for your door will contain the requirements for your torsion spring. If you choose to proceed with the project yourself, you can rent a winding bar at a garage door installation company. Never substitute a metal dowel, screwdriver, or any other tool for a genuine winding bar that's shaped to fit the lugs on your door.

(continued)

With the help of another person, remove both locking pliers from the door tracks and carefully lower the old door to the floor. Be aware that, without springs installed, you'll bear the entire weight of the door as you lower it. Garage doors can weigh 200 to 400 lbs., so use extreme caution.

Starting at the top panel, unbolt the top hinges and door roller hardware and lift the top door section out of the tracks. Repeat for the other sections, removing only one section's worth of hardware at a time. After you have removed all door sections, unbolt both track assemblies from the door jambs and dismantle the tracks. These can be discarded. Do not remove the perforated hanger brackets that hold the rear end of the tracks to the ceiling framing or roof trusses. Unless these are damaged, they can usually be reused for the new door tracks.

How to Install a New Garage Door

Measure the width of the existing top header, the headroom clearance to the ceiling, and the inside opening of the doorway. Check these measurements against the minimum requirements outlined in the instruction manual that comes with your new door. Depending on the design of the new door and spring system, you may need to first install a wider header or make other modifications to your framing or garage door opener height to accommodate the new door.

Working on the floor, assemble the vertical tracks, jamb brackets, and flag angle hardware. Install the roller and hinge hardware on the bottom door section.

Set the bottom door section into position against the side jambs, and adjust it left or right until the side jambs overlap it evenly. Check the top of the door section for level. Place shims beneath the door, if necessary, to level it. Have a helper hold the door section in place against the jambs until it is secured in the tracks.

Slip the left vertical track over the door section rollers and against the side jamb. Adjust it for plumb, then fasten the jamb brackets to the side jamb with lag screws. Carefully measure, mark, and install the right vertical track now as well.

Depending on your door design, you may need to attach lift cables to the bottom door section at this time. Follow the instructions that come with your door to connect these cables correctly.

Fasten the end and intermediate hinges to the bottom door section, and then install roller brackets and hinges to the other door sections. Attach hinges to the top edges of each door section only. This way, you'll be able to stack one section on top of the next during assembly.

(continued)

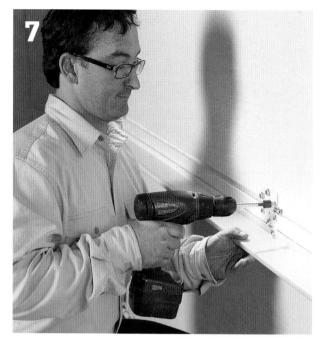

Slip the second door section into place in the door tracks and on top of the first section. Connect the bottom hinges to the second door section. Repeat the process until you have installed all but the top door section.

The top door section may require additional bracing, special top roller brackets, and a bracket for securing a garage door opener. Install these parts now, following the door manufacturer's instructions.

Set the top door section in place and fasten it to the hinges below it. Hold it in place temporarily with a few nails driven at an angle up into the top door header.

Fasten horizonal door tracks to the flag angle brackets on top of the vertical tracks. Check the horizontal tracks for level, and inspect their rear connection points to the hanger brackets you left from the previous door. *Note: If you need to modify or replace the old hanger brackets, do this now and connect the horizontal tracks to the brackets to complete the track installation. Do not attempt to open the new door.*

11

Assemble the torsion spring components and mount any required support brackets to the top door jamb. Set the torsion spring into place on its jamb brackets and fasten it. Secure the winding cables to the spring winding drums (see Warning, page 203).

12

Attach a locking pliers or clamp to each door track to prevent the door from raising when you wind the counter-balance springs. Follow the instructions that come with your door kit to wind each torsion spring correctly. You need winding bars to do this. You can rent ot borrow these bars from a garage door dealer or installer (see Warning, page 203).

13

Before fully raising the door, carefully check the alignment of the door tracks to one another and the spacing between the door and tracks. Adjust the roller brackets, if needed. Attach the door's emergency disconnect handle, door lock, lift handles, and other hardware, depending on your door kit.

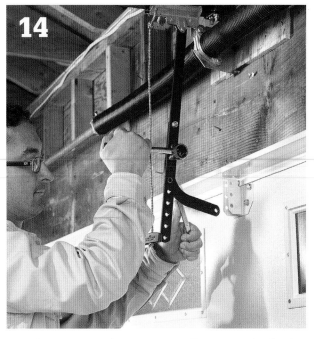

14

Attach the garage door opener trolley arm to the door's operator bracket. You may need to adjust the length of the arm by changing the arrangement of the parts to retrofit it to the new door. Test the action and travel of the new door and then install an electric garage door opener (optional). Finally, measure, cut, and nail stop moldings in place and add a garage door sweep (also optional).

Maintenance

Windows and doors must withstand the effects of weather, temperature extremes, insect damage, and the wear and tear that happens with normal use. So, it's only logical that now and again you'll need to repair them. The good news is, window and door fix-it projects are fairly straightforward and easy to do. If you tend to those sticky mechanisms, loose hinges, or deteriorating finishes before they lead to bigger problems, your windows and doors may last for decades. Granted, these little maintenance jobs may not be as satisfying as installing a state-of-the art skylight or dramatic new entry door, but your efforts will pay dividends in the amount of money you save when you don't have to replace them prematurely, due to neglect.

This chapter includes:

- Replacing Broken Window Glass
- Improving Window Operation
- Replacing Insulating Glass Units (IGUs)
- Painting Windows & Doors
- Graining Entry Doors
- Shortening Interior Doors
- Solving Common Door Problems
- Replacing Thresholds
- Fixing Sliding Screen Doors
- Repairing & Maintaining Storm Windows & Doors
- Tuning Up Garage Doors

Replacing Broken Window Glass

For people who live in new, well-made houses, the windows from the ground to the ridge are bound to be double-glazed units that perform with commendable energy efficiency. This is a good thing, mostly. But these hi-tech units can break just like their older single-pane siblings. People who live in older houses have it better. Their single pane sash and storm windows are easier to repair. If you have just one pane to replace, most people can finish up the job in a couple of hours. Usually the hardest part of this chore is working off a ladder. You'll need one to remove the storm windows to fix a regular sash because the repair needs to be made on the outside of the window.

Replacing a broken glass pane isn't nearly as common an occurrence today as it was a decade or two ago, before most homes had double-pane windows. But it's still a great skill to have for owners of older homes.

A clean putty knife (A), glazing compound (B,) and a package of glazier's points (C) are essential tools and materials for replacing window glass.

Tool Tip ▸

One way to be sure your glass supplier will cut your new glass panes accurately is if you provide a cardboard template that matches the pane size you need. Take this with you when ordering the glass.

Each glass pane in a typical wood sash is held in place in pockets on the muntins that form the sash and on the outside by glazing compound. This compound is a soft, caulk-like material when it's installed. But it hardens over time to form a durable seal that keeps the glass in the frame and the water out. If you wiggle the pieces of broken glass in and out, this will loosen the compound and you can pull the shards out.

How to Fix a Broken Windowpane

Wearing heavy leather gloves, remove the broken pieces of glass. Then, soften the old glazing compound using a heat gun or a hair dryer. Don't hold the heat gun too long in one place because it can be hot enough to scorch the wood or crack adjacent panes of glass.

Once a section of compound is soft, remove it using a putty knife. Work carefully to avoid gouging the wood frame. If a section is difficult to scrape clean, reheat it with the heat gun. Soft compound is always easy to remove.

Once the wood opening is scraped clean, seal the wood with a coat of linseed oil or primer. If the wood isn't sealed, the dry surface will draw too much moisture from the glazing compound and reduce its effectiveness.

Apply a thin bed of glazing compound to the wood frame opening and smooth it in place with your thumb.

Press the new pane into the opening, making sure to achieve a tight seal with the compound on all sides. Wiggle the pane from side to side and up and down until the pane is seated. There will be some squeeze-out, but do not press all the compound out.

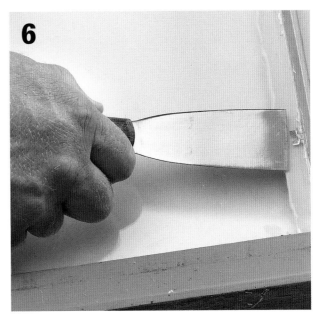

Drive glazier's points into the wood frame to hold the pane in place. Use the tip of a putty knife to slide the point against the surface of the glass. Install at least 2 points on each side of the pane.

Make a rope of compound (about ½" dia.) by rolling it between your hands. Then press it against the pane and the wood frame. Smooth it in place by drawing a putty knife, held at a 45° angle, across its surface. Scrape off excess.

Allow the glazing compound at least one week to dry completely. Then prime and paint it to match the rest of the sash. Be sure to spread the paint over the joint between the compound and the glass. This will seal the joint completely. When the paint is dry, scrape off the extra with a razor blade paint scraper.

Improving Window Operation

Many of us have experienced difficulty with opening windows due to swelled wood or painted channels. Almost as frequent, windows won't stay open because of a broken sash cord or chain. To avoid difficulties with windows, regular maintenance is crucial. Double-hung windows with spring-loaded sash tracks require cleaning and an occasional adjustment of the springs in (or behind) the tracks. Casement windows are often faulty at the crank mechanisms. If cleaning doesn't fix the problem, the crank mechanism must be replaced. For storm windows, the window track must be clean, and greaseless lubricant must be applied each time the windows and screens are removed.

Tools & Materials ▶

Screwdrivers	Toothbrush
Paint zipper or utility knife	Paint solvent
	Rags
Hammer	Sash cord
Vacuum	Lubricant
Small pry bar	Wax candle
Scissors	String
Stiff brush	All-purpose grease

Windows endure temperature extremes, house setting, and all sorts of wear and tear. Sooner or later you'll need to perform a bit of maintenance to keep them working properly.

How to Adjust Windows

Spring-loaded windows have an adjustment screw on the track insert. Adjust both sides until the window is balanced and opens and closes smoothly.

Spring-lift windows operate with the help of a spring-loaded lift rod inside a metal tube. Adjust them by unscrewing the top end of the tube from the jamb, then twisting the tube to change the spring tension: clockwise for more lifting power; counterclockwise for less. Maintain a tight grip on the tube at all times to keep it from unwinding.

Cut the paint film if the window is painted shut. Insert a paint zipper or utility knife between the window stop and the sash, and slide it down to break the seal.

Place a block of scrap wood against the window sash. Tap lightly with a hammer to free the window.

Clean the tracks on sliding windows and doors with a hand vacuum and a toothbrush. Dirt buildup is common on storm window tracks.

Clean weatherstrips by spraying with a cleaner and wiping away dirt. Use paint solvent to remove paint that may bind windows. Then apply a small amount of lubricant to prevent sticking.

Lubricate wood window channels by rubbing them with a white candle, then open and close the window a few times. Do not use liquid lubricants on wood windows.

How to Replace Broken Sash Cords

1

Cut any paint seal between the window frame and stops with a utility knife or paint zipper. Pry the stops away from the frame, or remove the molding screws.

2

Bend the stops out from the center to remove them from the frame. Remove any weatherstripping that's in the way.

3

Slide out the lower window sash. Pull knotted or nailed cords from holes in the sides of the sash (see step 9).

4

Pry out or unscrew the weight pocket cover in the lower end of the window channel. Pull the weight from the pocket, and cut the old sash cord from the weight.

5

Tie one end of a piece of string to a nail and the other end to the new sash cord. Run the nail over the pulley and let it drop into the weight pocket. Retrieve the nail and string through the pocket.

6

Pull on the string to run the new sash cord over the pulley and through the weight pocket. Make sure the new cord runs smoothly over the pulley.

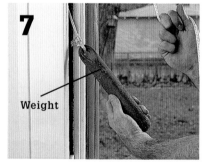

7

Attach the end of the sash cord to the weight using a tight double knot. Set the weight in the pocket. Pull on the cord until the weight touches the pulley.

8

Rest the bottom sash on the sill. Hold the sash cord against the side of the sash, and cut enough cord to reach 3" past the hole in the side of the sash.

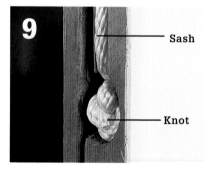

9

Knot the sash cord and wedge the knot into the hole in the sash. Replace the pocket cover. Slide the window and any weatherstripping into the frame, then attach the stops in the original positions.

How to Clean & Lubricate a Casement Window Crank

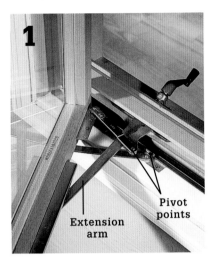
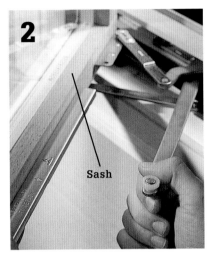
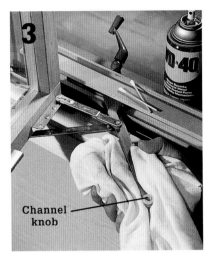

If a casement window is hard to crank, clean the accessible parts. Open the window until the roller at the end of the extension arm is aligned with the access slot in the window track.

Disengage the extension arm by pulling it down and out of the track. Clean the track with a stiff brush, and wipe the pivoting arms and hinges with a rag.

Lubricate the track and hinges with spray lubricant or household oil. Wipe off excess lubricant with a cloth, then reattach the extension arm. If that doesn't solve the problem, repair or replace the crank assembly (below).

How to Repair a Casement Window Crank Assembly

Disengage the extension arm from the window track, then remove the molding or cap concealing the crank mechanism. Unhinge any pivot arms connected to the window.

Remove the screws securing the crank assembly, then remove the assembly and clean it thoroughly. If the gears are badly worn, replace the assembly. Check a home center or call the manufacturer for new parts. Note which way the window opens—to the right or left—when ordering replacement parts.

Apply an all-purpose grease to the gears, and reinstall the assembly. Connect the pivot arms, and attach the extension arm to the window. Test the window operation before installing the cap and molding.

Replacing Insulated Glass Units (IGUs)

If you live in a newer home or have had your windows replaced at some point, chances are your windows contain double-pane, insulating glass units (IGU). IGU windows are much more energy efficient than the old, single-pane styles, but they aren't immune to the usual breakage calamities that affect glass. A more common problem with IGU windows, however, is leaky seals that can cause the glass to look foggy or etched.

The difficulty of changing an IGU depends on the window's design. IGUs are self-contained and fit inside the sash in one of two ways. Some window sash can be disassembled into sections. A gasket surrounds the IGU and fits into grooves in the sash members. If your sash has a screw at each corner, it may be this style, and it's easy for a do-it-yourselfer to repair. If there are no corner screws, chances are the sash is permanently assembled. With this style, the IGU is held in place with stop moldings and either specialized sealing tape or caulk. The stop moldings are attached to one side of the sash. On wood windows, look for filled nail holes in the trim area next to the glass; the putty hides the brads that hold the stop moldings in place. On vinyl or aluminum windows, the molding strips fit into channels in the sash frame. To locate the moldings on the sash, look for a slight color mismatch between the strips and the sash or tiny gaps around their edges that indicate these pieces are removable.

Tools & Materials ›

Hammer
Screwdriver or drill/driver
Thin-blade putty knives
Small paint scraper
Scrap blocks

Neutral-cure silicone caulk
Replacement stop moldings
IGU gaskets or setting tape
Pneumatic brad nails, as required

Insulating glass units (IGUs) contain a pair of glass panes that trap inert gas between them to increase efficiency. Repairing a broken IGU is considerably harder than replacing a single pane, but it can be done.

Replacement Parts ▶

Before you attempt to replace a leaky IGU, remove the sash and take it to a window repair shop to seek an expert's advice. You'll need to have the shop take measurements for the replacement IGU anyway, and they can supply you with new gaskets, stop moldings, or specialized setting tape that might be required for the job. A window shop can also determine how old the window is. If the seal has failed and the window is less than 10 years old, the manufacturer's warranty may still be in effect.

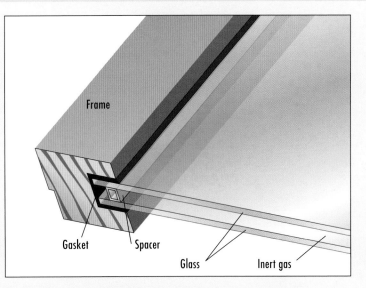

Some IGUs are made with wood frames that screw together, which presents a relatively easy fix for the DIYer. The new IGU is simply wrapped in a rubber gasket and reinstalled in the partially disassembled wood frame.

How to Replace an IGU in a Screw-type Sash

Use a screwdriver or drill/driver to remove two screws on the opposite corners of the sash frame. You can dismantle the frame into two L-shaped sections, which will make reassembly easier.

Pull the frame sections apart to remove the IGU. You may need to use a hammer to gently tap against a block of scrap wood to open the frame.

Peel the gasket off the old IGU. If it's undamaged, fit it around the new IGU, then slide the IGU in place between the sash sections. Reinstall the corner screws.

How to Replace an IGU in a Fixed-sash Frame

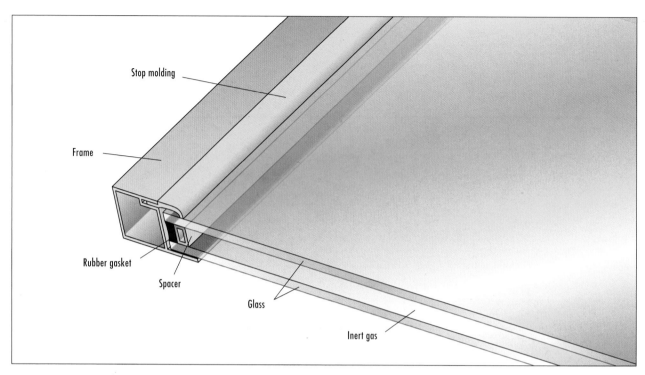

Stop molding

Frame

Rubber gasket

Spacer

Glass

Inert gas

Most newer IGU windows are built with a one-piece frame that has no corner fasteners. The glass unit is pinned into these fixed frames with removable stop molding.

Slide a thin-blade putty knife between one section of stop molding and the sash. Carefully pry the molding out of its channel. Once the first section is removed, the other pieces should be easier to pry free. If the moldings are held in place with brads, pull out the brads with pliers.

Flip the sash over, and slide a razor blade along the seam between the glass and the sash. You may have to do this in several deepening passes to break the bond between the caulk or sealing tape that holds the IGU in place. Work carefully to prevent damaging the sash.

3

Use a small paint scraper and mineral spirits to remove the old caulk or setting tape from the sash channel after removing the old IGU.

4

Apply new strips of sealing tape or a bead of neutral-cure silicone caulk to the sash channel. The tape or caulk should form a continuous seal all around the sash.

5

Position the new IGU in the sash channel, pressing it firmly into the tape or caulk to seat it. Make sure the IGU fits into the channel evenly. Use a razor blade to remove excess tape or caulk from the glass.

6

If the old stop molding strips have been damaged or are in bad repair, cut new ones. Press the stop molding pieces into their channels. Fasten wood stop moldings in place with 1" pneumatic brad nails. Drive the nails at a shallow angle into the sash to avoid hitting the glass.

Painting Windows & Doors

Start by painting the inside portions of trim and working out toward the larger flat areas. On windows, for instance, first paint the edges closest to the glass, then the surrounding face trim.

Doors should be painted quickly because of the large surface. To avoid overlap marks, always paint from dry surfaces back into wet paint. Plastic floor guards or a wide broadknife can help shield carpet and wood flooring from paint drips.

Either alkyd or latex enamel are good paint options for windows and doors. Always sand lightly between coats and wipe with a tack cloth so that the second coat bonds properly.

Tools & Materials ▸

Screwdriver
Hammer
Paintbrushes
Putty knife

Sawhorses
Broadknife
Alkyd or enamel paint
Wood sealer
Sanding paper

When painting trim, start with the inside edges closest to the glass first, then paint the surrounding face trim.

Painting double-hung windows is easier if you are able to remove them from their frames. Newer, spring-mounted windows are released by pushing against the frame.

Mount the window easel-style by inserting 2 nails into the legs of a wooden stepladder. Or, lay the window flat on a bench or sawhorses. *Note: Do not paint sides or bottom of sashes.*

How to Paint a Window

1

Using a tapered sash brush, begin by painting the wood next to the glass. Use the narrow edge of the brush, and overlap paint onto the glass to create a weather seal.

2

Clean excess paint off the glass with a putty knife wrapped in a clean cloth. Rewrap the knife often so that you always wipe with clean fabric. Leave 1/16" paint overlap from sash onto glass.

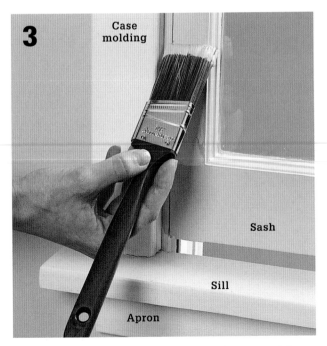

3

Case molding

Sash

Sill

Apron

Paint the flat portions of sash first, then the case moldings, sill, and apron. Use long brush strokes, and avoid getting paint between the sash and the frame.

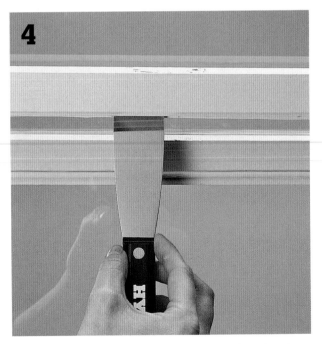

4

If you must paint windows in place, move the painted windows up and down several times during the drying period to keep them from sticking. Use a putty knife to avoid touching painted surfaces.

How to Paint a Door

Remove the door by driving the lower hinge pin out with a screwdriver and hammer. Have a helper hold the door in place. Drive out the center and upper hinge pins.

Place the door flat on sawhorses to paint. On paneled doors, paint in the following order: recessed panels (1), horizontal rails (2), and vertical stiles (3).

Let the door dry. If a second coat of paint is needed, sand lightly and wipe the door with a tack cloth before repainting.

Seal the unpainted edges of the door with clear wood sealer to prevent moisture from entering the wood. Water can cause wood to warp and swell.

Tips for Painting Trim ▸

Protect walls and floor surfaces with a wide taping knife or with a plastic shielding tool.

Wipe paint off of the taping knife or shielding tool each time it is moved.

Paint both sides of cabinet doors. This provides an even moisture seal and prevents warping.

Paint deeply patterned surfaces with a stiff-bristled brush, like this stenciling brush. Use small circular strokes to penetrate recesses.

Graining Entry Doors

Fiberglass and steel entry doors offer excellent durability against wear and the elements, but they have a hard time rivaling the richness and beauty of wood. While new technologies have made it possible for manufacturers to replicate real wood very closely on fiberglass doors, these high-end products tend to be quite expensive. If you have a plain steel or fiberglass door but prefer the appearance of wood, you can use a special wood-graining technique to paint on a finish that, with care and practice, will satisfy your needs. The technique shown here features a special wood-graining tool (available at paint stores and most home improvement centers), but if you're creative you can achieve a comparable effect with a dry bristle brush.

Tools & Materials ▸

Paintbrushes
Clean wiping cloths
Graining tool
    (optional)

Painter's tape
Wood stain
Polyurethane varnish

Give your fiberglass or steel door a wood-grain finish using stain and a wood-graining tool.

How to Paint on a Wood Grain Finish

1

Remove the door and lay it flat on sawhorses for best results. Also remove all hardware, and then wipe the door thoroughly with mineral spirits to clean the surfaces. Mask off glass panels with painter's tape. The staining sequence is important to getting a convincing result. Use the sequence indicated above, skipping steps for parts your door does not have.

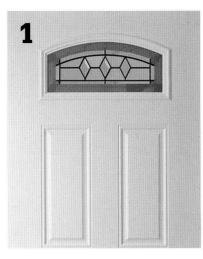

2

Use a foam brush to apply an even coat of wood stain to the center panels, following the wood-grain direction. Leave the excess stain. Choose a medium or dark wood tone (a dark oak stain is shown here).

3

Set the graining tool at the top of the panel and begin drawing it slowly but evenly toward the bottom. Apply light, downward pressure. *Note: It is a very good idea to practice the graining technique on some scrap until you're comfortable with it. Most graining tools have multiple faces that create different grain figures, and how you move the tool also impacts the grain, which can be made to appear to be face grain, quarter-sawn grain, or edge grain.*

4

Rock the tool downward into the stain, moving it slightly from side to side as you make your way down the panel. If, when you reach the bottom, you don't like the pattern, you can wipe up the stain and try again. Grain each panel individually. Let the grain coat dry overnight once you're done graining.

5

Apply the "tone coat" over the grain coat using a brush or soft cloth. Typically, the tone coat is applied with the same stain as the grain coat, but using a slightly different tone can have an interesting effect. The tone coat will even out the grain pattern. Apply a heavier coat for lowered contrast.

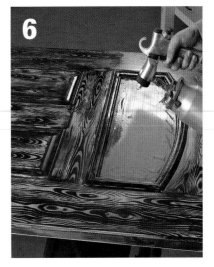

6

After the tone coat has dried, apply a protective coat of polyurethane varnish. Use a sprayer if you have one to avoid brush strokes and roller lines. Use an exterior-rated varnish if the door will be exposed to the elements. Hang the door after the top coat dries.

Shortening Interior Doors

There should be a ⅜ to ¾" gap between the bottom of interior doors and the finished floor. This lets the door swing without binding on new carpet or other floor coverings. But eventually, you may decide to recarpet or add new tile or wood flooring beneath an existing door, and you'll need to shorten the door to create the proper gap again. If you own a circular saw with a fine-tooth blade, it's a simple project for a do-it-yourselfer.

Most newer homes have solid-wood interior doors these days, but hollow-core doors are still fairly common, and they're typical on older homes. Shortening either door type is a similar task, but hollow-core doors will require a few more steps because the door consists of multiple pieces (see page 231).

Tools & Materials ▶

Hammer
Screwdriver
Utility knife
Sawhorses
Circular saw with fine-tooth blade

Straightedge
Clamps
File
Sanding block
Scrap plywood

Changing a floor covering is a great way to update the look of a room, but if the new floor covering is thicker than the old one, you can impede door swing. The solution is to shorten the door.

How to Shorten a Solid Wood Door

Set a strip of scrap plywood on the floor against the door, and trace along the plywood to create a reference line for cutting. The thickness of the plywood will set the amount of door gap, and it will help establish an even gap line. Do not press the plywood down into the carpet when drawing the line. If the flooring is uneven, open the door to where it rubs the most and use this spot to mark the gap.

Remove the door from the jamb by tapping out the hinge pins with a hammer and flat-blade screwdriver. If the hinge pins are fixed, you'll need to unscrew the hinge leaves from the jamb instead.

To prevent the saw from chipping the wood as it cuts, use a sharp utility knife to score along the cutting line. Guide the knife against a metal straightedge. Score both door faces and the edges.

(continued)

Clamp a straightedge to the door so the saw blade will cut about 1⁄16" on the waste side of your score line. The straightedge provides a guide for the edge of the saw base. Use the saw with a fine-tooth blade installed to check your setup.

Set the blade so the teeth project about 1⁄4" below the door, and guide the saw along the straightedge to saw off the door bottom. Use steady feed pressure, and slow down your cutting rate at the end to prevent splintering the door edge.

Use a file to soften the sharp edges of the cut and to form a very slight chamfer all around the door bottom. Switch to a sanding block and medium-grit sandpaper to smooth away any blade marks and roughness.

With the door in place, measure ⅜" up from the top of the floor covering and mark the door. Remove the door from the hinges by tapping out the hinge pins with a screwdriver and a hammer.

Mark the cutting line. Cut through the door veneer with a sharp utility knife to prevent it from chipping when the door is sawed.

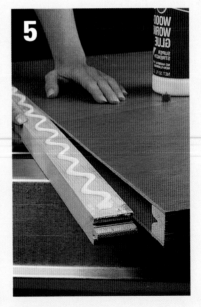

Lay the door on sawhorses and clamp a straightedge to the door as a cutting guide. Saw off the bottom of the door. The hollow core of the door may be exposed.

To reinstall a cutoff frame piece in the bottom of the door, chisel the veneer from both sides of the removed portion.

Apply wood glue to the cutoff piece. Insert the frame piece into the opening of the door and clamp it. Wipe away any excess glue and let the door dry overnight.

Solving Common Door Problems

The most common door problems are caused by loose hinges. When hinges are loose, the door won't hang right, causing it to rub and stick and throwing off the latch mechanism. The first thing to do is check the hinge screws. If the holes for the hinge screws are worn and won't hold the screws, try the repair on the next page.

If the hinges are tight but the door still rubs against the frame, sand or plane down the door's edge. If a door doesn't close easily, it may be warped; use a long straightedge to check for warpage. You may be able to straighten a slightly warped door using weights, but severe warpage can't be corrected. Instead of buying a new door, remove the doorstop and reinstall it following the curve of the door.

Door latch problems occur for a number of reasons: loose hinges, swollen wood, sticking latchbolts, and paint buildup. If you've addressed those issues and the door still won't stay shut, it's probably because the door frame is out of square. This happens as a house settles with age; you can make minor adjustments by filing the strike plate on the door frame. If there's some room between the frame and the door, you can align the latchbolt and strike plate by shimming the hinges. Or, drive a couple of extra-long screws to adjust the frame slightly (page 234, bottom left photo).

Common closet doors, such as sliding and bifold types, usually need only some minor adjustments and lubrication to stay in working order.

Door locksets are very reliable, but they do need to be cleaned and lubricated occasionally. One simple way to keep an entry door lockset working smoothly is to spray a light lubricant into the keyhole, then the key in and out a few times. Don't use graphite in locksets, as it can abrade some metals with repeated use.

Tools & Materials ▶

Screwdrivers	Spray lubricant
Nail set	Wooden golf tees or
Hammer	dowels
Drill	Wood glue
Utility knife	Cardboard shims
Metal file	3" wood screws
Straightedge	Finish nails
Pry bar	Paint or stain
Plane	Sandpaper
Paintbrush	Wood sealer

Tip ▶

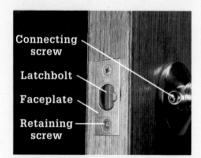

Latchbolts stick when they are dirty or in need of lubrication. Clean and lubricate locksets, and make sure the connecting screws aren't too tight—another cause of binding.

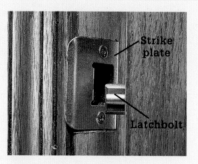

A misaligned latchbolt and strike plate will prevent the door from latching. Poor alignment may be caused by loose hinges, or the door frame may be out of square.

Sticking doors usually leave a mark where they rub against the door frame. Warped doors may resist closing and feel springy when you apply pressure. Check for warpage with a straightedge.

How to Remove a Door

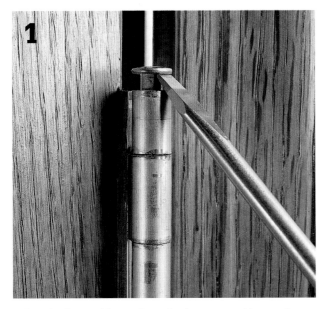

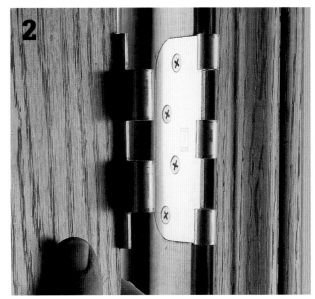

Drive the lower hinge pin out using a screwdriver and hammer. Have a helper hold the door in place, then drive out the upper (and center, if applicable) hinge pins. To help get the screwdriver tip under the pin head, use a nail set or small punch to tap the pin up from underneath.

Remove the door and set it aside. Clean and lubricate the hinge pins before reinstalling the door.

How to Tighten a Loose Hinge Plate

Remove the door from the hinges. Tighten any loose screws. If the wood won't hold the screws tightly, remove the hinges.

Coat wooden golf tees or dowels with wood glue, and drive them into the worn screw holes. If necessary, drill out the holes to accept dowels. Let the glue dry, then cut off excess wood.

Drill pilot holes in the new wood, and reinstall the hinge.

Check the door for a square fit. If the door is far out of square with the frame, remove it (page 233) and shim the top or bottom hinge (right). Or, drive long screws into one of the hinges (below).

Install a thin cardboard shim behind the bottom hinge to raise the position of the latchbolt. To lower the latchbolt, shim behind the top hinge.

Remove two hinge screws from the top or bottom hinge, and drive a 3" wood screw into each hole. The screws will reach the framing studs in the wall and pull the door jamb upward, changing the angle of the door. Add long screws to the top hinge to raise the latchbolt or to the bottom hinge to lower it.

Fix minor alignment problems by filing the strike plate until the latchbolt fits.

How to Straighten a Warped Door

Check the door for warpage using a straightedge. Or, close the door until it hits the stop and look for a gap (see below). The amount of gap between the door and the stop reveals the extent of the warpage. The stop must be straight for this test, so check it with a straightedge.

If the warpage is slight, you can straighten the door using weights. Remove the door (page 233), and rest the ends of the door on sawhorses. Place heavy weights on the bowed center of the door, using cardboard to protect the finish. Leave the weights on the door for several days, and check it periodically with a straightedge.

How to Adjust for a Severely Warped Door

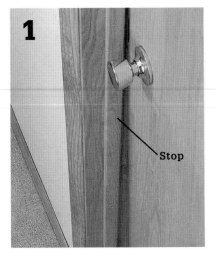

A severe warp cannot be corrected. Instead, you can adjust the doorstop to follow the shape of the door. If you touch up the door jamb with paint or stain after you've finished, no one will notice the repair.

Remove the doorstop using a small pry bar. If it's painted, cut the paint film first with a utility knife to prevent chipping. Avoid splintering by removing nails from the stop by pulling them through the back side of the piece. Pull all nails from the door jamb.

Close the door and latch it. Starting at the top, refasten the stop, keeping the inside edge flush against the door. Drive finish nails through the old holes, or drill new pilot holes through the stop. Set the nails with a nail set after you've checked the door's operation.

How to Free a Sticking Door

Tighten all of the hinge screws. If the door still sticks, use light pencil lines to mark the areas where the door rubs against the door jamb.

During dry weather, remove the door (page 233). If you have to remove a lot of material, you can save time by planing the door (step 3). Otherwise, sand the marked areas with medium-grit sandpaper. Make sure the door closes without sticking, then smooth the sanded areas with fine-grit sandpaper.

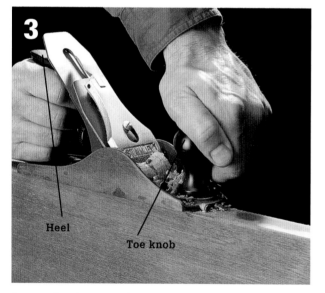

Heel

Toe knob

Secure the door on-edge. If the door has veneered surfaces, cut through the veneers with a utility knife to prevent splintering. Operate the plane so the wood grain runs "uphill" ahead of the plane. Grip the toe knob and handle firmly, and plane with long, smooth strokes. To prevent dipping, press down on the toe at the start of the stroke, and bear down on the heel at the end of the stroke. Check the door's fit, then sand the planed area smooth.

Apply clear sealer or paint to the sanded or planed area and any other exposed surfaces of the door. This will prevent moisture from entering the wood and is especially important for entry doors.

How to Maintain a Sliding Door

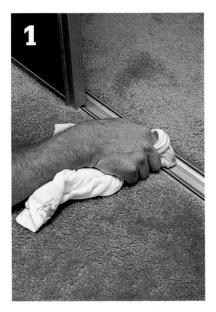

Clean the tracks above and below the doors with a toothbrush and a damp cloth or a hand vacuum.

Spray a greaseless lubricant on all the rollers, but do not spray the tracks. Replace any bent or worn parts.

Check the gap along the bottom edge of the door to make sure it is even. To adjust the gap, rotate the mounting screw to raise or lower the door edge.

How to Maintain a Bifold Door

Open or remove the doors and wipe the tracks with a clean rag. Spray the tracks and rollers or pins with greaseless lubricant.

Check closed doors for alignment within the door frame. If the gap between the closed doors is uneven, adjust the top pivot blocks with a screwdriver or wrench.

Adjustable pivot blocks are also found at the bottom of some door models. Adjust the pivot blocks until the gap between the door and the frame is even.

Replacing Thresholds

While construction varies from home to home, the part of a door that is generally referred to as the "threshold" is actually made up of two separate components: a sill, which serves as the bottom of the door frame and diverts water and dirt away from the home, and the threshold or saddle, which is attached to the sill and helps to seal the air space under a door. Due to constant traffic and exposure to the elements, sills and saddles may eventually require replacing.

Modern prehung doors often have a cast metal sill with an integrated saddle and are installed directly on top of the subfloor. Older homes often have thick wooden sills that are installed lower than metal sills, flush with the floor framing, with a separate saddle bridging the gap between the sill and the finished floor. Saddles are available in several styles and materials, such as wood, metal, and vinyl. Because the design of entry thresholds can vary, it is important to examine the construction of your door threshold to determine your needs. In this project, we replaced a deteriorating wooden sill and saddle with a new oak sill and a wooden weatherstripped saddle.

Besides replacing a deteriorating threshold, you might also choose to replace an existing threshold for increased accessibility. While standard thresholds are designed to keep mud and dirt out of a home, they deny access to people in wheelchairs and can cause people to trip if they are unsteady on their feet. See page 241 for tips on making thresholds accessible.

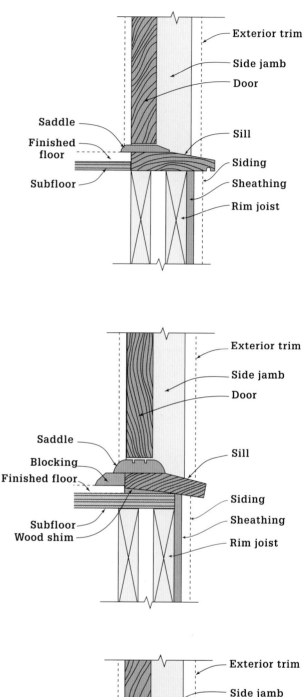

Tools & Materials ▸

Reciprocating saw
Pry bar
Hammer
Drill with
   countersink bit
Pencil
3" galvanized screws
   or 10d galvanized
   casing nails
1½" galvanized screws
   or 8d galvanized
   nails
Shims
Putty
Silicone caulk
Sealer/protectant

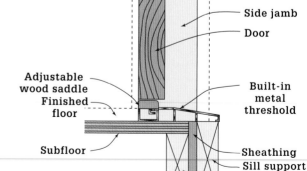

How to Replace an Exterior Door Threshold

Remove the old saddle. This may be as easy as unscrewing the saddle and prying it out. If necessary, cut the old saddle in two using a reciprocating saw, then pry out the saddle. Be careful not to damage the flooring or door frame. Note which edge of the saddle is more steeply beveled; the new saddle should be installed the same way.

Examine the sill for damage or deterioration. If it needs replacing, use a reciprocating saw to cut the sill into three pieces, cutting as close to the jambs as possible. Pry out the center piece, then use a hammer and chisel to split out the pieces directly beneath the jambs. Remove any remaining nails from beneath the jambs using a reciprocating saw with a metal cutting blade.

Measure and cut the new sill to size. If possible, use the salvaged end pieces from the old sill as a template to mark the notches on the new sill. Cut the notches using a jigsaw.

Test-fit the new sill, tapping it into place beneath the jambs using a hammer and wood block to protect the sill. Remove the sill and, if necessary, install long wood strips (or tapered shims) beneath the sill so it fits snugly beneath the jambs with a gentle slope away from the home.

(continued)

5

Apply several beads of caulk to the area beneath the sill. Tap the sill back in place. Drill countersunk pilot holes every 4 to 5" and fasten the sill with 10d galvanized casing nails or 3" screws.

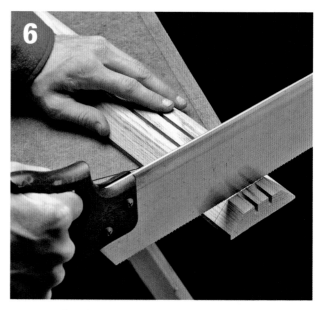

6

Measure the distance between the jambs and cut the new saddle to length. Test-fit the saddle. Mark the ends and cut notches to fit around the door jamb stops using a jigsaw. Apply caulk to the bottom of the saddle and position it so it covers the gap between the sill and the finished floor. Fasten the saddle using 1½" galvanized screws.

Variation ▶

If you are installing a metal saddle, instead of cutting notches in the saddle, use a hammer and chisel to notch the jamb stops to fit.

Tip ▶

A threshold insert seals the gap between the door and the saddle. A door sweep attaches to the door bottom to help seal out drafts.

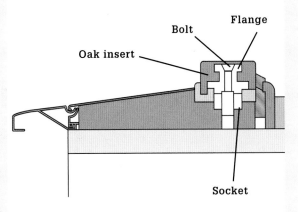

Adjustable sills: Many prehung doors have an aluminum sill with an adjustable wood saddle. Some versions can be made accessible without additional modification by lowering the saddle as far as possible. Other types can be adapted by recessing the sill into the subfloor.

Standard Installation (Inaccessible)

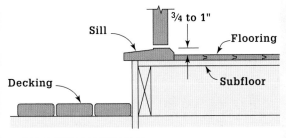

Accessible Installation

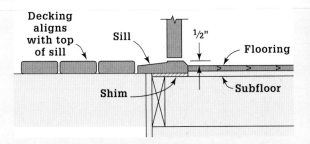

Accessible thresholds: There are many ways to modify standard thresholds for accessibility. Often, the first step is to raise the exterior surface or decking to the same level as the threshold. Entry thresholds should be no higher than ¼" for square-edged sills and ½" high for beveled sills.

Mini-ramps: The slide channels on most sliding glass doors present a major obstacle for wheelchair users. The height difference can be as much as 2" from the bottom to the top of the track. Commercially available mini-ramps can make standard sliding glass door thresholds accessible.

Fixing Sliding Screen Doors

Sliding screen doors easily fall victim to pets and children and often need repair. First you'll need to remove the screen door panel. It is held in grooves by four spring-loaded wheels, one on each corner of the door. Take a short section of the old spline to a hardware store or home center and buy new spline material that matches the diameter of the old one. Also buy replacement screening and an installation tool designed for the size of spline you are installing. These tools come with a roller on both ends: one convex-shaped to force the screen into the door groove, the other concave-shaped to force the spline over the screen.

Screen doors are extremely vulnerable to damage from feet, pets, and a host of other hazards. But fixing them is a breeze with the right tools and a few supplies.

Tools & Materials ▸

Screening material
Mineral spirits
Screwdrivers

Masking tape
Utility knife
Spline roller
Spline cord

Screen Material ▸

Window screening (technically, it's called insect mesh) is woven from three different materials: galvanized wire, aluminum wire, and black fiberglass strands. Each has its advantages and drawbacks: galvanized wire is inexpensive and easy to find, but can become misshapen or rusty; aluminum is less common, but it is strong and won't discolor as easily; fiberglass is easy to work with and won't rust or corrode, but it is prone to tearing. The best advice is simply to buy screening that matches the windows on the rest of your house.

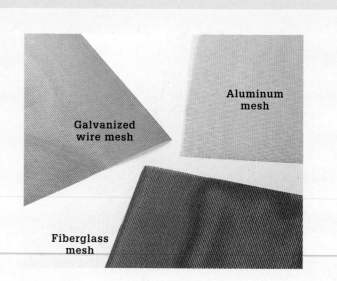

Galvanized
wire mesh

Aluminum
mesh

Fiberglass
mesh

How to Fix a Sliding Screen Door

You can't remove the screen door until you release the tension on the roller wheels. Loosen the adjustment screws, then lift the door out of the channel that holds it captive.

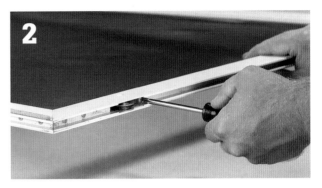

Remove the door rollers using a screwdriver. Sometimes these rollers can just be pried out. Other times you'll have to remove a small screw.

Clean the rollers with mineral spirits and an old paintbrush. Once all the dirt and grime is removed, dry the rollers and lubricate them with light oil.

Pry up one corner of the old spline and then gently pull it out of the screen channel. If this plastic spline is still soft and flexible, it can be reused for the new screen.

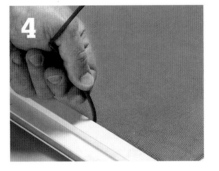

Tape the new screen onto the door frame with masking tape. Then make a diagonal cut at each corner to remove the excess screen. This will keep the screen from bulging at the corner when it is pressed into its channel.

Force the screen into the door groove using the convex wheel on the spline roller installation tool. Don't force the screen in with a single pass. Rather, make several lighter passes until the screen reaches the bottom of the channel.

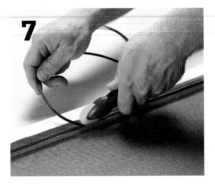

Once the screen is in the channel, install the spline material. Use the concave wheel and work slowly to make sure the spline is forced all the way into the channel. Several passes may be required.

Trim off any excess screening with a sharp utility knife. Do not cut the spline. Reinstall the wheels and replace the panel in the door.

Repairing & Maintaining Storm Windows & Doors

Compared to removable wood storm windows and screens, repairing combination storm windows is a little more complex. But there are several repairs you can make without too much difficulty, as long as you find the right parts. Take the old corner keys, gaskets, or other original parts to a hardware store that repairs storm windows so the clerk can help you find the correct replacement parts. If you cannot find the right parts, have a new sash built.

Tools & Materials ▸

Tape measure
Screwdriver
Scissors
Drill
Utility knife
Spline roller

Nail set
Hammer
Spline cord
Screening, glass
Rubber gasket
Replacement hardware

Remove the metal storm window sash by pressing in the release hardware in the lower rail then lifting the sash out. Sash hangers on the corners of the top rail should be aligned with the notches in the side channels before removal.

How to Replace Screening in a Metal Storm Window

Pry the vinyl spline from the groove around the edge of the frame with a screwdriver. Retain the old spline if it is still flexible, or replace it with a new spline.

Stretch the new screen tightly over the frame so that it overlaps the edges of the frame. Keeping the screen taut, use the convex side of a spline roller to press the screen into the retaining grooves.

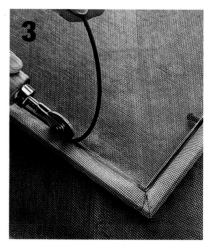

Use the concave side of the spline roller to press the spline into the groove (it helps to have a partner for this). Cut away excess screen using a utility knife.

How to Replace Glass in a Metal Storm Window

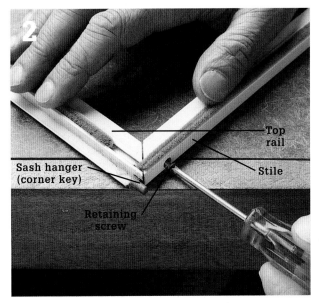

Remove the sash frame from the window, then completely remove the broken glass from the sash. Remove the rubber gasket that framed the old glass pane and remove any glass remnants. Find the dimensions for the replacement glass by measuring between the inside edges of the frame opening, then adding twice the thickness of the rubber gasket to each measurement.

Set the frame on a flat surface, and disconnect the top rail. Remove the retaining screws in the sides of the frame stiles where they join the top rail. After unscrewing the retaining screws, pull the top rail loose, pulling gently in a downward motion to avoid damaging the L-shaped corner keys that join the rail and the stiles. For glass replacement, you need only disconnect the top rail.

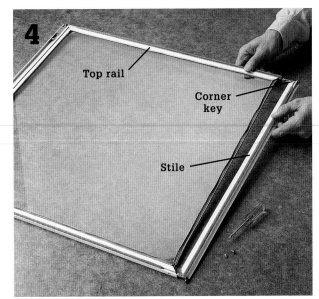

Fit the rubber gasket (buy a replacement if the original is in poor condition) around one edge of the replacement glass pane. At the corners, cut the spine of the gasket partway so it will bend around the corner. Continue fitting the gasket around the pane, cutting at the corners, until all four edges are covered. Trim off any excess gasket material.

Slide the glass pane into the channels in the stiles and bottom rail of the sash frame. Insert corner keys into the top rail, then slip the other ends of the keys into the frame stiles. Press down on the top rail until the mitered corners are flush with the stiles. Drive the retaining screws back through the stiles and into the top rail to join the frame together. Reinsert the frame into the window.

How to Disassemble & Repair a Metal Sash Frame

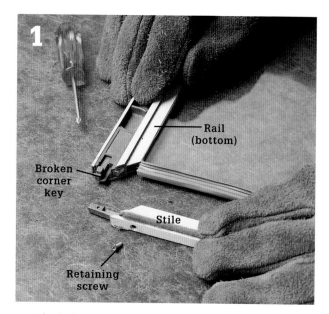

Metal window sash are held together at the corner joints by L-shaped pieces of hardware that fit into grooves in the sash frame pieces. To disassemble a broken joint, start by disconnecting the stile and rail at the broken joint—there is usually a retaining screw driven through the stile that must be removed.

Corner keys are secured in the rail slots with crimps that are punched into the metal over the key. To remove keys, drill through the metal in the crimped area using a drill bit the same diameter as the crimp. Carefully knock the broken key pieces from the frame slots with a screwdriver and hammer.

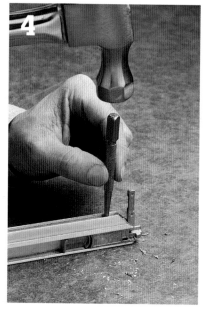

Locate matching replacement parts for the broken corner key, which is usually an assembly of two or three pieces. There are dozens of different types, so it is important that you save the old parts for reference.

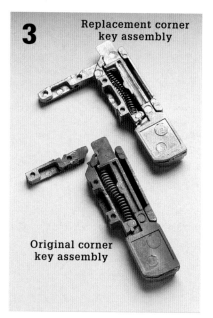

Insert the replacement corner key assembly into the slot in the rail. Use a nail set as a punch, and rap it into the metal over the corner key, creating a new crimp to hold the key in place.

Insert the glass and gasket into the frame slots, then reassemble the frame and drive in retainer screws (for screen windows, replace the screening).

Replace turnbuttons and window clips that do not hold storm windows tightly in place. Fill old screw holes with wood dowels and glue before driving the screws.

Lubricate the sliding assemblies on metal-framed combination storm windows or doors once a year using penetrating lubricant.

Replace deteriorated glazing around glass panes in wood-framed windows. Sound glazing makes windows more energy-efficient and more attractive.

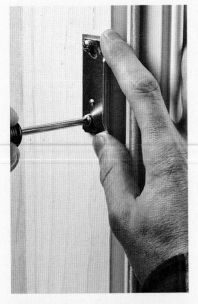

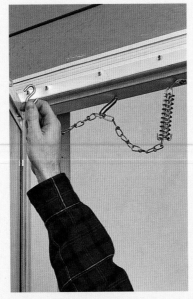

Tighten storm door latches by redriving loose screws in the strike plate. If the latch does not catch on the strike plate, loosen the screws on the strike plate, insert thin wood shims between the plate and the jamb, and retighten the screws.

Add a wind chain if your storm door does not have one. Wind chains prevent doors from blowing open too far, causing damage to the door hinges or closer. Set the chain so the door will not open more than 90°.

Adjust the door closer so it has the right amount of tension to close the door securely, without slamming. Most closers have tension-adjustment screws at the end of the cylinder farthest from the hinge side of the door.

Tuning Up Garage Doors

Imagine this: You're driving home late at night, it's pouring outside, and you're shivering because you've got the flu. Then, you turn into your driveway, punch a little button, and your garage door opens, a light comes on, you pull in, and you're HOME. You didn't have to get drenched, or lift a door that felt like heavy metal, or scream at the heavens for making you so miserable. Thanks to a well-maintained garage door and opener, you escaped all of this, and that is a good thing.

Unfortunately, over time, many good things become bad things, especially if they aren't well-maintained. An overhead garage door is no exception. To keep everything running smoothly requires effort on three fronts: the door, the opener, and the opener's electronic safety sensors. Here's what you need to know to keep all three in tiptop shape.

Tools & Materials ▸

Mineral spirits
Graphite spray
  lubricant
Garage door
  weather-stripping
Level
Soft-faced mallet

Penetrating lubricant
Toweling
Socket wrenches
Lightweight oil
Pliers
Open-end wrenches

A bit of routine maintenance now and again will help keep your garage door working exactly as it should, rain or shine.

How to Tune-Up a Garage Door

Begin the tune-up by lubricating the door tracks, pulleys, and rollers. Use a lightweight oil, not grease, for this job. The grease catches too much dust and dirt.

Remove clogged or damaged rollers from the door by loosening the nuts that hold the roller brackets. The roller will come with the bracket when the bracket is pulled free.

Mineral spirits and kerosene are good solvents for cleaning roller bearings. Let the bearing sit for a half-hour in the solvent. Then brush away the grime build-up with an old paintbrush or toothbrush.

(continued)

4

If the rollers are making a lot of noise as they move over the tracks, the tracks are probably out of alignment. To fix this, check the tracks for plumb. If they are out of plumb, the track mounting brackets must be adjusted.

5

To adjust out-of-plumb tracks, loosen all the track mounting brackets (usually 3 or 4 per track) and push the brackets into alignment.

6

It's often easier to adjust the brackets by partially loosening the bolts and tapping the track with a soft-faced mallet. Once the track is plumb, tighten all the bolts.

7

Sometimes the door lock bar opens sluggishly because the return spring has lost its tension. The only way to fix this is to replace the spring. One end is attached to the body of the lock; the other end hooks onto the lock bar.

8

If a latch needs lubrication, use graphite in powder or liquid form. Don't use oil because it attracts dust that will clog the lock even more.

Alternative: Sometimes the lock bar won't lock the door because it won't slide into its opening on the door track. To fix this, loosen the guide bracket that holds the lock bar and move it up or down until the bar hits the opening.

(continued)

Worn or broken weather stripping on the bottom edge of the door can let in a lot of cold air and stiff breezes. Check to see if this strip is cracked, broken, or has holes along its edges. If so, remove the old strip and pull any nails left behind.

Measure the width of your garage door, then buy a piece of weather stripping to match. These strips are standard lumber-yard and home center items. Sometimes they are sold in kit form, with fasteners included. If not, just nail the stripping in place with galvanized roofing nails.

If the chain on your garage door opener is sagging more than ½" below the bottom rail, it can make a lot of noise and cause drive sprocket wear. Tighten the chain according to the directions in the owner's manual.

13

On openers with a chain, lubricate the entire length of the chain with lightweight oil. Do not use grease. Use the same lubricant if your opener has a drive screw instead.

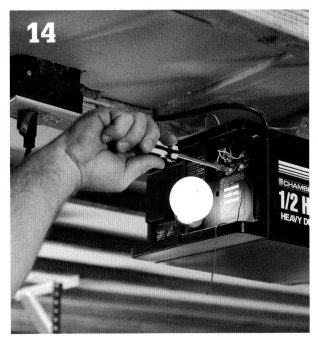

14

Test the door's closing force sensitivity and make adjustments at the opener's motor case if needed. Because both the sensitivity and the adjustment mechanism vary greatly between opener models, you'll have to rely on your owner's manual for guidance. If you don't have the owner's manual, you can usually download one from the manufacturer's website.

15

Check for proper alignment on the safety sensors near the floor. They should be pointing directly at one another and their lenses should be clean of any dirt and grease.

16

Make sure that the sensors are "talking" to the opener properly. Start to close the door, then put your hand down between the two sensors. If the door stops immediately and reverses direction, it's working properly. If it's not, make the adjustment recommended in the owner's manual. If that doesn't do the trick, call a professional door installer and don't use the door until it passes this test.

Weatherizing Windows & Doors

Windows and doors do more than enhance the beauty of your home or help you keep an eye on the weather. They also create important thermal barriers to help control your annual heating and cooling costs. If you are concerned about the ever-rising price of energy or the impact our consumption has on the environment, consider having an energy audit performed on your home. Make it your first window and door weatherizing project. That way, you'll know exactly where to focus your efforts.

The secret to energy-tight windows and doors is blocking air movement. On windows, this involves creating a sealed-off dead air space between interior and exterior glass panes. Modern double- and triple-paned windows often contain inert gasses to help create dead air spaces. You can accomplish the same effect on older windows by using weather stripping and a good storm window or plastic window sheeting to block air movement. For exterior doors, consider adding storm doors if your home doesn't already have them. Then, be sure door jambs are sealed with metal or neoprene weather stripping and an adjustable threshold. This chapter will acquaint you with weatherizing and energy-efficiency issues and show you how to install a variety of weather stripping products properly.

This chapter includes:

- Overview of Weatherizing Issues
- Detecting Energy Loss
- Replacing Storm Windows

Overview of Weatherizing Issues

No matter whether you live in a hot or a cold climate, weatherizing your home's windows and doors can pay off handsomely. Heating and cooling costs may account for over half of the total household energy bill.

Before buying a basement window well cover, measure the widest point of the window well and note its shape.

Since most weatherizing projects are relatively inexpensive, you can recover your investment quickly. In fact, in some climates, you can pay back the cost of a weatherproofing project in one season.

If you live in a cold climate, you probably already understand the importance of weatherizing. The value of keeping warm air inside the house during a cold winter is obvious. From the standpoint of energy efficiency, it's equally important to prevent warm air from entering the house during summer.

Weatherizing your home is an ideal do-it-yourself project, because it can be done a little at a time, according to your schedule. In cold climates, the best time of the year to weatherize is the fall, before it turns too cold to work outdoors.

Whether you're concerned about the environment or want to spend less on your utility bills, some simple adjustments around your home can help you accomplish your goal.

Most weatherizing projects deal with windows (pages 259 to 261) and doors (pages 262 and 263), because these are the primary areas of heat loss in most homes. Here are a few simple suggestions you might consider for the exterior of your home:

Use a caulk that matches your home exterior to seal the window and door frames.

A felt door sweep can seal out drafts, even if you have an uneven floor or a low threshold.

Minimize heat loss from basement window wells by covering them with plastic window well covers (left, top). Most window well covers have an upper flange designed to slip under the siding. Slip this in place, then fasten the cover to the foundation with masonry anchors and weigh down the bottom flange with stones. For extra weatherizing, seal the edges with caulk.

Adding caulk is a simple way to fill narrow gaps in interior or exterior surfaces. It's also available in a peelable form that can be easily removed at the end of the season.

When buying caulk, estimate half a cartridge per window or door, four for an average-sized foundation sill, and at least one more to close gaps around vents, pipes, and other openings.

Caulk around the outside of the window and door frames to seal any gaps. For best results, use a caulk that matches or blends with the color of your siding.

There are many different types of caulk and weather stripping materials. All are inexpensive and easy to use, but it's important to get the right materials for the job, as most are designed for specific applications.

Generally, metal and metal-reinforced weather stripping is more durable than products made of plastic, rubber, or foam. However, even plastic, rubber, and foam weather stripping products have a wide range of quality. The best rubber products are those made from neoprene rubber—use this whenever it's available.

A door sweep (previous page, bottom) attaches to the inside bottom of the door to seal out drafts. A felt or bristle sweep is best if you have an uneven floor or a low threshold. Vinyl and rubber models are also available.

A threshold insert fits around the base of the door (page 240). Most have a sweep on the interior side and a drip edge on the exterior side to direct water away from the threshold.

A threshold insert seals the gap between the door and the threshold. These are made from vinyl or rubber and can be easily replaced (see pages 238 to 241).

Self-adhesive foam strips (below) attach to sashes and frames to seal the air gaps at windows and doors. Reinforced felt strips have a metal spine that adds rigidity in high-impact areas, such as doorstops.

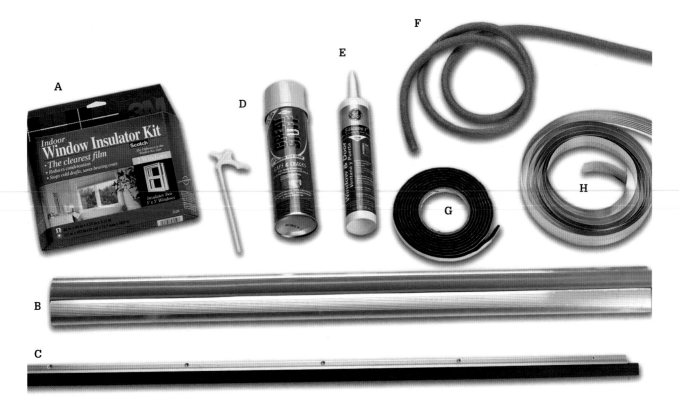

Weatherizing products commonly found in home centers include: A clear film, heat-shrink window insulator kit (A); an aluminum door threshold with vinyl weatherstripping insert (B); a nail-on, rubber door sweep (C); minimal expanding spray foam (D); silicone window and door caulk (E); open-cell foam caulk-backer rod (F); self-adhesive, closed-cell foam weatherstripping coil (G); flexible brass weatherstripping coil, also called V-channel, (H).

Detecting Energy Loss

Some of the indications that your home is not energy-efficient will be obvious, such as draftiness, fogged or frosted windows, ice dams, gaps around windows in the foundation wall, and high energy bills. However, it can be more difficult to detect problems such as inadequate wall insulation or the loss of warm air around attic vents. The following are some ways to identify where your home may be losing energy:

- Measure the temperature in different parts of a room. A difference of more than one or two degrees indicates that the room is poorly sealed. The solution is to update the weather stripping around the windows and doors (page 257).
- Check for drafts around windows and doors by holding a tissue next to the jambs on a windy day. If the tissue flutters, the weather stripping is inadequate. Another sign is outside light coming in around the jambs.
- Conduct an energy audit. Most power companies will provide you with an audit kit or conduct an audit for you.
- Monitor your energy usage from year to year. If there's a significant increase that can't be explained by variations in the weather, consider hiring a professional to conduct an energy audit.

The average home has many small leaks, which collectively may add up to the equivalent of a 2-ft. hole in the wall. The air that leaks through these cracks can account for as much as one-third of your total energy loss.

Condensation or frost buildup on windows is a sign of poor weather stripping and an inadequate storm window.

Weather stripping and insulation may begin to deteriorate. Telltale signs include crumbling foam or rubber.

Energy audits done by power companies may use a blower door to measure airflow and detect leaks.

Tips for Weatherizing a Window ▶

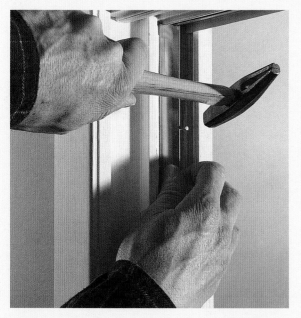

Sliding windows: Treat side-by-side sliding windows as if they were double-hung windows turned 90°. For greater durability, use metal tension strips, rather than self-adhesive compressible foam, in the sash track that fit against the edge of the sash when the window is closed.

Casement windows: Attach self-adhesive foam or rubber compression strips on the outside edges of the window stops.

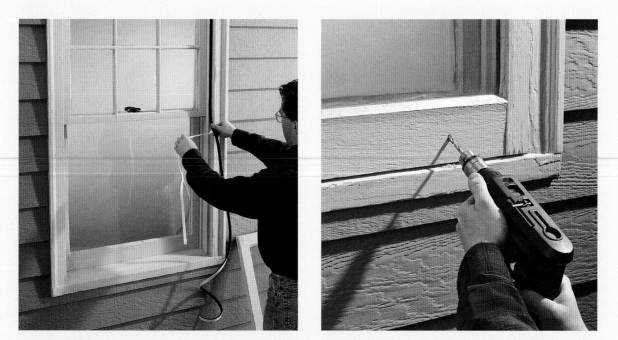

Storm windows: Create a tight seal by attaching foam compression strips to the outside of storm window stops. After installing the storm window, fill any gaps between the exterior window trim and the storm window with caulk backer rope (left). Check the inside surface of the storm window during cold weather for condensation or frost buildup (facing page). If moisture is trapped between the storm window and the permanent window, drill one or two small holes through the bottom rail (right) to allow moist air to escape. Drill at a slightly upward angle.

How to Weatherstrip a Window

Cut metal V-channel to fit in the channels for the sliding sash, extending at least 2" past the closed position for each sash (do not cover sash-closing mechanisms). Attach the V-channel by driving wire brads (usually provided by the manufacturer) with a tack hammer. Drive the fasteners flush with the surface so the sliding sash will not catch on them.

Flare out the open ends of the V-channels with a putty knife so the channel is slightly wider than the gap between the sash and the track it fits into. Avoid flaring out too much at one time—it is difficult to press V-channel back together without causing some buckling.

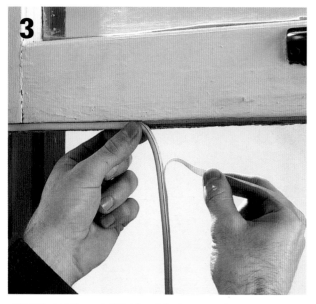

Wipe down the underside of the bottom window sash with a damp rag, and let it dry; then attach self-adhesive compressible foam or rubber to the underside of the sash. Use high-quality hollow neoprene strips, if available. This will create an airtight seal when the window is locked in position.

Bottom sash (raised)

Top sash (lowered)

Seal the gap between the top sash and the bottom sash on double-hung windows. Lift the bottom sash and lower the top sash to improve access, and tack metal V-channel to the bottom rail of the top sash using wire brads. Tip: The open end of the "V" should be pointed downward so moisture cannot collect in the channel. Flare out the V-channel with a putty knife to fit the gap between the sash.

Replacing Storm Windows

As old removable storm windows wear out, many homeowners elect to replace them with modern, combination storm windows. Designed to mount permanently in the existing opening, retrofit combination storm windows are very easy to install and are fairly inexpensive.

Most retrofit storm windows attach to the outside edges of the window stops on the sides and top of the window opening. Most windows do not have a bottom stop. Secure the bottom rail of the new window with caulk. Common window sizes are stocked at most building centers, but you may need to order custom-made windows. Have the exact measurements when you order the windows. You also will be asked to choose a finish color and a style. If you have operating double-hung windows, choose three-sash windows so you have the option of opening the top storm sash.

Tools & Materials ▸

Screwdriver	Replacement storm
Drill	windows
Tape measure	Caulk or panel
Screws	adhesive

Retrofit storm windows attach to the window stops in the existing window opening. The easiest way to size them is to use the dimensions of old storm windows. Otherwise, measure the narrowest point between the side jambs to find the width, and measure the shortest point from the header to the sill (where it meets the front edges of the stops) to find the height.

How to Install a New Combination Storm Window

Buy replacement storm windows to fit your window openings. Test-fit before installing them. To install, first apply a bead of exterior-grade panel adhesive or caulk to the outside edges of the window stops at the top and sides.

Drill pilot holes for the fasteners in the mounting flanges, spaced 12" apart, making sure they will be centered over the stops. Press the new storm window into the opening, centered between the side stops, with the bottom rail resting on the windowsill.

Drive the fasteners (#4 × 1" sheet-metal screws work well), starting at the top. Make sure the window is squarely in the opening, then fill in the fasteners on the side stops. Apply caulk along the bottom rail, leaving a ¼"-wide gap midway as a weep hole.

Tips for Weatherizing Doors ▸

Door weather stripping is prone to failure because it undergoes constant stress. Use metal weather stripping that is tacked to the surfaces whenever you can—especially around door jambs. It is much more durable than self-adhesive products. If your job calls for flexible weather stripping, use products made from neoprene rubber, not foam. Replace old door thresholds (see pages 238 to 241) or threshold inserts as soon as they begin to show wear.

Install a storm door to decrease drafts and energy loss through entry doors. Buy an insulated storm door with a continuous hinge and seamless exterior surface.

Adjust the door frame to eliminate large gaps between the door and jamb. Remove the interior case molding and drive new shims between the jamb and framing member on the hinge side, reducing the size of the door opening. Close the door to test fit, and adjust as needed before reattaching the case molding.

Patio door: Use rubber compression strips to seal the channels in patio door jambs, where movable panels fit when closed. Also install a patio door insulator kit (plastic sheeting installed similarly to plastic sheeting for windows) on the interior side of the door.

Garage door: Attach a new rubber sweep to the bottom outside edge of the garage door if the old sweep has deteriorated. Also check the door jambs for drafts, and add weather stripping, if needed.

How to Weatherize an Exterior Door

Cut two pieces of metal tension strip or V-channel the full height of the door opening, and cut another to full width. Use wire brads to tack the strips to the door jambs and door header on the interior side of the doorstops. *Tip: Attach metal weather stripping from the top down to help prevent buckling.* Flare out the tension strips with a putty knife to fill the gaps between the jambs and the door when the door is in the closed position (do not pry too far at a time).

Add reinforced felt strips to the edge of the doorstop on the exterior side. The felt edge should form a close seal with the door when closed. Tip: Drive fasteners only until they are flush with the surface of the reinforcing spine—overdriving will cause damage and buckling.

Attach a new door sweep to the bottom of the door on the interior side (felt or bristle types are better choices if the floor is uneven). Before fastening it permanently, tack the sweep in place and test the door swing to make sure there is enough clearance.

Tip ▸

Fix any cracks in wooden door panels with epoxy wood filler or caulk to block air leaks. If the door has a stain finish, use tinted wood putty, filling from the interior side. Sand and touch up with paint or stain.

Appendix: Preparation

Adding a new window or door to your home requires careful prep work at the beginning of the project, followed by some degree of patching and finishing at the end. Preparing your work area involves checking for hidden wiring, plumbing, or ductwork and locating nearby wall framing. Identifying and rerouting or disconnecting hidden mechanicals will prevent costly mistakes and even possible injury. Once you're certain about what's hidden behind the wall, you can lay out your new window or door location confidently and remove the wall coverings to create a new opening.

After your new window or door is in place, you'll probably have to repair the surrounding interior and exterior wall coverings. When done well, careful patching should help your new door or window look as though it's been there forever.

This chapter includes:

- Preparing for Projects
- Supporting Load-bearing Walls
- Removing Windows & Doors
- Removing Wallboard
- Removing Plaster
- Removing Exterior Surfaces
- Installing & Finishing Wallboard
- Patching Exterior Walls

Preparing for Projects

When planning a door or window installation—or any carpentry project—you will need to consider and choose from dozens of design and construction options.

Consider hiring professionals for some parts of your project if you are unsure of your own skills.

Organize your project into stages, such as layout and planning, permit application (if required), shopping, site preparation, construction, and inspection. Smaller stages help you work efficiently and let you break large projects into a series of smaller, daily tasks.

If your project requires permits from the local building inspector, do not begin work until the inspector has approved your plans and issued the permits. Shopping is easier once you've obtained permits required for the job. Make a detailed materials list and make all of your purchases at the outset.

During the preparation phase, try to salvage or recycle materials when possible. Window and door units that are in good shape can be used elsewhere or sold to salvage yards. Most raw metals, such as the frames on old aluminum storm windows, are accepted at recycling centers.

Most carpentry projects share the same basic preparation techniques and follow a similar sequence. Start by checking for hidden mechanicals in the work area and shutting off and rerouting electrical wiring, plumbing pipes, and other utility lines. If you are not comfortable performing these tasks, hire a professional.

Test all electrical outlets before beginning any demolition of walls, ceilings, or floors. Shovel all demolition debris away from the work area. Clear away the debris whenever materials begin to pile up during the construction of a project. For larger jobs, consider renting a dumpster.

Tools & Materials ▸

Screwdrivers	Channel-type pliers
Broom	Finish nails
Flat pry bar	Masking tape
Trash containers	Building paper
Neon circuit tester	Plywood
Electronic stud finder	Drop cloths

How to Prepare the Work Area

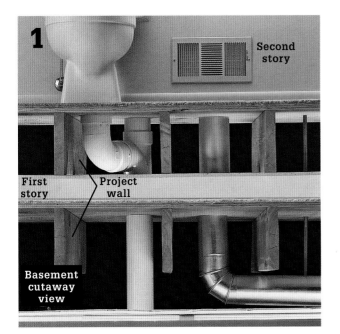

Check for hidden plumbing lines, ductwork, and gas pipes before you cut into a wall to create or enlarge a door or window opening. To determine the location of the pipes and ducts, examine the areas directly below and above the project wall. In most cases, pipes, utility lines, and ductwork run through the wall vertically between floors.

Disconnect electrical wiring before you cut into walls. Trace the wiring back to a fixture outside the cutout area, then shut off the power and disconnect the wires leading into the cutout area. Turn the power back on and test for current with a circuit tester before cutting into walls.

Locate framing members using a stud finder or by knocking on the wall and feeling for solid points. Verify the findings by driving finish nails through the wall surface. After finding the center of one stud, measure over 16" to locate neighboring studs.

Shovel debris through a convenient window into a wheelbarrow to speed up demolition work. Use sheets of plywood to cover shrubs and flower gardens next to open windows and doors. Cover adjoining lawn areas with sheets of plastic or canvas to simplify cleanup.

Supporting Load-bearing Walls

If your project requires you to remove more than one stud in a load-bearing wall, temporary supports will be needed while you do the framing. The technique for making temporary supports varies, depending on your house's construction.

Removal of load-bearing interior walls requires temporary support on both sides of the wall. To make temporary supports for platform framing, use hydraulic jacks or a temporary stud wall. The stud wall method is a better choice if the supports must remain in place for more than one day.

To make temporary supports for balloon framing, see below and page 271. The project shown involves working on an exterior wall on the first floor of a balloon-framed house. Consult a professional if you want to alter an interior load-bearing wall or an exterior wall on an upper floor of a balloon-framed house. Hire a professional to remove any wall over 12 ft. long.

Tools & Materials ▸

Tape measure
Level
Circular saw
Hammer
Ratchet
Drill and spade bit

Hydraulic jacks
2 × 4 lumber, shims
3 and 4" lag screws
2" wallboard screws
10d nails
Cloth

Temporary supports for a platform-framed house must support the ceiling joists, since the ceiling platform carries the load of the upper floors. Platform framing can be identified by the sole plate to which the wall studs are nailed.

Temporary supports for a balloon-framed house support the wall studs, which carry the upstairs load. The temporary support header, called a whaler, is anchored to the wall studs above the planned rough opening and is supported by wall studs and bracing adjacent to the rough opening. Balloon framing can be identified by long wall studs that pass uncut through the floor to a sill plate resting on the foundation.

How to Support Platform Framing with Hydraulic Jacks (Joists Perpendicular to Wall)

Measure the width of the planned rough opening and add 4 ft. so the temporary support will reach well past the rough opening. Cut three 2 × 4s to length. Nail two of the 2 × 4s together with 10d nails to make a top plate for the temporary support; the remaining 2 × 4 will be the sole plate. Place the temporary sole plate on the floor, 3 ft. from the wall, centering it on the planned rough opening.

Set the hydraulic jacks on the temporary sole plate, 2 ft. in from the ends. (Use three jacks if the opening will be more than 8 ft. wide.) For each jack, build a post by nailing together a pair of 2 × 4s. The posts should be about 4" shorter than the distance between the ceiling and the top of the jacks. Attach the posts to the top plate, 2 ft. from the ends, using countersunk lag screws.

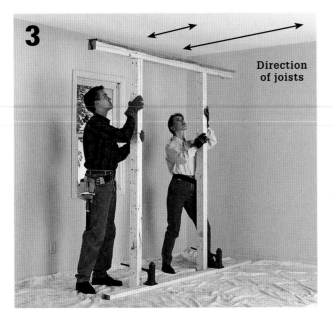

Cover the top of the plate with a thick layer of cloth to protect the ceiling from marks and cracks, then lift the support structure onto the hydraulic jacks.

Adjust the support structure so the posts are exactly plumb, and raise the hydraulic jacks until the top plate just begins to lift the ceiling. Do not lift too far, or you may damage the floor or ceiling.

How to Support Platform Framing with a Temporary Stud Wall (Joists Perpendicular to Wall)

Build a 2 × 4 stud wall that is 4 ft. wider than the planned wall opening and 1¾" shorter than the distance from floor to ceiling.

Raise the stud wall and position it 3 ft. from the wall, centered on the planned rough opening.

Slide a 2 × 4 top plate between the temporary wall and the ceiling. Check to make sure the wall is plumb, and drive shims under the top plate at 12" intervals until the wall is wedged tightly in place.

How to Support Platform Framing with Hydraulic Jacks (Joists Parallel to Wall)

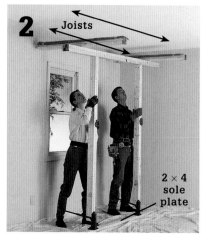

Follow directions on page 269, except: Build two 4-ft.-long cross braces using pairs of 2 × 4s nailed together. Attach the cross braces to the double top plate, 1 ft. from the ends, using countersunk lag screws.

Place a 2 × 4 sole plate directly over a floor joist, then set hydraulic jacks on the sole plate. For each jack, build a post 8" shorter than the jack-to-ceiling distance. Nail posts to the top plate, 2 ft. from the ends. Cover braces with cloth, and set the support structure on jacks.

Adjust the support structure so the posts are exactly plumb, and pump the hydraulic jacks until the cross braces just begin to lift the ceiling. Do not lift too far, or you may damage the ceiling or floor.

How to Support Balloon Framing

Remove the wall surfaces around the rough opening from floor to ceiling. Make a temporary support header (called a whaler) by cutting a 2 × 8 long enough to extend at least 20" past each side of the planned rough opening. Center the whaler against the wall studs, flush with the ceiling. Tack the whaler in place with 2" screws.

Cut two lengths of 2 × 4 to fit snugly between the bottom of the whaler and the floor. Slide the 2 × 4s into place at the ends of the whaler, and attach them with nailing plates and 10d nails.

Drill two ³⁄₁₆" holes through the whaler and into each stud it spans. Secure the whaler with ³⁄₈ × 4" lag screws.

Drive shims between the bottom of each 2 × 4 and the floor to help secure the support structure.

Removing Windows & Doors

If your remodeling project requires removing old windows and doors, do not start this work until all preparation work is finished and the interior wall surfaces and trim have been removed. You will need to close up the wall openings as soon as possible, so make sure you have all the necessary tools, framing lumber, and new window or door units before starting the final stages of demolition. Be prepared to finish the work as quickly as possible.

Windows and doors are removed using the same basic procedures. In many cases, old units can be salvaged for resale or later use, so use care when removing them.

Tools & Materials ▸

Utility knife
Flat pry bar
Screwdriver
Hammer

Reciprocating saw
Plywood
Masking tape
Screws

Masking tape used to keep windows from shattering

Removing windows or doors is a similar process and often easier with a helper. Use care when removing large windows or patio doors, which can be very heavy.

How to Remove Doors

1

Using a pry bar and hammer, gently remove the interior door trim. Save the trim to use after the new door is installed.

2

Cut away the old caulk between the exterior siding and the brick molding on the door frame using a utility knife.

3

Use a flat pry bar or a cat's paw to remove the casing nails securing the door jambs to the framing. Cut stubborn nails with a reciprocating saw (see step 2, below). Remove the door from the opening.

How to Remove Windows

1

Carefully pry off the interior trim around the window frame. For double-hung windows with sash weights, remove the weights by cutting the cords and pulling the weights from the weight pockets near the bottom of the side jambs.

2

Cut through the nails holding the window jambs to the framing members using a reciprocating saw. Place tape over the windowpanes to prevent shattering, then remove the window unit from the opening.

Nailing flange

Variation: For windows and doors attached with nailing flanges, cut or pry loose the siding material, then remove the nails holding the unit to the sheathing. See pages 282 to 284 for more information on removing siding.

Applying Caulk

Once you've patched exterior surfaces around a new window or door project, the final step is to apply a bead of caulk to seal the joint. Caulk will prevent moisture from penetrating behind your siding and damaging the jambs, framing, or insulation. It also keeps insects out.

Applying caulk is one of those do-it-yourself projects that really isn't difficult, but it definitely takes practice. The secret is to avoid the urge to apply too much caulk, which quickly makes a big mess and is annoying to clean up. The goal is to create a bead just large enough to cover the gap and both sides of the joint. At the same time, you want to apply the caulk smoothly so it requires minimal—or even no—touch-up once in place.

To prepare the tube and gun for use, cut the tip of the nozzle off at 45° to create a hole no larger than about ¼". Poke a nail down through the nozzle to break the inner seal, releasing the caulk, then load the tube in the gun. Push the plunger on the gun forward until it makes contact with the back of the tube, and twist the angled end of the plunger up to engage its teeth with the gun's trigger.

Squeeze the trigger a few times, and the caulk should begin to flow. Now, press the nozzle against the joint and pull the gun along slowly while gently squeezing the trigger to create an even, smooth bead. When you want to stop the flow, twist the plunger's end down again to release it.

If excess caulk begins to accumulate around the nozzle, stop the flow and wipe off the nozzle before starting again. Try to keep the nozzle area clean as you go along to maintain a uniform bead.

Caulk guns are used to deliver a wide range of household products, not simply caulk. The guns are tricky to use at first, but with practice you'll get the hang of it.

Many specialized caulks exist, but the best type for window and door projects is silicone acrylic. It stays flexible and cleans up easily with soap and water.

Tools & Materials ▸

Putty knife	Paintbrush
Utility knife	Primer
Caulk gun	Paint
Caulk	

How to Caulk a Window or Door

Before applying new caulk, it's a good idea to prime the crack with exterior primer. This is especially important when caulking around new brick molding or wood-framed windows.

After the primer dries, caulk the joint and smooth the bead with your finger or a putty knife.

Finish up the job by brushing on two coats of paint. Allow the caulk to dry, according to the manufacturer's instructions, before you paint.

Removing Wallboard

You must remove interior wall surfaces before starting the framing work for many window and door projects. Most often, the material you'll be removing is wallboard. Demolishing a section of wallboard is a messy job, but it is not difficult. Before you begin, shut off the power and inspect the wall for wiring and plumbing.

Remove enough surface material so that there is plenty of room to install the new framing members. When framing for a window or door, remove the wall surface from floor to ceiling and all the way to the first wall studs on either side of the planned rough opening.

Note: If your walls are covered in wood paneling, remove it in full sheets if you intend to reuse it. It may be difficult to find new paneling to match the old style.

Tools & Materials ▸

Screwdrivers
Tape measure
Pencil
Stud finder
Chalk line
Utility knife
Pry bar
Circular saw with
    demolition blade
Hammer
Protective eyewear

Tool Tip ▸

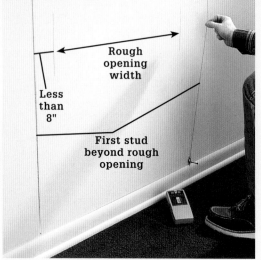

If the rough opening is less than 8" from the next stud, you will not have room to attach an extra stud. Use a chalk line to mark the cutting line down the center of the wall stud. The exposed portion of the stud will provide a surface for attaching new wallboard when finishing the room.

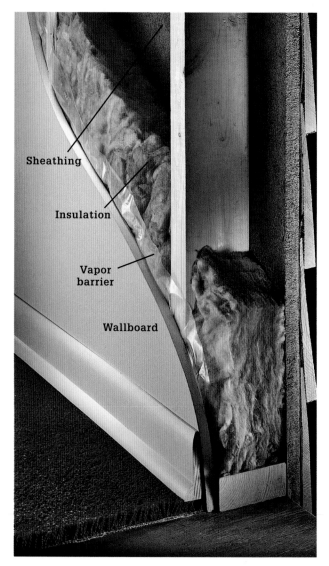

Before removing wallboard from an exterior wall, study this cross section to familiarize yourself with the typical components that make up the wall.

How to Remove Wallboard

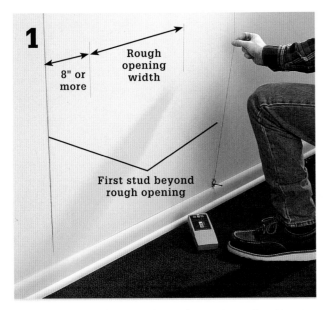

1

Rough opening width

8" or more

First stud beyond rough opening

Mark the width of the rough opening on the wall and locate the first stud on either side of the planned rough opening. If the rough opening is more than 8" from the next stud, use a chalk line to mark a cutting line on the inside edge of the stud. During framing, an extra stud will be attached to provide a surface for anchoring the new wallboard.

2

Remove baseboards and other trim, and prepare the work area (pages 266 and 267). Make a ½"-deep cut from floor to ceiling along both cutting lines using a circular saw. Use a utility knife to finish the cuts at the top and bottom and to cut through the taped horizontal seam where the wall meets the ceiling surface.

3

Insert the end of a pry bar into the cut near one corner of the opening. Pull the pry bar until the wallboard breaks, then tear away the broken pieces. Take care to avoid damaging the wallboard outside the project area.

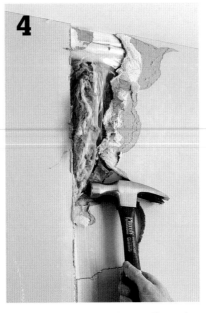

4

Continue removing the wallboard by striking the surface with the side of a hammer and pulling the wallboard away from the wall with the pry bar or your hands.

5

Remove nails, screws, and any remaining wallboard from the framing members using a pry bar. Remove any vapor barrier and insulation.

Removing Plaster

Plaster removal is a dusty job, so always wear eye protection and a particle mask during demolition, and use sheets of plastic to protect furniture and to block open doorways. Plaster walls are very brittle, so work carefully to avoid cracking the plaster in areas that will not be removed.

If the material being removed encompasses most of the wall surface, consider removing the whole interior surface of the wall. Replacing the entire wall with wallboard is easier and produces better results than trying to patch around the project area.

Tools & Materials ▸

Straightedge
Pencil
Chalk line
Pry bar
Utility knife
Particle mask
Hammer

Aviation snips
Work gloves
Reciprocating saw or jigsaw
Protective eyewear
Masking tape
Scrap 2 × 4

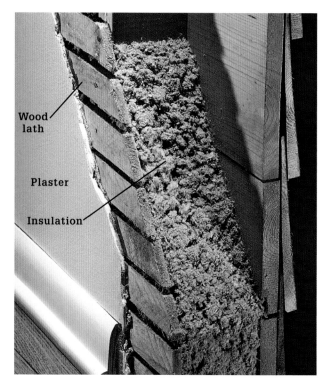

Before removing plaster from an exterior wall, study this cross section to familiarze yourself with the typical components that make up the wall.

How to Remove Plaster

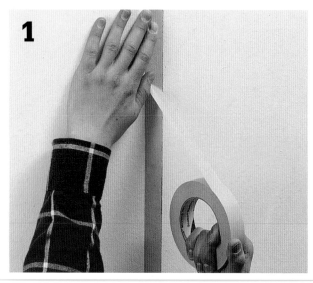

1

Shut off the power and inspect the wall for wiring and plumbing. Mark the wall area to be removed. Apply a double layer of masking tape along the outside edge of each cutting line.

2

Score each line several times with a utility knife using a straightedge as a guide. Scored lines should be at least ⅛" deep.

3

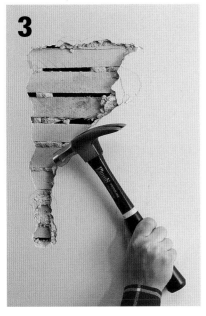

Beginning at the top of the wall
in the center of the planned opening,
break up the plaster by striking the wall
lightly with the side of a hammer. Clear
away all plaster from floor to ceiling to
within 3" of the marked lines.

4

Break the plaster along the edges by
holding a scrap piece of 2 × 4 on edge
just inside the scored line and rapping it
with a hammer. Use a pry bar to remove
the remaining plaster.

5

Cut through the lath along the edges
of the plaster using a reciprocating saw
or jigsaw.

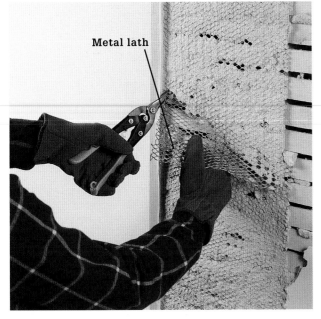

Metal lath

Variation: If the wall has metal lath laid over the wood lath,
use aviation snips to clip the edges of the metal lath. Press the
jagged edges of the lath flat against the stud. The cut edges of
metal lath are very sharp; be sure to wear work gloves.

6

Remove the lath from the studs using a pry bar. Pry
away any remaining nails, and remove any vapor barrier and
insulation.

Removing Exterior Surfaces

Exterior surfaces must be removed when you create or enlarge an opening for a window or door in an exterior wall. Determine the best method for your project based on the exterior surface you have and the type of window or door unit you plan to install.

Wood siding can be cut in place or removed in full pieces to expose the area for the window or door opening. For windows and doors with brick molding, you can temporarily set the unit in place, trace around the brick molding onto the wood siding, then cut the siding to fit exactly around the molding. This method is shown on pages 58 and 59.

An alternative method is to remove the brick molding from the window and door unit, then cut the siding flush with the framed rough opening. After the unit is installed, temporarily set the molding in place and trace around it onto the siding. Cut the siding, then permanently attach the molding to the unit frame. Use this method to install a window with nailing flanges, but be sure to remove enough siding during the initial cut to provide room for the flanges (pages 55 to 57).

With vinyl or metal siding, it's best to remove whole pieces of siding to expose the opening, then cut

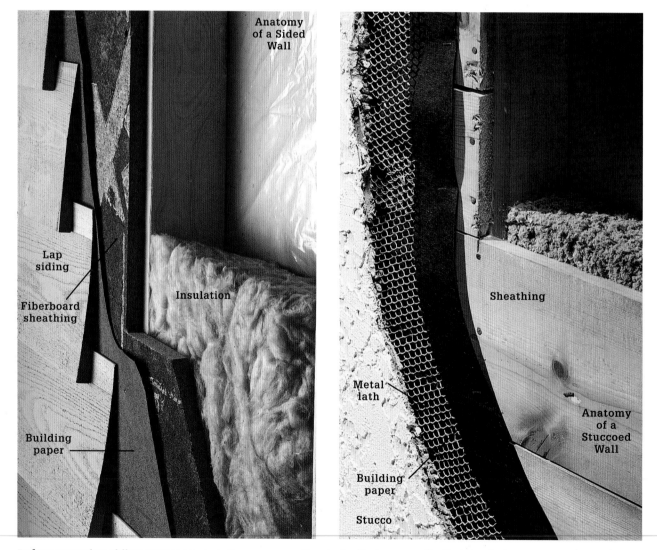

Anatomy of a Sided Wall

Lap siding

Fiberboard sheathing

Insulation

Building paper

Anatomy of a Stuccoed Wall

Sheathing

Metal lath

Building paper

Stucco

Before removing siding or stucco, study these cross sections to familiarize yourself with the typical components that make up the wall.

them to fit after the unit and molding are installed. Be aware that vinyl and metal siding typically require special trim around openings. Check with the siding manufacturer before cutting anything to make sure all of the necessary pieces are available.

Stucco surfaces can be cut away so the brick molding is recessed into the wall surface and makes contact with the sheathing. Or, you can use masonry clips (see page 57) and install the unit with the molding on top of the stucco.

If you're installing a window and door in a new framed opening, don't remove the exterior surface until the framing is complete.

Tools & Materials ▸

Stapler	Masonry chisel and
Flat pry bar	hammer
Zip tool	Masonry-cutting blade
Drill	Masonry bit
Chalk line	Aviation snips
Circular saw	Building paper
Reciprocating saw	Nails, 1 × 4

Brick molding comes pre-attached to most wood-frame window and door units. To remove molding, pry along the outside of the frame to avoid marring exposed parts of the jambs and molding.

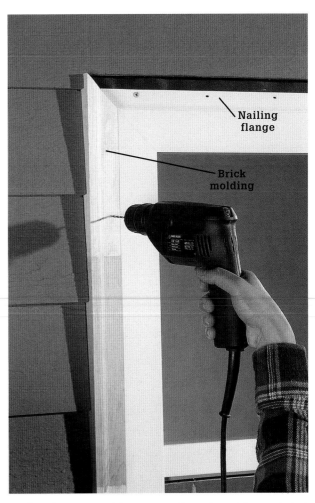

Nailing flanges provide a means of attachment for most vinyl windows. After installation, the nailing flanges are covered with brick molding, 1× exterior trim, or channel trim for vinyl or metal siding.

Siding shown cut away for clarity

To remove a piece of wood siding, start by prying up the piece above using a flat pry bar near the nail locations. Knock the top piece back down with a hammer to expose the raised nails, then pull the nails. Insert spacers between the siding and sheathing to make it easier to access the work areas. Use a hacksaw blade or a cold chisel to shear any difficult nails.

Vinyl and metal siding pieces have a locking J-channel that fits over the bottom of the nailing strip on the piece below. Use a zip tool (inset) to separate siding panels. Insert the zip tool at the overlapping seam nearest the removal area. Slide the zip tool over the J-channel, pulling outward slightly to unlock the joint from the siding below. Remove nails from the panel, then push the panel down to unlock it.

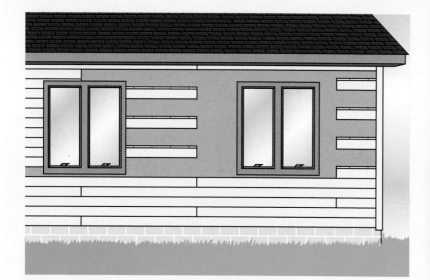

Remove whole pieces of siding to expose the area around a window or door opening. Siding is installed in a staggered pattern so that joints between successive rows do not line up. Number the siding pieces as you remove them to simplify reinstallation.

Patch-in building paper after removing the siding. Loosen the building paper above the patch area, slip the top of the patch underneath, and attach it with staples. Use roofing cement to patch small holes or tears.

How to Make an Opening in Wood Siding

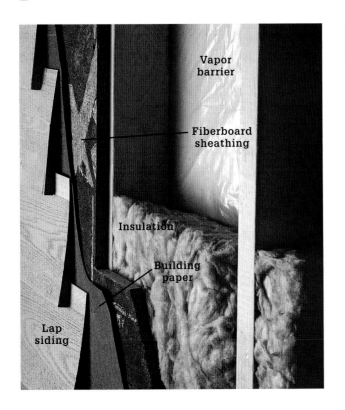

- Vapor barrier
- Fiberboard sheathing
- Insulation
- Building paper
- Lap siding

Tip ▸

Always shut off the power and reroute utility lines, remove any interior surfaces, and frame-in the new opening before removing an exterior surface. To protect the wall cavities against moisture, enclose the new opening as soon as you remove the old siding.

Tools & Materials ▸

Drill with an 8"-long 3/16" twist bit
Hammer
Tape measure
Chalk line

Circular saw with remodeling blade
Reciprocating saw
Eye protection
8d casing nails
Straight 1 × 4

1

From inside the home, drill through the wall at the corners of the framed opening. Push casing nails through the holes to mark their location. For round-top windows, drill holes around the curved outline (see pages 58 and 59).

2

Measure the distance between the nails on the outside of the home to make sure the dimensions are accurate. Mark cutting lines with a chalk line stretched between the nails. Push the nails back through the wall.

3

Nail a straight 1 × 4 flush with the inside edge of the right cutting line. Sink nail heads with a nail set to prevent scratches to the foot of the saw. Set the depth of the circular saw so it cuts through the siding and sheathing.

(continued)

Rest the saw on the 1 × 4, and cut along the marked line using the edge of the board as a guide. Stop the cuts about 1" short of the corners to keep from damaging the framing members.

Reposition the 1 × 4, and make the remaining straight cuts. Drive nails within 1½" of the inside edge of the board, because the siding under this area will be removed to make room for window or door brick moldings.

Variation: For round-top windows, make curved cuts using a reciprocating saw or jigsaw. Move the saw slowly to ensure smooth, straight cuts. To draw an outline for round-top windows, use a cardboard template (page 58).

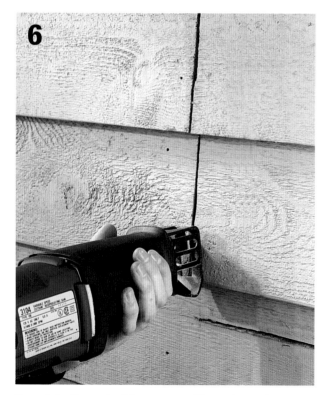

Complete the cuts at the corners with a reciprocating saw or jigsaw. Be careful not to cut beyond the corner marks and keep both hands on the saw while operating it.

Remove the cut wall section. If you wish, remove the siding pieces from the sheathing and save them for future use.

How to Make an Opening in Stucco

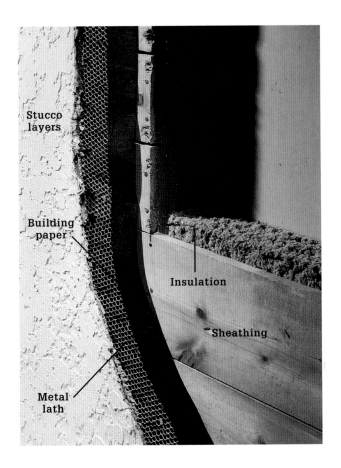

Stucco layers

Building paper

Insulation

Sheathing

Metal lath

Tip ▸

Stucco is a multiple-layer cement product applied to metal lath. Building paper is sandwiched between the metal lath and the sheathing to create a waterproof barrier. Stucco is extremely durable due to its cement base. But if you don't do the removal carefully, it's easy to crack the stucco past the outline for the new window or door.

Tools & Materials ▸

Drill with an 8"-long, 3/16" twist and masonry bits
Tape measure
Chalk line
Compass
Masonry hammer
Eye and ear protection

Circular saw and blades (masonry-cutting and remodeling)
Masonry chisels
Pry bar
Aviation snips
8d casing nails

From inside the home, drill through the wall at the corners of the framed opening. Use a twist bit to drill through the sheathing, then use a masonry bit to finish the holes. Push casing nails through the holes to mark their locations.

On the outside wall, measure the distance between the nails to make sure the rough opening dimensions are accurate. Mark cutting lines between the nails using a chalk line.

(continued)

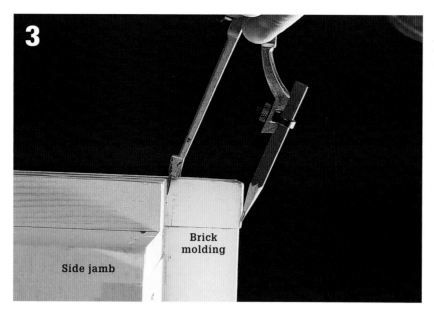

Match the distance between the side jambs and the edge of the brick molding on a window or door with the legs of a compass.

3

Brick molding

Side jamb

Drill corners and mark cutting lines with a chalk line. Measure out from the chalk line the same distance as the width of the molding on the window or door unit. Make a second set of lines at the outer marks (the added margin will allow the brick molding to fit tight against the wall sheathing). Score the stucco surface around the outer lines using a masonry chisel and hammer. The scored grooves should be at least $1/8$" deep.

4

Make straight cuts using a circular saw and masonry-cutting blade. Make several passes with the saw, gradually deepening the cuts until the blade just cuts through the metal lath, causing sparks to fly. Stop the cuts just ahead of the corners to avoid damaging the stucco past the cutting line; complete the cuts with a masonry chisel.

5

Variation: For round-top windows, mark the outline on the stucco using a cardboard template (page 58), and drill a series of holes around the outline using a masonry bit. Complete the cut with a masonry chisel.

Break up the stucco with a masonry hammer or sledgehammer, exposing the underlying metal lath. Use aviation snips to cut through the lath around the opening. Use a pry bar to pull away the lath and attached stucco.

Outline the rough opening on the sheathing using a straightedge as a guide. Cut the rough opening along the inside edge of the framing members using a circular saw or reciprocating saw. Remove the cut section of sheathing.

Installing & Finishing Wallboard

Use wallboard panels both to finish new walls and to patch existing wall areas exposed during the installation of a window or door.

Openings in smooth plaster walls can usually be patched with wallboard, but if you need to match a textured plaster surface, it is best to hire a plasterer to do the work.

Wallboard panels are available in 4 × 8-ft. or 4 × 10-ft. sheets and in ³⁄₈", ¹⁄₂", and ⁵⁄₈" thicknesses. For new walls, ¹⁄₂" thick is standard.

Use all-purpose wallboard compound and paper joint tape. Lay out the wallboard panels so that the seams fall over the center of the openings, not at the sides, or use solid pieces at the openings. Insulate all of the framing cavities around each opening.

Tool Tip ▸

Score wallboard face paper with a utility knife using a wallboard T-square as a guide. Bend the panel away from the scored line until the core breaks, then cut through the back paper (inset) with a utility knife, and separate the pieces.

Tools & Materials ▸

Tape measure	6 and 12" wallboard knives	1¼" coarse-thread wallboard
Utility knife	150-grit sanding sponge	screws
Wallboard T-square	Wallboard	Wallboard compound
	Wallboard tape	Metal inside corner bead

How to Install & Finish Wallboard

Install panels with their tapered edges butted together. Fasten with 1¼" screws, driven every 8" along the edges and every 12" in the field. Drive screws deep enough to dimple the surface without ripping the face paper (inset).

Finish the seams by applying an even layer of compound over the seam, about ⅛" thick using a 6" taping knife.

3

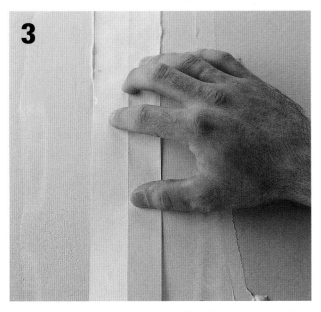

Center the tape over the seam and lightly embed it into the compound, making sure it's smooth and straight.

4

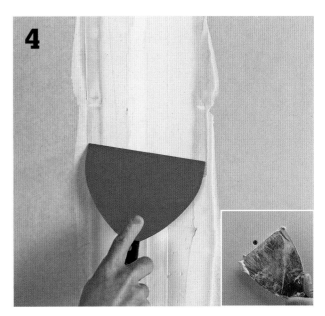

Smooth the tape with the taping knife. Apply enough pressure to force the compound from underneath the tape, leaving the tape flat and with a thin layer underneath. Cover all exposed screw heads with the first of three coats of compound (inset). Let the compound dry overnight.

5

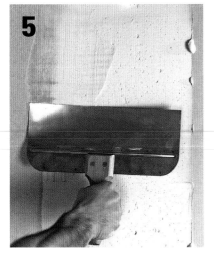

Second-coat the seams with a thin, even layer of compound using a 12" knife. Feather the sides of the compound first, holding the blade almost flat and applying pressure to the outside of the blade so that the blade just skims over the center of the seam.

6

After feathering both sides, make a pass down the center of the seam, leaving the seam smooth and even, the edges feathered out to nothing. Completely cover the joint tape. Let the second coat dry, then apply a third coat using the 12" knife. After the third coat dries completely, sand the compound lightly with a drywall sander or a 150-grit sanding sponge.

Tip ▶

Finish any inside corners using paper-faced metal inside corner beads to produce straight, durable corners with little fuss. Embed the bead into a thin layer of compound, then smooth the paper with a taping knife. Apply two finish coats to the corner, then sand the compound smooth.

Patching Exterior Walls

Many remodeling projects involve patching or repairing exterior wall surfaces, and the key to a successful job is to follow the original work. This will help you determine the best installation method and make sure the patch blends in with the surrounding area.

To patch siding, use a staggered pattern so that vertical end joints are not aligned between rows. If you've installed a window or door into an existing opening, you may have to remove some siding pieces before patching in new ones to maintain the staggered installation.

Wood siding generally is easy to match with new material from a lumberyard. Vinyl and metal siding can be more difficult to match, so contact the siding manufacturer before making any changes to your existing surfaces. It's also important that you have the right trim pieces to make sure the patch looks good and creates a weatherproof barrier.

Windows and doors with nailing flanges must be covered with wood or metal molding, usually purchased separately. After the window is installed, hold trim pieces in place, then mark an outline around the trim onto the siding. Trim the siding to fit.

Tools & Materials ▸

Circular saw
Flat pry bar
Aviation snips
Trowel
Scratching tool
Whisk broom
Exterior-wall
   sheathing

Building paper
Siding
6d siding nails
Paintable silicone caulk
Stucco mix, tint
   (optional)
Self-furring metal lath
Spray bottle

Tips for Installing Vinyl Siding Tip ▸

Cut vinyl siding using a circular saw, metal snips, or a utility knife. Outfit a circular saw with a plywood blade (fine-toothed), and install the blade backward so the teeth point down. Make the cuts slowly, using standard cutting techniques. *Note: Do not cut any material other than vinyl siding with the saw blade installed backward. When cutting siding with a utility knife, score the panels using a framing square as a guide, then snap along the scored line.*

Attach siding panels so they can expand and contract with temperature changes. Lock the bottom edge underneath the nailing strip of the panel below using a zip tool (see page 282), if necessary. Hold the panel flat to the sheathing without stretching it upward and nail through the centers of the nailing-strip slots, leaving about 1/32" between the nail head and the panel. Fasten the middle of the panel first, and space the nails following manufacturer's instructions.

How to Patch Wood Lap Siding

Cover the patch area with sheathing and building paper, if not already present. If the bottom row of siding is missing, nail a starter strip cut from a piece of siding along the bottom of the patch area using 6d siding nails. Leave a ¼" gap at each joint in the starter strip to allow for expansion.

Use a flat pry bar to remove lengths of lap siding on both sides of the patch area, creating a staggered pattern. When new siding is installed, the end joints will be offset for a less conspicuous appearance.

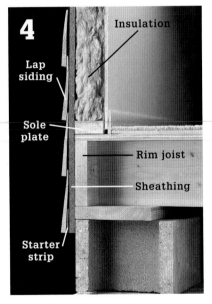

Cut the bottom piece of lap siding to span the entire opening, and lay it over the starter strip. Allow a ¼" expansion gap between board ends. Attach the siding with pairs of 6d siding nails driven at each stud location.

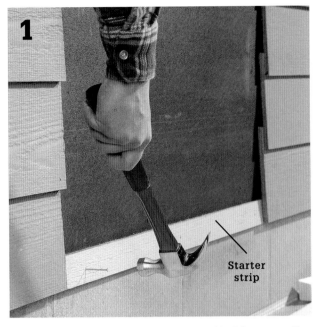

Cut and install succeeding rows of siding, nailing only near the top of the siding at stud locations. Work upward from the bottom to create the proper overlap.

Fill joints between the siding pieces with paintable silicone caulk. Repaint the entire wall surface as soon as the caulk dries to protect the new siding against weather.

Ingredients of Scratch (base) Coat and Brown Coat Stucco

- 3 parts sand
- 2 parts portland cement
- 1 part masonry cement
  water

Ingredients of Finish Coat Stucco

- 1 part lime
- 3 parts sand
- 6 parts white cement
- tint (as desired)
- water

For small jobs, use premixed stucco, available at building centers. For best results, apply the stucco in two or three layers, letting each layer dry completely between applications. Premixed stucco can also be used on larger areas, but it is more expensive than mixing your own ingredients.

For large jobs, combine dry stucco mix with water, following the manufacturer's directions, or use the ingredients lists shown here. A stucco finish typically contains two or three layers, depending on the application (see below). The mixtures for the base and brown coats should be just moist enough to hold their shape when squeezed (inset). A finish-coat mix requires slightly more water than other coats. If you need to color the finish coat, mix test batches first, adding measured amounts of tint to each batch. Let the test batches dry for at least an hour to get an accurate indication of the final color.

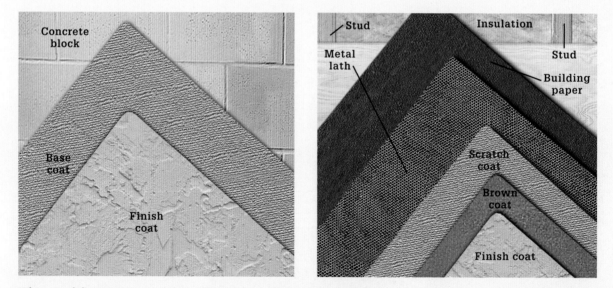

When applying stucco over brick or block (left), use two coats: a ⅜"-thick base coat and a ¼"-thick finish coat. Do not apply stucco directly over painted concrete block. On wood-frame construction or an insulation-board surface (right), first cover the area with building paper and metal lath. Then apply three coats of stucco: a scratch coat (⅜ to ½" thick), a brown coat (⅜" thick), and a finish coat (⅛" thick). Both the base coat on masonry walls and the scratch coat on wood-frame walls should be "scratched" after they are applied. This involves etching horizontal grooves into the partially set stucco using a scratching tool. You can make your own scratching tool by driving a row of 1½" wire nails through a piece of 1 × 2. The grooves provide a gripping surface for the next stucco layer.

How to Patch Stucco

Cover the patch area with sheathing and building paper, if not already present. Cut self-furring metal lath using aviation snips, and attach it to the sheathing with 1½" galvanized roofing nails driven into the wall studs every 6". Overlap pieces of lath by 2". *Note: If patch area extends to the base of the wall, install a metal stop bead at the bottom of the wall.*

Mix a batch of stucco for the scratch coat (facing page). Apply a ⅜"-thick layer of stucco over the lath using a trowel. Press firmly to fill any voids, and cover the lath completely. Let the stucco dry until it will hold the impression of a thumbprint, then use a scratching tool to make shallow grooves across the entire surface. Let the stucco set for two days, dampening it every few hours with fine spray to help it cure evenly.

Mix a batch of stucco for the brown coat (facing page), and apply it in a ⅜"-thick layer or until the patch area is within ¼ to ⅛" of the surrounding surface. Let the coat cure for two days, dampening it every few hours.

Mix a stucco finish coat (facing page). Dampen the wall, then apply the finish coat to match the surrounding stucco. The texture for the finish coat above was dashed on with a flick of a whisk broom, then flattened with a trowel. Keep the finish coat damp for a week while it cures. Let the stucco dry for several more days if you plan to paint it.

Glossary

Apron — Flat trim piece placed just below a windowsill or stool.

Backband — Trim surrounding window or door casing, usually for the purpose of increasing depth.

Balloon framing — A type of framing construction in which each exterior wall stud runs from the sill plate on the foundation to the roof framing in one continuous piece. Used most commonly in house construction before 1930.

Bevel cut — An angled cut through the width or thickness of a board or other piece of stock.

Brick molding — A thick, exterior wood casing traditionally used with brick, which covers the frame and the exterior finish.

Buck — Lumber pieces used to serve as a window frame for fastening a window to concrete or concrete block.

Building code — A set of building regulations and ordinances governing the way a house may be built or modified. Most building codes are controlled by the local municipality.

Casing — The interior and exterior trim surrounding the frame of a window or door.

Cladding — A skin or sheathing, typically vinyl or metal, covering the exterior portions of a door or window unit.

Clerestory — A window near the top of a wall. Typically several are arranged in a series to provide indirect lighting.

Cornice — A wooden frame used as a window top treatment.

Cripple stud — The short wall studs that fall over window and door headers and beneath windowsills.

Dormer — A building element that projects from a sloping roof and contains a vertical window.

Drip edge — Preformed weather flashing installed above door or window trim.

Egress window — A window meeting specific requirements for use as an emergency exit.

Elevation drawing — An architectural drawing showing the side view of a room or exterior, usually with one wall per drawing.

Endnailing — Joining two boards by driving nails through the face of one board and into the end of another.

Facenailing — Joining two boards by driving nails through the faces of both boards.

Flashing — A thin sheet, usually metal or plastic, designed to divert water from a joint or building surface.

Floor plan — An architectural drawing showing a room as seen from above.

Furring strip — Wood strips used to level or add thickness to a surface.

Gable wall — The triangular exterior end wall underneath a two-sided pitched roof.

Grille — Ornamental or simulated window muntins that don't actually divide the glass.

Head — The area at the top of a window or door.

Header — A horizontal framing member over a window or door opening that supports the structural load above.

Jack stud — A wall-framing member used to support a header in a doorway or window opening.

Jambs — The pieces that make up a window or door frame.

Joist — The horizontal framing member of a floor or ceiling.

King stud — The first stud on either side of a framed opening to span from the sole plate to the top plate.

Level — Perfectly horizontal.

Light (or lite) — Glazing (glass) framed by muntins and/or sash in a window or door.

Low-E glass — Glass that has low emissivity due to a film or metallic coating restricting the passage of radiant heat.

Miter cut — A 45° angled cut in the end of a piece of molding or a framing member.

Mullion (or mullion post) — A vertical member that divides multiple windows within a single unit.

Muntin — A smaller, secondary member that divides the glass or openings in a sash or door.

Nail set — A pointed metal rod used in finish carpentry for driving finish nails or casing nails below the wood surface.

Platform framing — A type of framing construction in which the studs only span a single story, and each floor acts as a platform to build and support the next level. Used in most homes built after 1930.

Plumb — Standing perfectly vertical. A plumb line is exactly perpendicular to a level surface.

Prehung door — A door already mounted with hinges in a frame.

R-value — The measure of resistance of a material to the passage of heat.

Rail — The horizontal member of a window sash or door panel frame.

Rough opening — An opening in framing made to fit a manufactured unit such as a window or door.

Saddle — The shaped strip or board that lays over the doorsill and seals the gap beneath the door.

Sash — The outermost frame that holds glass in a window unit.

Sash cord — A rope connecting the window sash to a weight inside the window frame. The cord travels on a pulley that rotates as the window is opened or closed.

Sheathing — A layer of plywood or other sheet good covering the wall or roof framing of a house.

Shim — Wood wedge used to align a window or door unit in its rough opening.

Sidelight — A tall, narrow window beside a door.

Sill — The framing member at the bottom of a window or door or the sloped exterior base of a window or door unit.

Sole plate — A 2 × 4 or 2 × 6 board nailed flat on the floor to support the bottom ends of wall studs.

Stile — The vertical side member of a window sash or door panel frame.

Stool — A horizontal shelf-like trim piece at the interior base of a window.

Stop — Small molding strips attached to window or door jambs to guide moving sashes and stop swinging doors.

Stud — The vertical member of a wall.

Threshold — The base of any exterior door frame, made up of the sill and saddle. Also, the saddle itself.

Toenailing — Joining two boards at a right angle by driving nails at an angle through one board and into the other.

Wallboard (or drywall) — Paper-covered gypsum panels used for most interior wall and ceiling surfaces.

Weatherstripping — Strips of metal, plastic, felt, or other material used to seal windows and doors to prevent air leakage and water intrusion.

Whaler — A temporary support beam used in the modification of balloon framing.

Resources

Access One, Inc.
800 561 2223
www.beyondbarriers.com

AGI Group, Inc.
800 823 6677
www.agigroup.com

American Institute of Architects
800 242 3837
www.aia.org

American Society of Interior Designers
202 546 3480
www.asid.org

Andersen Windows, Inc.
800 426 4261
www.andersenwindows.com

Atrium
Windows and patio doors
800 935 2000
www.home.atrium.com

Bilco Company
203 934 6363
www.bilco.com

Cherry Tree Design
Doors, lighting, mirrors
800 634 3268
www.cherrytreedesign.com

CLOPAY Doors
Garage doors
800 225 6729
www.clopaydoor.com

Construction Materials
   Recycling Association
630 548 4510
www.cdrecycling.org

Craftmaster Manufacturing, Inc.
800 405 2233
www.craftmasterdoorsdesign.com

Designer Doors
715 426 1100
www.designerdoors.com

Emtek Products, Inc.
800 356 2741
www.emtek.com

Endura
800 447 8442
www.endura-flooring.com

Energy & Environmental
   Building Association
952 881 1098
www.eeba.org

FLOR
Inspired modular floor coverings
866 281 3567
www.FLOR.com

Hunter Douglas
800 265 1363
www.hunterdouglas.com

International Conference of
   Building Officials
800 284 4406
www.icbo.com

JELD-WEN, Inc.
800 877 9482
www.jeld-wen.com

Kohler
800 456 4537
www.kohler.com

Kolbe & Kolbe Millwork Co., Inc.
800 955 8177
www.kolbe-kolbe.com

Kwikset Corporation
714 535 8111
kwikset.com

Larson Manufacturing
800 411-larson
www.larsondoors.com

Madawaska Doors, Inc.
800 263 2358
www.madawaska-doors.com

Marvin Windows and Doors
888 537 8268
www.marvin.com

Milgard Windows
*Featuring Hoffman York
   decorative glass*
800-MILGARD
www.milgard.com

Nostalgic Warehouse
Grandeur by Nostalgic Warehouse
www.nostalgicwarehouse.com
www.grandeur-nw.com

National Association of the Remodeling
   Industry (NARI)
847 298 9200
www.nari.org

Peachtree Doors and Windows
800 732 2499
www.peach99.com

Pittsburgh Corning Corporation
800 732 2499
www.pittsburghcorning.com

Roto Frank of America
800 787 7709

Schlage, Ingersoll Rand Security
   Technologies
*Security devices for both residential and
   commercial applications*
800 847 1864
www.schlage.com

Simpson Door Company
800 952 4057
www.simpsondoor.com

Suntunnel Skylights
800 369 7465
www.suntunnel.com

Thermatru
*Fiberglass entry doors, as featured on pages
   126 to 129, and patio door systems available
   through a national network of distributors,
   lumberyards, and home centers*
800 537 8827
www.thermatru.com

US Environmental Protection Agency
www.epa.gov

VELUX America, Inc.
800 888 3589
www.velux-america.com

Vetter
Windows and patio doors
www.vetterwindows.com

Wayne Dalton
*Garage doors and door openers, as
   featured on pages 202 to 207*
www.wayne-dalton.com

Wheatbelt, Inc.
800 264 5171
www.rollupshutter.com

Wood Harbor
Doors and cabinetry
641 423 0444
www.woodharbor.com

Woodport Interior Doors
715 526 2146
www.woodport.com

Univeral Design Resources

ABLEDATA
800 227 0215
www.abledata.com

Adaptive Environments
   Center, Inc.
617 695 1225
www.adaptenv.org

American Association of
   Retired Persons (AARP)
800 424 3410
www.aarp.org

Center for Inclusive Design &
   Environmental Access
School of Architecture and
   Planning, University of Buffalo
716 829 3485
www.ap.buffalo.edu

Center for Universal Design
NC State University
919 515 3082
www.design.ncsu.edu/cud

National Association of Home
   Builders (NAHB)
800 638 8556
www.nahbrc.org

Weathershield Windows & Doors
800 538 8836
www.weathershield.com

Woodharbor
Doors and cabinetry
641 423 0444
www.woodharbor.com

Photography Credits

p. 4 Flynn (film), 13 (top & lower) photos © Brian Vanden Brink

p. 6, 15 (lower) photos © Eric Roth

p. 8, 15 (top), 62 photos courtesy of Kolbe

p. 9 (lower right), 12 (top left) photo courtesy of Peachtree Doors and Windows

p. 9 (top & lower left), p. 22 (lower middle) photos courtesy of ThermaTru

p. 10 (lower), 11 (lower) photos © M. Eric Honeycutt, www.istockphoto.com

p. 11 (top) photo courtesy of Weathershield Windows & Doors

p. 12 (top right) photo courtesy of Atrium

p. 12 (lower), 22 (lower left) photos courtesy of Hoffman York

p. 14 (top & lower), 18 (lower), 19 (top), 20 (top middle) photos courtesy of Marvin

p. 18 (top) photo courtesy of Milgard Windows

p. 19 (lower), photo courtesy of Morgan Door, part of the JELD-WEN family; 20 (top & lower right) courtesy of Caradco Windows, part of the JELD-WEN family, 20 (lower middle) courtesy of Summit Windows, part of the JELD-WEN family

p. 20 (lower left), 21 (top middle & right, lower middle), 27 (top right) photos © Brad Daniels

p. 21 (top left) photo © Andrea Rugg

p. 21 (lower right), 34 photos courtesy of Simpson Door company

p. 21 (lower left), 80 photos courtesy of VELUX America

p. 22 (top middle) photo courtesy of Cherry Tree Design

p. 22 (top right), p. 116 photos courtesy of Woodharbor

p. 23, 29 photos courtesy of CLOPAY

p. 24 (top right) photo courtesy of Emtek, (middle two far right) Nostalgic, (lower three far right) Schlage

p. 37 photo courtesy of Dave Regel Construction / Access One, Inc.

p. 90 (top) photo courtesy of SunTunnel Systems, Inc.

p. 118 photo courtesy of FLOR

p. 180 © Jerry Koch Photography, www.istockphoto.com

Conversion Charts

Metric Conversions

To Convert:	To:	Multiply by:
Inches	Millimeters	25.4
Inches	Centimeters	25.4
Feet	Meters	0.305
Yards	Meters	0.914
Square inches	Square centimeters	6.45
Square feet	Square meters	0.093
Square yards	Square meters	0.836
Ounces	Milliliters	30.0
Pints (U.S.)	Liters	0.473 (Imp. 0.568)
Quarts (U.S.)	Liters	0.946 (Imp. 1.136)
Gallons (U.S.)	Liters	3.785 (Imp. 4.546)
Ounces	Grams	28.4
Pounds	Kilograms	0.454

To Convert:	To:	Multiply by:
Millimeters	Inches	0.039
Centimeters	Inches	0.394
Meters	Feet	3.28
Meters	Yards	1.09
Square centimeters	Square inches	0.155
Square meters	Square feet	10.8
Square meters	Square yards	1.2
Milliliters	Ounces	.033
Liters	Pints (U.S.)	2.114 (Imp. 1.76)
Liters	Quarts (U.S.)	1.057 (Imp. 0.88)
Liters	Gallons (U.S.)	0.264 (Imp. 0.22)
Grams	Ounces	0.035
Kilograms	Pounds	2.2

Converting Temperatures

Convert degrees Fahrenheit (F) to degrees Celsius (C) by following this simple formula: Subtract 32 from the Fahrenheit temperature reading. Then, multiply that number by $\frac{5}{9}$. For example, 77°F - 32 = 45. 45 × $\frac{5}{9}$ = 25°C.

To convert degrees Celsius to degrees Fahrenheit, multiply the Celsius temperature reading by $\frac{9}{5}$. Then, add 32. For example, 25°C × $\frac{9}{5}$ = 45. 45 + 32 = 77°F.

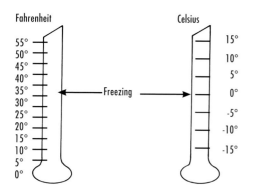

Metric Plywood Panels

Metric plywood panels are commonly available in two sizes: 1,200 mm × 2,400 mm and 1,220 mm × 2,400 mm, which is roughly equivalent to a 4 × 8-ft. sheet. Standard and Select sheathing panels come in standard thicknesses, while Sanded grade panels are available in special thicknesses.

Standard Sheathing Grade		Sanded Grade	
7.5 mm	($\frac{5}{16}$ in.)	6 mm	($\frac{4}{17}$ in.)
9.5 mm	($\frac{3}{8}$ in.)	8 mm	($\frac{5}{16}$ in.)
12.5 mm	($\frac{1}{2}$ in.)	11 mm	($\frac{7}{16}$ in.)
15.5 mm	($\frac{5}{8}$ in.)	14 mm	($\frac{9}{16}$ in.)
18.5 mm	($\frac{3}{4}$ in.)	17 mm	($\frac{2}{3}$ in.)
20.5 mm	($\frac{13}{16}$ in.)	19 mm	($\frac{3}{4}$ in.)
22.5 mm	($\frac{7}{8}$ in.)	21 mm	($\frac{13}{16}$ in.)
25.5 mm	(1 in.)	24 mm	($\frac{15}{16}$ in.)

Lumber Dimensions

Nominal - U.S.	Actual - U.S. (in inches)	Metric
1 × 2	$\frac{3}{4}$ × 1$\frac{1}{2}$	19 × 38 mm
1 × 3	$\frac{3}{4}$ × 2$\frac{1}{2}$	19 × 64 mm
1 × 4	$\frac{3}{4}$ × 3$\frac{1}{2}$	19 × 89 mm
1 × 5	$\frac{3}{4}$ × 4$\frac{1}{2}$	19 × 114 mm
1 × 6	$\frac{3}{4}$ × 5$\frac{1}{2}$	19 × 140 mm
1 × 7	$\frac{3}{4}$ × 6$\frac{1}{4}$	19 × 159 mm
1 × 8	$\frac{3}{4}$ × 7$\frac{1}{4}$	19 × 184 mm
1 × 10	$\frac{3}{4}$ × 9$\frac{1}{4}$	19 × 235 mm
1 × 12	$\frac{3}{4}$ × 11$\frac{1}{4}$	19 × 286 mm
1$\frac{1}{4}$ × 4	1 × 3$\frac{1}{2}$	25 × 89 mm
1$\frac{1}{4}$ × 6	1 × 5$\frac{1}{2}$	25 × 140 mm
1$\frac{1}{4}$ × 8	1 × 7$\frac{1}{4}$	25 × 184 mm
1$\frac{1}{4}$ × 10	1 × 9$\frac{1}{4}$	25 × 235 mm
1$\frac{1}{4}$ × 12	1 × 11$\frac{1}{4}$	25 × 286 mm
1$\frac{1}{2}$ × 4	1$\frac{1}{4}$ × 3$\frac{1}{2}$	32 × 89 mm
1$\frac{1}{2}$ × 6	1$\frac{1}{4}$ × 5$\frac{1}{2}$	32 × 140 mm
1$\frac{1}{2}$ × 8	1$\frac{1}{4}$ × 7$\frac{1}{4}$	32 × 184 mm
1$\frac{1}{2}$ × 10	1$\frac{1}{4}$ × 9$\frac{1}{4}$	32 × 235 mm
1$\frac{1}{2}$ × 12	1$\frac{1}{4}$ × 11$\frac{1}{4}$	32 × 286 mm
2 × 4	1$\frac{1}{2}$ × 3$\frac{1}{2}$	38 × 89 mm
2 × 6	1$\frac{1}{2}$ × 5$\frac{1}{2}$	38 × 140 mm
2 × 8	1$\frac{1}{2}$ × 7$\frac{1}{4}$	38 × 184 mm
2 × 10	1$\frac{1}{2}$ × 9$\frac{1}{4}$	38 × 235 mm
2 × 12	1$\frac{1}{2}$ × 11$\frac{1}{4}$	38 × 286 mm
3 × 6	2$\frac{1}{2}$ × 5$\frac{1}{2}$	64 × 140 mm
4 × 4	3$\frac{1}{2}$ × 3$\frac{1}{2}$	89 × 89 mm
4 × 6	3$\frac{1}{2}$ × 5$\frac{1}{2}$	89 × 140 mm

Liquid Measurement Equivalents

1 Pint	= 16 Fluid Ounces	= 2 Cups
1 Quart	= 32 Fluid Ounces	= 2 Pints
1 Gallon	= 128 Fluid Ounces	= 4 Quarts

Drill Bit Guide

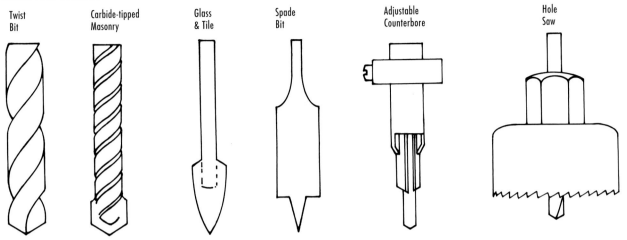

Twist Bit | Carbide-tipped Masonry | Glass & Tile | Spade Bit | Adjustable Counterbore | Hole Saw

Nails

Nail lengths are identified by numbers from 4 to 60 followed by the letter "d," which stands for "penny." For general framing and repair work, use common or box nails. Common nails are best suited to framing work where strength is important. Box nails are smaller in diameter than common nails, which makes them easier to drive and less likely to split wood. Use box nails for light work and thin materials. Most common and box nails have a cement or vinyl coating that improves their holding power.

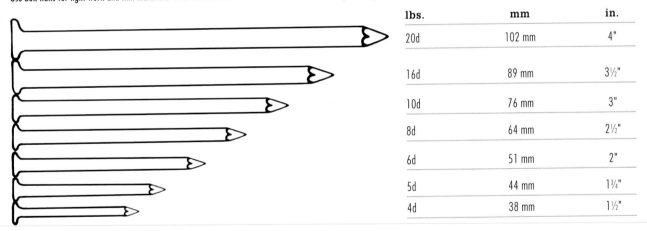

lbs.	mm	in.
20d	102 mm	4"
16d	89 mm	3½"
10d	76 mm	3"
8d	64 mm	2½"
6d	51 mm	2"
5d	44 mm	1¾"
4d	38 mm	1½"

Counterbore, Shank & Pilot Hole Diameters

Screw Size	Counterbore Diameter for Screw Head (in inches)	Clearance Hole for Screw Shank (in inches)	Pilot Hole Diameter	
			Hard Wood (in inches)	Soft Wood (in inches)
#1	.146 (⁹/₆₄)	⁵/₆₄	³/₆₄	¹/₃₂
#2	¼	³/₃₂	³/₆₄	¹/₃₂
#3	¼	⁷/₆₄	¹/₁₆	³/₆₄
#4	¼	⅛	¹/₁₆	³/₆₄
#5	¼	⅛	⁵/₆₄	¹/₁₆
#6	⁵/₁₆	⁹/₆₄	³/₃₂	⁵/₆₄
#7	⁵/₁₆	⁵/₃₂	³/₃₂	⁵/₆₄
#8	⅜	¹¹/₆₄	⅛	³/₃₂
#9	⅜	¹¹/₆₄	⅛	³/₃₂
#10	⅜	³/₁₆	⅛	⁷/₆₄
#11	½	³/₁₆	⁵/₃₂	⁹/₆₄
#12	½	⁷/₃₂	⁹/₆₄	⅛

Index

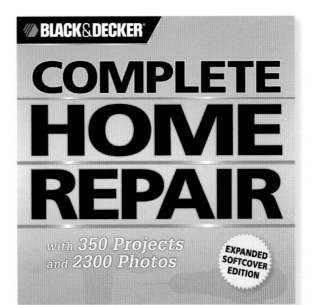

Also From CREATIVE PUBLISHING international

ISBN 1-58923-331-X

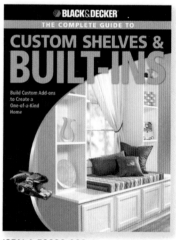

ISBN 1-58923-303-4

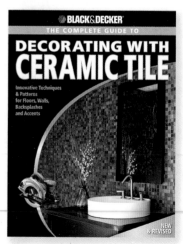

ISBN 1-58923-333-6

Creative Publishing
international

400 First Avenue North • Suite 300 • Minneapolis, MN 55401 • www.creativepub.com